An Appeal to Justice
Litigated Reform of Texas Prisons

AN APPEAL TO JUSTICE

Litigated Reform of Texas Prisons

*Ben M. Crouch
and James W. Marquart*

Foreword by John Irwin

 University of Texas Press, Austin

First Edition, 1989

Requests for permission to reproduce material from this work
should be sent to Permissions, University of Texas Press,
Box 7819, Austin, Texas 78713–7819.

Library of Congress Cataloging-in-Publication Data

Crouch, Ben M.
    An appeal to justice.

    Bibliography: p.
    Includes index.
    1. Prisons—Texas. 2. Prison administration—Texas.
3. Prisons—Law and legislation—Texas. 4. Prisoners—
Legal status, laws, etc.—Texas. I. Marquart, James W.
(James Walter), 1954–   . II. Title.
HV9475.T4C76   1989   364'.973   88-29476
ISBN 0-292-70407-0

⊗ The paper used in this publication meets the minimum
requirements of American National Standard for Information
Sciences–Permanence of Paper for Printed Library Materials,
ANSI Z39.48–1984.

Contents

Foreword   vii

Preface   ix

1. Prison Order and Litigated Reform   1

2. From Anarchy to Order   13

3. Stability and Control, Texas Style   46

4. Co-optation of the Kept   85

5. Justice Comes to Texas Prisons   117

6. Changing of the Guards   151

7. Prisoner Crisis and Control   185

8. A New Prison Order   221

Notes   239

Bibliography   261

Index   275

Tables

1. Racial Distribution of Prisoners on Eight Prison
   Farms, 1927   17

2. Reasons for Discharging Officers, 1927–1937 25

3. Official Deviance That Did Not Preclude Rehiring,
   1927–1937   26

4. Prisoner Offenses That Were Sanctioned by Whipping 28

5. Good Time Classification of Inmates by Race
   (in Percent)   69

6. Monthly Flat-Rate Overtime Schedule, 1929
   (in Hours)   89

7. Changes in Prisoner Rule Violations   152

8. Statewide Infractions for Marijuana and Alcohol 190

9. Serious Assaultive Behavior Rates, Eight Key Units,
1983–1987   201
10. Gang Membership and Offense of Record (in Percent)   208
11. Inmate Perceptions of Personal Safety, 1970–1987   216
12. Model of Litigated Reform in TDC and Variations in
Major Structural Dimensions   222

Foreword

BEN CROUCH and James Marquart have written a valuable book about the drastic changes in the Texas prison system in the last forty years. Until World War II, Texas, along with many other southern states, suffered from penological retardation. The cruelty of Texas prison regimens (from 1944 to 1948, 341 prisoners mutilated themselves by severing their Achilles tendons, breaking their arms, or cutting off their feet or hands to avoid the brutal work routines) was characteristic of other American prisons in the middle of the nineteenth century. In the late 1940s, Texas finally experienced its belated reform. The system's new director, Oscar Ellis, removed most of the excessive cruelty, although he continued to guide Texas in its own directions. Instead of adopting the rehabilitative ideal and transforming prisons into "correctional institutions," which many eastern, midwestern, and western states had done, Texas established a highly disciplined, harsh prison routine built around a profitable agricultural enterprise. Also, Texas kept its convict boss system. In several southern states, convict bosses, called building tenders in Texas, had been very important in maintaining control of prisoners. Although Ellis suppressed most of the extremely cruel, even murderous activities of the "BTs," he still chose to continue with BTs as a key control device.

The Texas system under Ellis and his successor, George Beto, experienced twenty years of stability and profitability. It was well known by those familiar with it for being rigid, austere, even mean and for not putting much effort into rehabilitating prisoners. However, other states' penologists recognized that the Texas prison agricultural program greatly reduced the cost of the system and that Texas maintained order among prisoners (no small accomplishment).

Texas' assault and murder rates, between prisoners and between prisoners and between prisoners and guards, remained low while they escalated in many other states. Also, Texas did not experience the prisoner strikes and riots that swept across the country in the late sixties and early seventies. What was not appreciated was the extent to which this order was maintained by the administration extending power to the building tenders, who ran roughshod over the general prison population, and by the guards applying physical force—"tune ups" and "ass whippings."

By the end of the 1970s, Texas was increasingly seen by other state prison administrators and state legislators as the model system. Most other states had given up on rehabilitation and were spending more and more money to house expanding, factious, gang-ridden prison populations, which they were unable to control. After he turned the administration over to W. J. Estelle in 1972, George Beto was increasingly called upon by desperate legislators and prison administrators in other states to advise them on how to run their prison systems.

However, the Texas system came apart in the 1980s. Two factors caused this. The first was overcrowding. Like those in many other states, Texas prison populations expanded rapidly and the state was unwilling to spend the money required to keep up with this expansion. Second, a 1972 lawsuit charging cruel and unusual punishment filed by one of the prisoner writ writers—David Ruiz—received the careful attention of William W. Justice, judge of the Federal District Court of the Eastern District of Texas. Judge Justice then presided over a protracted judicial review of the Texas system (which still continues) that forced Texas to drastically alter its prison system.

With considerable resistance and pain, Texas made the changes dictated by the courts and has stepped into the age of modern penology. In making this leap, the state has apparently coped with the new realities of prison administration: close judicial scrutiny, a drastically expanded prisoner population, and the invasion of nonwhite and female guards into the exclusive circle of white, rural "good ole boy" guards. Crouch and Marquart have described in great detail this difficult transition and the new system that has emerged. Many other states are experiencing the same strains as Texas and will have to make drastic changes in their prison systems. Perhaps the Texas system *will* be a model for other states and this book may become a valuable guide for prison change.

JOHN IRWIN

Preface

FEDERAL COURT intervention radically transformed one prison system, the Texas Department of Corrections (TDC). While we focus
on litigation as the change agent, our primary concern is with the
impact of that process on prison organization, the prisoners, and the
staff. As such, the book is much more about the functioning of a
prison than that of a court.

Our account presents what Texas prisons were like prior to reform, why and how they changed, and what they have become after
years of litigation. Critical to this account, of course, is rich and accurate information about preform TDC; without such information we could not confidently characterize the extent and nature of
change. The detailed analysis of conditions in TDC prior to the reforms does not derive from some natural experiment we had the wit
to devise. Instead, we were simply in the right place at the right
time, doing research in TDC years before the litigation became
salient.

Our analysis draws on data and field notes from as early as 1973,
when Crouch conducted a short survey of prison officers, the first in
a series of projects involving guards and the general problem of control in prisons. In 1976, he spent half the summer employed as a uniformed officer in TDC's Ferguson prison unit. Then, through 1979
and 1980, with the help of Marquart, he conducted a series of surveys and interviews of recruits at TDC's Training Academy and of
veterans on most prison units. From 1981 through 1983, Marquart
worked as a uniformed officer in TDC's Eastham Unit. Beyond developing insight into daily prison rounds, he gained a unique understanding of how the inmate guard, or "building tender" (BT), system
operated. The timing of this participant observation at Eastham

allowed him to observe and record the dismantling of the BT system and the unit's initial efforts to comply with the court's directives. In addition to these specific projects, in the late 1970s and early 1980s we regularly visited many units and conducted hundreds of informal, unstructured interviews with TDC administrators, officers, and prisoners. The understanding of TDC's organizational culture, as well as the informant contacts that we developed over these years, proved invaluable as we focused on the impact of the reforms.

Because of the special contacts made in the Eastham Unit and because that unit was, according to both prison officials and court monitors, representative of the "old" TDC, we conducted a series of structured interviews there in late 1984 and early 1985. Seventy prisoners and forty officers were selected on a quasi-random basis for taped, in-depth interviews about the impact of the reforms. Although these interviews were done in a single unit, the insights gained were confirmed through many less formal interviews in other units across the system. Indeed, between 1984 and 1986, we interviewed staff and prisoners in nearly all TDC units, with the only exceptions being the few very low security units and the female units. Consequently, all data and references pertain to male prisoners and officials.

We augmented these interviews with data from two surveys designed to tap staff and prisoner perceptions of the reforms. The officer survey, completed in late 1986, involved 439 respondents from across the system (a 51 percent return rate). In early 1987, we completed a survey of 460 prisoners in eight of TDC's largest and most secure units, those with which the court was most concerned. Prisoners who had entered TDC between 1978 and 1982 constituted the population from which the ultimate sample was drawn on each unit. Of the approximately 75 prisoners randomly selected per unit, 10 to 15 percent either refused to participate or, more often, could not be easily brought from a work station or other activity. We looked to these quantitative data to corroborate insights developed from interviews.

Finally, we utilized a wide range of documentary data. Information on the early history of Texas prisons came in large part from newspapers and institutional records contained in the Texas prison museum located at Sam Houston State University. Invaluable in developing details and an accurate chronology of events from the late 1970s was a complete file of prison-related newspaper clippings maintained in the Texas Collection of the Houston Public Library. From TDC we secured institutional records on personnel changes, prison populations, disciplinary infractions, "death logs," and prison

Location of prison units of the Texas Department of Corrections.

gang membership and activities. From the special master's office came reports on compliance progress and problems.

These varied sources of information provided windows through which we viewed a complex and diverse institution undergoing change at all levels in over two dozen units. Though through the book TDC is spoken of as a wholistic system, its component units reflect much diversity in size and character. Our conclusions are thus not equally applicable to every unit and do not apply to the female units at all. Moreover, there were many streams of change and not all progressed at the same pace. We thus faced the difficult and regularly frustrating task of trying to capture the modal or most fundamental elements of change, of trying to discern general patterns among the welter of discrete, situation-specific events. This, of course, is the perennial problem of longitudinal research on organizational change. The results are never perfect, and our effort is certainly no exception. We tried, however, to present a balanced perspective and to project comprehensibly the details of individual experiences against the broader organizational and political realities that mark litigated prison reform.

If we offer a balanced and useful account of the Texas prison experience, it is in large part due to the generous assistance of a number of people. Those who read and reacted to all or part of the manuscript include John DiIulio, Neal Shover, Jim Estelle, George Beto, Geoff Alpert, Jim Burk, David Ward, Fred Wolinsky, Andy Collins, Steve Dial, and Mike Brodsgaard. Nancy Crouch edited various drafts of the manuscript. The Public Policy Resources Laboratory at Texas A&M University and the Criminal Justice Center at Sam Houston State University each provided financial and other support at various times during the research.

There are also many people who over the years have been especially valuable in helping us understand the world of TDC and who regularly gave us reality checks for our ideas. A number of present and former TDC staff members deserve special mention: Oscar "Slim" Savage, Leonard Peck, David Myers, Billy McMillian, Ricky McMillian, Ed Turner, Keith Price, Jim MacDonald, James Warren, J. R. Minyard, Kevin Dover, Mike Hallmark, Junior Herring, and Gary Kessler. Former and current prisoners whose help should be specifically acknowledged include Paul Maness, Vernon Johnson, Raymond Hafti, Steve Wilson, Leroy Lafoon, Toby Galloway, Benny Strickland, Jack Friday, Tom Pederson, and Leroy Curlin. Without the cooperation of these and many others, this book would not have been possible.

We gratefully acknowledge the contributions to our work made by each of these people and organizations. Of course, responsibility for any errors contained herein is our own.

Through the years of work on various parts of the project, and especially during the past three when most of the writing was done, we received tremendous support from our families. Thus, to Nancy, Caren, and Amy and to Cecelia, John, and Jessica we dedicate this book.

An Appeal to Justice
Litigated Reform of Texas Prisons

1.

Prison Order and Litigated Reform

As the rights model expands the rights of service recipients, the autonomy of service providers is correspondingly reduced. [Providers] are required entirely to restructure their behavior and their services.[1]

SINCE THE early 1960s, prison reform advocates have aggressively used the courts to extend prisoners' rights and generally improve life behind the walls. Reflective of a broader societal trend to seek legal remedies for personal and collective problems,[2] the number of suits filed against prison authorities has grown dramatically. In 1966, for example, 219 suits were filed by prisoners; by the late 1970s, nearly 10,000 were being filed annually.[3] With at least 80 percent of the state prison systems having experienced some type of court order to reform, judicial intervention has become a widespread correctional reality.[4]

Court intervention in prisons has certainly had a significant impact on prison organizations, prisoners, and correctional staff. But there is little consensus on the nature of that impact. In a recent analysis, John DiIulio points out several different characterizations of intervention outcomes.[5] Some observers see judicial activism as highly disruptive, promoting instability and violence. Others credit the courts with improving prison conditions. Still others draw attention to the marked bureaucratization of prisons that seems to follow intervention. None of these characterizations of court activism is adequate alone; at the same time, depending on the nature and extent of intervention, they may all be, in some measure, correct.

Although court activism has extensively influenced prisons, we have relatively little systematic information on the process and the consequences of that activism. Some intervention research in specific prisons is, of course, available.[6] That work, however, varies widely in scope and depth while offering little insight into how prisons and prison relations change over a protracted period of decree implementation. Thus, there is a need, as Malcolm Feely and Roger Hanson argue,[7] for in-depth case studies of the impact of judicial reform within individual prison systems. Accordingly, we present a case study of the litigated reform of the Texas prison system.

Prison Reform in Texas

In 1972, a Texas prisoner named David Ruiz filed a suit against the Texas Department of Corrections (TDC) and its director, W. J. Estelle, Jr. In that suit, Ruiz complained that the state's prisons were, among other things, physically deteriorated, dangerous for prisoners, and overcrowded. That suit, *Ruiz v. Estelle*,[8] would become the most comprehensive civil action suit in correctional law history.

After years of legal conflict and a lengthy trial, presiding Federal District Judge William W. Justice ruled in favor of the plaintiff. In his written opinion, the judge attacked a public agency that had developed a reputation for being austere but fair, highly efficient, safe, and orderly. That reputation derived from good public relations and nearly thirty years of relative tranquility at the time of the trial. Indeed, from the early 1950s through the late 1970s, legislators, citizens, and the media in Texas generally approved of TDC's traditional philosophy that hard work and strict discipline were good for the state and for the prisoners.

Judge Justice, however, found little in TDC that was good for prisoners. His scathing opinion detailed, among other problems, TDC's denial of adequate legal and medical services and failure to protect prisoners from the brutality of guards and inmate elites, called "building tenders," all in overcrowded facilities. For the judge, these conditions rendered unconstitutional TDC's control system, management style, and physical structure. He thus ordered reforms involving conditions of confinement (fire and work safety, sanitation), overcrowding, access to courts, medical care, discipline procedures, and prisoner supervision and control. The judge appointed a special master to oversee the reform process. Implementation of these reforms set in motion fundamental transformations of prison relations, organizational and control structures, and TDC's public image.

The *Ruiz* intervention in TDC is remarkable for the range of issues addressed and for the fact that ultimate reform altered almost every aspect of prison operation. But it is remarkable for another reason as well, namely, the extent to which the decrees were resisted by prison officials at all levels and, at least in the beginning, by state officials. That resistance cost millions in legal fees to fight the intervention, and the agency's credibility with the legislature suffered. It also contributed to hundreds of injuries and dozens of deaths within the prisons.

Our study of this complex and often painful reform process is guided by several basic questions. The first concerns the organizational, political, and cultural factors that affect compliance and resistance to court-ordered reform. As we previously noted, in Texas, resistance to change was great and, in turn, costly. We will examine the basis for that resistance and the conditions that ultimately prompted compliance.

The second question concerns the stages and dynamics of the reform process. Of particular interest here will be the impact that court-ordered changes have on the keepers and the kept. Staff and prisoner accommodations to mandated changes, especially control structures, can mean uncertainty at best and heightened danger at worst. We will also look at the organizational problem of balancing constitutional law and prison order. In a democratic society, law and order in the justice system are always, at least potentially, in conflict.[9] We will explore how this problem was "solved" before and during the decree implementation process.

The final question concerns the nature of the prison social order that is emerging in the postlitigation period in TDC. We will describe that order and how it differs from past prison orders. A key issue will be whether changes as perceived by officials and prisoners after years of litigation constitute fundamental or only superficial reform.

Texas prisons, for several reasons, offer a particularly appropriate setting for examining questions about the impact of litigated reform. First, TDC is one of the largest state prison systems in the country, second in size only to the California system. Because of its size and complexity, the Texas system faces the political, economic, and demographic exigencies that all large state prison systems face. Second, although Texas prisons certainly experienced pressures from overcrowding in the late 1970s, reforms resulted almost exclusively from Judge Justice's orders. The opportunity exists then to examine reforms that are primarily traceable to court intervention. Third, TDC enjoyed, both in the state and across the nation, a reputation for organizational efficiency and effective prisoner control. That reputation not only encouraged resistance to change but also ensured state and national attention for the implementation process.[10]

Finally, the Texas prison experience of moving by court order in a relatively short period from isolation, autonomy, and paternalism toward a more constitutional prison parallels the experience of other state prisons over the past twenty-five years. In this respect, TDC arguably serves as a microcosm for American corrections. To the extent that it does, an examination of the Texas experience provides the basis for a better understanding of how court decrees have actually changed prisons.

The Courts and American Prisons

Prior to the 1960s, the judiciary took a "hands off" approach toward prisons, viewing prisoners as "slaves of the state" who lost all rights upon conviction.[11] Bolstering this posture among federal and state judges were the beliefs that intervention might encourage so many cases that the judiciary would be swamped, that court officials lacked the expertise to direct prison change, and that judicial tinkering would undermine prison order and control. The most persuasive rationale for the limited court interest in prison conditions was the separation of powers doctrine, which might be violated if the courts (judicial branch) intervened in prisons (executive branch).[12] At the same time, some prison administrators successfully cultivated an institutional image that "everything was OK" and, therefore, that prisoners' complaints or suits were not only frivolous but also the work of malcontents and troublemakers.

That courts actively avoided intervention had fundamental implications for prison conditions. Citizens, and most of their elected representatives, have historically been uninterested in prison conditions as long as the facilities were orderly, quiet, and not too expensive.[13] Sensing the public's priorities, legislators spent little time or money on prisons, and wardens understood that order came first; prisoner amenities and programs were a very distant second. As a result, physical deterioration, absence of due process, poor medical care, abuse, and despair among prisoners were often the rule in American prisons, at least through the first half of this century.[14]

The hands off doctrine of the courts also indirectly shaped the way prison staff related to and controlled prisoners. Legal isolation meant not only few rights and poor living conditions for prisoners but also autonomy for prison officials. This autonomy typically translated into extreme discretion for the security staff in handling prisoner problems and problem prisoners. Strict obedience was expected, and prisoners were regularly subjected to highly particularistic treatment and coercion of all types.[15] The practices of Joseph Ragen and his minions at Stateville prison in Illinois or those of officials in the traditional Alabama and Arkansas prisons well illustrate this discretion, especially in regard to prisoner control.[16]

Of course, although officials prior to court intervention often employed various types of force to gain prisoner compliance, that force could never achieve complete compliance. There were then, and now, limits to the use of force.[17] Guards were always outnumbered by inmates, and the too frequent use of force could be counterproductive to maintaining order.

In reality, then, officer-prisoner relations usually involved some negotiation and were more calculative than coercive. This meant that prisoners in the past were certainly not powerless, despite the discretion of authorities to use almost any means to gain compliance. Simply stated, prisoners derived their power from the fact that guards informally depended on them to help maintain order.[18] That dependence allowed prisoners to exert some influence over staff and to erode subtly official authority.[19] Through the 1960s, however, such power that individual prisoners acquired through negotiation and wit paled compared to that of prison officials. The reason was that, while guards depended on prisoners to some degree, prisoners depended on their keepers for everything, essentials as well as such amenities as officials thought prisoners deserved.

The legal autonomy that encouraged official discretion also fostered conditions in which strong prisoners could prey on the weak. In that closed world, the strong or elite inmates regularly cooperated with officials to maintain order and the power status quo. This cooperation was most often informal. In exchange for the latitude they needed to run prison rackets and reduce their own deprivations, these prisoner elites provided officials with information and with assurances that there would be no "trouble." Since strong inmates benefited materially (contraband) and socially (power) from such informal arrangements, they had a vested interest in maintaining the status quo.[20] In some prisons, especially in the south, this cooperation was more institutionalized. Until courts intervened, select prisoners in Louisiana, Mississippi, and Arkansas, for example, were armed and charged with supervising other prisoners. The practice of using a cadre of strong prisoners to control their fellows was a central element in TDC's traditional control system, an element of special concern to Judge Justice.

Two or three decades ago in state prisons, the mass of prisoners perceived their incarceration experience primarily in terms of immediate deprivations and spent their time trying to minimize those deprivations. These efforts produced an elaborate inmate social system, including a convict code and a set of inmate roles, which generally rewarded prisoners for not cooperating with the authorities.[21] That prison world could be characterized as pitting the "cons" against the "hacks."[22] Essentially powerless to change broad prison conditions, prisoners relied on manipulation, guile, and secrecy to counter the power of officials and blunt their personal deprivations.

Significantly, this relationship between the keepers and the kept, part interdependence and part conflict, fostered institutional stability.

With no third party, such as a court, to turn to and with few rights, prisoners collectively lived at the bottom of the prison caste system. That status had important implications for prisoner identity. Through midcentury, at least, inmates had no option in most state prisons but to see themselves as unquestionably subordinate to prison authorities. In that regimented and closed environment, the "prisoner" identity tended to overshadow all others. Racial and ethnic identities were relatively unimportant, for example, as bases for defining the self and the incarceration experience. Although racial and ethnic identities certainly influenced microrelations in prison, their significance was minimized through the late 1950s by the fact that every prisoner was a "slave of the state."[23]

Through the middle of the twentieth century, then, state prisons were socially, as well as legally, isolated. This arrangement allowed much discretion among prison officials in the care and custody of prisoners. Certainly, discretion did not always lead to poor living conditions and abuse, but such conditions probably prevailed, if only because of limited money and interest in the free world for prisoners. This situation began to change, however, with the rise of the prisoners' rights movement.

The Prisoners' Rights Movement

By the mid-1960s, prison conditions began to be seen as falling within the court's purview for the first time. In that decade, social activists on behalf of a number of minority groups, youth, women, the poor, and the mentally retarded attacked those institutions that maintained the societal status quo. With the power of the judiciary to change racial segregation in schools demonstrated by *Brown v. Board of Education*, these activists began to look to the courts as the most effective means for reforming institutions, including prisons.[24]

Judicial activism was encouraged by the progressive philosophy of the U.S. Supreme Court under Chief Justice Earl Warren. Through a series of rulings extending civil rights to persons under arrest or in adjudication, the Supreme Court signaled that the federal judiciary might also intervene in prisons on behalf of prisoners. The traditional hands off doctrine began to crumble when, in 1964, the high court ruled in *Cooper v. Pate*[25] that inmates have the right to bring legal action against prison officials under Section 1983 of the Civil Rights Act of 1871. From that beginning, the number of suits filed by prisoners increased dramatically.[26]

The majority of these remedy cases have been filed under Section 1983, in which a prisoner claims that an official of the state has deprived him of a right or a privilege guaranteed by constitutional law. There are other remedy options available to prisoners, including state or federal habeas corpus writs, state or federal tort suits, and the Civil Rights of Institutionalized Persons Act of 1980. But Section 1983 suits have been the primary mechanism of litigated prison reform.[27]

On whatever basis it intervenes, however, a court can be a potent change agent. Once a judge orders a reform measure (e.g., access to court, improvements in prisoner classification, disciplinary procedures, mail privileges, or religious freedom) that order is difficult to resist. It draws authority from the constitution, from the tradition of case law, and from the prestige of the court as a moral force in society. This authority, backed by the power of contempt, is what gives courts the capacity to bring about major institutional reforms. Moreover, federal judges, appointed for life, are theoretically impervious to political pressure. Once courts became inclined to intervene and brought their power to bear, litigated reform produced major changes in American prison organizations.

The Impact of Litigated Reform on American Prisons

There is great variation in the nature and impact of court intervention on behalf of prisoners.[28] Many court orders are narrowly drawn, affecting only those specific prison conditions identified in a lawsuit (e.g., inmate mail and religious practices). Since the court responds only to those conditions brought before it, remedial orders in such narrow cases usually have little effect on overall prison organization and operations. In other actions, in which prisoners point to an array of problems, a judge may find that many aspects of a prison system are legally unacceptable ("totality of conditions" cases). Reform orders in these cases obviously have a much broader impact on prison operation and interaction, as the Texas prison experience illustrates.

Predictably, reactions by prison officials vary with the nature of the intervention. Generally, intervention on specific issues is less likely to be resisted if for no other reason than that the organizational impact of the remedial order will probably be limited. Some orders may even be welcomed by prison administrators since decrees can provide the leverage needed to secure from a stingy legislature the funding for long recognized shortcomings. When court orders are more sweeping, affecting almost every aspect of the prison system, however, official resistance and negative, unanticipated consequences are more likely.

One of the most persistently noted negative consequences of court intervention is disorder and increased danger. Though courts have eliminated many of the brutal punishments and privations of years past, the impression persists that, despite reforms, the quality of prisoner life has deteriorated. Several observers have noted that, though "reformed" through intervention, prisons are marked even more by uncertainty, fear, and violence. In short, litigation often paradoxically seems to worsen the quality of prison life.[29] As Charles Silberman concludes: "Prison rights suits have served to protect inmates from their keepers: but . . . they have left inmates more vulnerable to intimidation and brutality on the part of other inmates."[30]

The argument here is that litigation upsets the informal relations on which prison order has traditionally rested. Emboldened by court action against prison officials, prisoners have become politicized, pressing for and gaining more freedoms either through direct litigation or by default as officials became uncertain of what they could do to control inmates. Freed from traditional controls, prisoners may then use new liberties to prey on other inmates. For example, court orders that limit official intrusiveness into inmates' lives and that liberalize visitation and communication among inmates can also facilitate drug trafficking and growth of prison gangs. Thus, court intervention fosters disorganization of the prisoner social system and promotes inmate-inmate violence.[31]

Relatedly, evidence suggests that court-mandated reforms have also increased officer-inmate confrontations and the likelihood of prisoner violence aimed at officials. Thirty years ago, confrontations between inmates and staff were relatively rare. Inmates tended to accept their subordinate and deprived status and tried to make the best of it. Reforms altered this situation such that by the mid-1970s in many state prisons inmate confrontations with staff were frequent and even considered to be status conferring, especially among the younger, more aggressive inmates.[32] Court intervention gives inmates a sense of rising expectations,[33] as well as a rhetoric and a method for promoting change. Feeling justified in their claims for change, inmates become increasingly willing to resort to violence to achieve them. A direct consequence is officer demoralization and frustration both with court intervention and with administrators who seem to have given in to court pressure.[34]

Besides promoting prisoner politicalization and violence, court intervention can also alter prison organization.[35] Court-ordered reform addresses organizational means rather than ends. That is, courts do not question such broad, institutional objectives as rehabilitation, inmate care, societal safety, order maintenance, or organizational efficiency. Instead, courts are concerned with whether the means employed by prison officials to pursue those objectives unduly harm or limit the rights of prisoners. Thus, when a court prescribes new means of operation and control, the goal is ultimately to change the behavior of prison officials.

The most effective type of staff control in these circumstances is bureaucracy. Administrative compliance with court mandates typically requires an elaboration of rules and explicit procedures so that staff may be held closely accountable.[36] The proliferation of rules and the requirement that they be strictly followed is intended to limit staff discretion significantly. This emphasis on rules and staff accountability may restrain coercion, but it may also produce an overly formalized, legalistic work setting.

Since officials committed to traditional prison modes of operation often find it difficult either to embrace decrees or to ensure compliance with them, administrative succession often follows court intervention. But whether traditionally oriented administrators "see the light" or are replaced by more progressive directors, line officers may withdraw support from any administration that suddenly pushes new policies. If they sense that the front office will not support them as it did in the past, line officers may experience even greater demoralization.[37] Such feelings have been an important reason for the unionization of many state prison guard forces in recent years.[38]

Structural changes that follow judicial intervention can also alter the power relations between prisoners and staff. Court intervention can reduce the extent to which inmates depend solely on prison officials to define the conditions of their confinement. Accordingly, inmate power increases in relation to that of the keepers. Greater power can lead to an increase in the prisoners' questioning of policies, diminished respect for staff and rules, and more open conflict.

Constrained by bureaucratic standards and accountability, officers may find they must make do with new and, seemingly, more limited control devices. Informal alliances between officials and inmates involving information exchange[39] and cooperation of elite inmates usually diminish. These changes in control structures, plus a more confrontational posture among prisoners, are the basis for the most frequent lament among correctional officers in contemporary prisons, namely, that their power and control are either drastically limited or lost altogether.[40]

Formalization also seems to have affected relations among prisoners themselves. An emphasis on procedural due process not only equalizes, to some extent, prisoners and staff but also tends to place prisoners on even footing with each other. One indirect, but important, consequence of this equalization through formal treatment has been the rise in racial and ethnic conflict among prisoners. In the past, race and ethnicity played only a small role in prisoner relations. This was due to both the traditional subordination of minorities in the larger society and the fact that the status of "prisoner" overshadowed other statuses. In some states, moreover, black and white prisoners were segregated and had limited contact.

The significance of minority, and especially racial, status in prison began to change in the early 1960s, however, when Black Muslim prisoners in California pressed in court their complaints against religious restrictions by prison officials. Their victory, plus the growing racial awareness in the larger society, encouraged other minority prisoners to reject their traditional, doubly subordinate status. As a result, black prisoners became increasingly threatening to white prisoners, as well as to the overwhelmingly white prison guard forces.

Racial pride and white fear grew through the 1960s and 1970s as prison populations became younger, seemingly more violence prone, and even more disproportionately black.[41] Assaults, especially sexual assaults, by black prisoners on whites fueled racial tensions.[42] As racial conflict grew, so too did prisoner gangs whose memberships were defined along strict racial and ethnic lines. Although court intervention was not solely responsible for this conflict,[43] legal rules did become tools used by minority inmates to redefine their prison status and to negate the traditional inmate social system.

Conclusion

In the above discussion we sketched prison conditions and relations in state prisons through the first five or six decades of this century. We then reviewed what available research tells us about the impact of court intervention in prisons. Both discussions represent a distillation of fragmentary evidence from several state prisons at different points in time. Nonetheless, that evidence provides some insight into what prelitigation prison relations might be like, as well as some reasonable hypotheses about at least the short-term impact that reform orders have on prison organizations and on those who live and work there.

What is missing in these discussions is any consideration of a postlitigation phase, what prisons become after extensive court involvement. Although prisons continue to function through years of decree implementation, we do not have a very good idea about what difference litigation makes, whether it works, and whether it is worth the pain and expense involved.

Overview of the Analysis

The following chapters constitute an analytic description of how one prison system was transformed by court order. From the outset we recognized that a full understanding of the process of change and of the results of that change required a detailed account of TDC conditions and relations prior to court intervention. The behavior and reactions of TDC and state officials must be seen against that background.

Accordingly, we begin in Chapter 2 with a history of Texas prisons through the 1970s. Throughout much of the twentieth century, Texas prisons reflected the horrible conditions so characteristic of many state prisons in this period. Beginning in the late 1940s and 1950s, however, primarily due to the presence of strong agency leadership, real improvements occurred. Under that leadership, TDC experienced nearly thirty years of marked stability, maintained by an elaborate, authoritarian control system.

The next two chapters examine that control system in detail. Chapter 3 first considers how guards were controlled by a strong officer subculture and then explores the formal and informal means that guards used to control inmates in that period. Chapter 4 explores how elite inmates controlled other inmates through the building tender system. Though control elements, such as the use of force by guards and the building tender system, existed prior to the 1950s in TDC, they were refined and legitimized in the period from 1950 to 1980.

The next three chapters focus on the consequences of the reform orders handed down in 1981 by Judge Justice. Chapter 5 examines the litigation that marked the turning point in TDC's organizational life. In addition to an account of the *Ruiz v. Estelle* case and trial, this chapter presents an overview of the implications of the judge's rulings for administrative policies, organizational structure, and operational procedures. In Chapter 6 we examine the reactions of correctional officers to changes in their subculture and in their relations with prisoners and administrators. In Chapter 7 we explore links between decree implementation and the emergence of prisoner violence and gangs.

As TDC managers and staff achieved greater compliance with the court's mandates and became more accustomed to them, a new order emerged in prison. Chapter 8 explores the dimensions of that new order, what it suggests about TDC and about "reformed" prisons in America.

2

From Anarchy to Order

*In those days, employees and inmates worked from "can to can't"
six days a week. They worked in rain, sleet, snow, and cold. It
didn't get too bad to turn out the force. The line kept working as
long as they could see.* —TEXAS PRISON EMPLOYEE

*I came to prison on February 2, 1927. The prison was really rough
then. We almost starved to death. There was no worst meal. They
were all the same and bad. The only thing we had was beans, peas,
sow belly, and cornbread. The bread had weevils in it. We had
only three decent meals a year: Thanksgiving, Christmas, and
Juneteenth.* —TEXAS INMATE[1]

IN THE 1840s, the criminal justice apparatus in the Republic of
Texas was most ineffective. Poor jails and often corrupt local
sheriffs faced increases in immigration and violent crime.[2] The frequent escapes of prisoners were frustrating to citizens and sometimes led to vigilantism.[3] Responding to political and media pressures, the Texas legislature passed a bill in 1842 providing for the
construction of a state penitentiary to improve crime control. After
several years of haggling over the proposed location, state officials
finally selected the East Texas town of Huntsville in 1846 as the site
for the penitentiary.[4] Land was purchased, and construction began
in 1849.

Early supporters of the prison advocated a design based on the
"Auburn model," namely, a walled building where inmates worked
to produce goods under strict control. Profits made from those goods
were a source of state revenue. This model was attractive in part because it was progressive, a requisite for a new, developing state. Self-
sufficiency, however, was the most attractive feature of the model.

But prison self-sufficiency would prove an illusive goal through
the nineteenth and much of the twentieth century. For example, in
the early years, prison efforts to produce cotton and wool commer-
cially failed to generate expected revenues. These failures exacerbated already serious financial problems in the state. In 1871, Texas
officials followed other southern states and began to lease prison labor to the private sector.

Leasing and Contract Era

The earliest form of leasing prisoners in Texas involved private farmers and railroad and mining companies.[5] The state simply transferred prisoners to these businesses, which were responsible for the full range of their care. In practice, prisoners were worked, housed, and cared for at the whim of the camp overseers or contractors. Though the state saved money, neglect and brutality were so extreme that this arrangement was discontinued in 1876, and a second type of leasing was tried. This type involved prison officials supervising, housing, and disciplining inmates on the contract job sites. Unfortunately, this scheme also led to deplorable living conditions, brutality, and escapes.

Several legislative investigations of the prison took place in the late 1870s, and numerous accounts surfaced in the media of inmates being bitten by guard dogs, whipped, and even killed by guards. Medical care and sanitation were virtually nonexistent in the camps, and inmates died with alarming regularity. For example, between 1876 and 1899, 2,142 prisoners died of various causes throughout the contract camps and state penitentiaries.[6] In this period 3,075 men chose to flee rather than die from disease, sunstroke, or brutality at the hands of the sergeants. In 1876 alone there were 382 escapes in a prisoner population of only 2,367. The horrible living conditions are reflected in the following description by an inmate who worked in a contract coal mine: "He has on no underwear. Just two top pieces. Coat or shirt may have been washed a couple of years ago. He has no bottom nor button holes either in front or on the sleeves. Greasy black in appearance. All stripes obliterated by reason of the dirty grease, etc. Trousers black in appearance and dirty, greasy, and smutty, without any buttons. Fastened around the waist with a horseshoe nail, without belt or suspenders. Too large in the waist by six or eight inches or more. Sleeves or the shirt without buttons and ragged. Shirt fastened in front with a match."[7]

Even though contract leasing was often criticized, it persisted against strong objections for several reasons. First, the prison investigators charged with checking the work sites were often incompetent, corrupt, or both. Not only were these state agents ignorant of the rules governing the care of contract prisoners, but also they often took bribes from the contractors to look the other way and did not report on the barbaric living conditions. Second, the wealthy planters and mining interests had sufficient political clout to maintain a system of cheap (or free) labor. Third, through leasing, roads were built, ore was extracted, and railroad lines were established with minimal state financing. Fourth, the leasing arrangement was a moneymaking operation, and the prison system as a whole was self-sufficient. Finally, life for most Texans in the last quarter of the nineteenth century was very hard, and people had little sympathy for convicted criminals who "got what they deserved." A nineteenth-century observer noted that, for most citizens, "to punish crime, no matter how, is to deter crime; that when broken laws are avenged that is the end; that it is enough to have the culprit in limbo, if only he is made to suffer and not to cost."[8]

By the late 1890s, prisoner leasing scandals had become so regular and embarrassing that officials began to consider other sources of revenue. One attractive alternative was to follow the industrialization of northern prisons. To this end prison officials established a foundry to manufacture iron, but it failed miserably. By 1912 the iron foundry had incurred a debt of over $2 million.

A much sounder plan, however, called for the prison to turn to agriculture. The plan was to create a plantation system that involved using inmate labor to farm state-owned land. Actually, the Harlem unit, a 5,000-acre facility, which also boasted a brick plant, was already operating in this way.[9] Besides making a profit, the plantation plan offered a means of dealing with the increasing numbers of freed slaves who violated state laws. The plan was readily accepted by economy-minded state officials and interested citizens because farming was cost effective (the goal of self-sufficiency) and took the care of prisoners away from exploitative private interests (the humanitarian goal).

The Making of the Prison Farms

Penitentiary officials purchased large tracts in Brazoria County (southwest of Houston), a region that had long produced cotton and sugar. The land was both inexpensive and fertile. Ten Brazoria County plantations became prison sites between 1899 and 1918.[10] In December 1899, three plantations were purchased to form the Clemens farm; five formed the Ramsey farm in 1908; and one plantation each became the Darrington and the Retrieve farms in 1918. The prison board bought land elsewhere as well. In 1907, for example, it bought the 13,000-acre Eastham plantation in Houston County, forty miles northeast of Huntsville. At the same time, officials acquired the Imperial and Blue Ridge farms in 1908 in Fort Bend County, northwest of Houston.

The first two decades of the prison's agricultural operation produced only limited economic success. Then, between 1912 and

1918, the prison system slowly emerged from debt and showed some profit. But the gain was short-lived. By 1923 the prison system was once again in severe debt and continued to operate at a loss until 1947.[11]

The farming venture was no more successful at improving the quality of inmate life than it was at making money. Legislative investigations of the prison system in 1910, 1913, and 1917 revealed guard favoritism, prejudice, neglect, and severe whippings with the "bat," a wooden-handled whip with a three-foot leather strap. The evils of the lease system continued under the prison-plantation system. Criticism continued unabated from the media and from reform-minded citizens. Although some progress was made during the brief tenure of Prison Manager Lee Simmons (1930–1935), inmate living conditions actually deteriorated from 1900 to 1940. During World War II the conditions became so bad that by 1947 Texas prisons were labeled as the nation's worst.

Life on the Farms: 1900–1948

The most striking feature of the newly purchased farms was their extreme isolation. Crude wooden prison buildings with steel latticed windows were erected miles from any towns or cities and most were not even visible from the adjacent highways. These farms were so remote that fencing was not even put up around the camps to forestall escapes. Most of the units had two, three, and even four camps scattered over the farm with total inmate populations of less than 600.

Racial segregation was also practiced. The 1927 inmate distribution for eight farms is indicated in Table 1. Racial segregation in the prison was an official policy in accordance with a 1911 state law. Indeed, the 1921 Rules, Regulations, and Statutory Laws of the Texas Prison System stated on page 32 that "white and negro prisoners shall not be worked together when it can be avoided, and shall be kept separate when not at work."

The "Evil of the Tanks"

Living conditions in the farm camps deteriorated from 1900 to 1947, particularly from 1937 to 1947. Legislative and media investigations documented extensive inmate abuse. Of all the criticisms, none surpassed those aimed at the "evil of the tanks." The only cells in the prison system at this time were at the main prison in Huntsville, or

Table 1 *Racial Distribution of Prisoners on Eight Prison Farms,*
        1927

Unit	Race	Number
Blue Ridge	Whites and hispanics	399
Clemens	Blacks	285
Darrington	Blacks	187
Eastham	Whites	337
Harlem	Whites and blacks	385
Imperial	Whites and blacks	399
Ramsey	Whites and blacks	593
Retrieve	Blacks	214

Source: Annual report, Texas Prison Board, 1927.

Walls Unit. Inmates on the farms lived in large open rooms (40' ×
100') called "tanks," which were filled with bunkbeds.
Physical Features.   Each prison building had between two and four
tanks designed to house 40 to 60 inmates. However, these living
areas were typically overcrowded, and it was not uncommon to find
75, 100, or 150 inmates living in a single tank. Beds, sometimes
stacked four high, often stood right next to each other, and inmates
could actually crawl from one bed to another without touching the
floor. Some inmates with untreated venereal diseases lived among
the others. Not all inmates received a bunk, and some had to sleep
on the floor. Blankets, shoes and socks, straw mattresses, and underwear were also in short supply; sheets were a luxury. An observer at
the Darrington Unit, one of the worst in the system, recalled the ap-
palling conditions. "The Darrington men were cold. The heating
system was out of order [this was in December] and they had few
clothes. The plumbing was leaking everywhere. Of sixteen commodes in the four main tanks there was not a one that was not defective. As for showers, the men had one or two open pipes to the tanks
that housed 59 to 80 men."[12] When the steam heating pipes did
work, they often leaked, keeping the floors wet and the tanks damp.
On the worst farms such as Darrington and Retrieve, inmates bathed
every other week because soap was in such short supply.
Laundry.   When soap was available, laundry facilities were so primi-
tive on the farms that clean clothes were rare. Some farms had no
laundry facilities at all, and inmates had to wash their clothes under
the showers or in sinks. On farms with laundry facilities, washing
clothes was done outdoors in huge iron pots atop brick furnaces

fired by logs.[13] Generally, since inmates received only two clean sets of clothes per week, they regularly worked in the same dirty and wet clothes for several days. In one extreme case, a prison board member was touring a farm and found some inmates who had worn the same set of clothes for five weeks. He commented in disbelief: "It was so rotten and filthy I pulled it to shreds with my thumb and index finger."[14]

Food.   Investigation consistently found the food to be awful. Inmates were supposed to receive one pound of meat per day, but shortages were frequent, and the available meat usually went into a stew to make it go further. In the mid-1940s, oxen used for plowing on one farm were slaughtered and served to the prisoners.[15] Hard biscuits (made from baking powder), "stale beans," and a "slimy stew" made up the usual daily monotonous fare.[16] Although the prison system had dairy cattle, fresh milk was seldom available because many cows were diseased and the farms lacked pasteurization equipment.[17] These terrible conditions sparked frequent food and work strikes among the prisoners.

Cliques, Perversion, and Contraband.   Because the tanks were chronically overcrowded, the guards, who feared the inmates, stayed out of the living areas altogether and generally patrolled outside the building to prevent escapes. To maintain some degree of control and order, the guards utilized convict guards called "building tenders" to enforce order. These inmate guards walked the tanks with sawed-off baseball bats, some openly wore knives, and most maintained order through fear, extortion, and violence.

The lack of a classification program facilitated gang rule, as well as a host of other problems. Even though each unit housed different inmates (e.g., Clemens housed young black first offenders, while the Eastham unit had "incorrigible and vicious whites" over twenty-five), new arrivals were basically thrown into the tanks and expected to survive on their own. No attempts were made to segregate the unsophisticated from hardened criminals. It was not uncommon for weak first offenders or mentally impaired inmates to be housed in tanks with older, aggressive homosexuals, psychopaths, and violent inmates. Uncontrolled exploitation prevailed, and newcomers in general suffered at the hands of veteran, dominant inmates. Perversion was rampant and very open, as testimony during a 1947 legislative investigation reveals: "By large and far, the Captain told us that the greatest crime going on in the prison was sodomy among the men. One inmate related to us that he was attacked at night by 28 men and had been held with a knife at his throat and made to submit. Many men have their girls and fight over them."[18] After touring a prison farm, a prison board member told the media of "vicious sex-perversion" in the tanks: "The tank was filled with older prisoners, incurably hardened criminals. There, on their bunks, were 12 or 15 of these veteran prisoners, each with a young man on his lap, being caressed and fondled. These boys were their 'sweethearts.' . . . [W]ith the arrival of each new youth, he immediately was 'courted' by the older prisoners, who vied with each other to possess him."[19]

The tanks were jungles that precipitated an unusual number of fights, beatings, knifings, and killings, as well as extortion rackets. Inmates strong enough to protect themselves survived, but those who could not were made into "punks."

Narcotics and other forms of contraband were readily available in the tanks if one had the money. Prior to 1948, inmates were allowed to carry five dollars to spend each week at the prison commissary. Money aided gambling, buying and selling of punks, drugs, or alcohol, purchasing of jobs other than fieldwork, and bribing guards.[20]

Three primary reasons account for the presence of illicit goods. First, guards earned between $100 and $130 a month, poor pay that was conducive to bribery and corruption. Second, unescorted inmate trusties drove the trucks that carried supplies between the various prison farms. These inmates made deals off prison grounds and then carried their goods back into the camps.[21] Third, visitors hid contraband on the prison grounds. After visiting hours, inmate trusties, who had access to the prison grounds, made pickups and then smuggled the items to the tanks. An inmate summarized the "wide-openness" of the prisons: "And during that time [1930s–1940s] there was a lot of cash, everything was cash money. . . . There was a lot of killing. A lot of killing over little petty debts, petty thefts, money, hustling money to gamble. Then you could buy whiskey from the trusties traveling back and forth outside. Used to be whiskey hid all in the fields, buried in the fields. Stash it out where you could go get a pint when you needed it. Send a trusty to get it."[22]

Douglas W. Stakes, prison manager in the 1940s, complained to the prison board about trusties driving trucks: "Inmates selected on the basis of their security alone, are now busied in transporting various commodities between units of the system. Very little, if any, supervision is had and such a course is conducive not only to escape but to smuggling various contraband items into the system. To illustrate that this was no light matter, one of our trucks disappeared several years ago and to this date, has not been found."[23]

Mortality and Violence.   Inmates died from such unusual causes as lightning, typhoid, drowning, and crushed skulls from tree-chopping accidents. Death came more frequently, however, from poor care, terrible conditions, and frequent violence. For example, between 1928 and 1945, 83 inmates died of pneumonia, 100 from gunshots, 52 from stabbings, and 37 from sunstroke.[24] Medical care was basically limited to emergencies and, excluding the hospital at the Walls Unit, no other facilities were available. The medical situation was so poor that in the 1940s an eighty-year-old doctor served about 2,000 inmates on the farms.[25] On some farms, aspirin was not even available.

The tank situation precipitated a wide variety of violence among the inmates. A good illustration of the tenor of the violence on the farms was the killing of Clarence William Redwine, the most celebrated inmate murder in Texas prison history. On December 12, 1948, an inmate kitchen worker decapitated Redwine with a cane knife as he sat at a table in the dining hall. The guards found Redwine's body sitting almost upright, his head on the table, and the fingers of one hand clutching a still-lit cigarette.[26] More than 200 inmates who were eating in the dining hall at the time "saw nothing." The tank arrangement made snitching a death sentence for a squealer. A kitchen worker, Ernest Jones, however, later confessed to the killing and stated that Redwine had threatened to kill him. Jones maintained: "It was either him or me and I wanted to get it over with."[27] When guards searched Redwine's body, they found a concealed knife.

Guards frequently shot their guns into the tanks and dining halls to scare and intimidate the prisoners. Inmates on one prison farm asked a visitor to "make [that guard up there] quit shooting down here among us." The visitor was shown .38-caliber slugs fired the previous day that had been dug out of the woodwork.[28] The following accounts from a prison board member come from the Darrington Unit.

> I stood beside a double-decker bunk in a Darrington "tank" and talked with a youngster whose ankle had been smashed by a .38-caliber slug fired into the tank by a guard to frighten another prisoner who had called him a dirty name.
>
> I saw a prisoner ruthlessly shot by a guard because he forgot to shout "Alley" before going into the latrine.[29]

It was not uncommon for guards to shoot out the tank windows or even to enter the inmate dining halls with their pistols drawn, cursing and threatening to kill inmates.[30]

Work Demands

Two established facts describe inmate life on the farms: everyone worked at some job, and if an inmate was not a trusty he labored in the fields. Inmates assigned to the field worked in the "field force," or "line," under an armed, mounted officer. Dog packs and a "high rider" (a guard armed with a carbine) were stationed at vantage points some distance from the squads to prevent escapes. The prisoners worked long hours, and the arduous work was done regardless of the heat, rain, sleet, or cold.

Mechanization on the farm was almost nonexistent. Prisoners used mules and hand tools to plow and plant seed. Sometimes equipment was homemade. When leather tack was in short supply, for example, the inmates wove harnesses and bridles out of corn shucks. The field force used large-bladed garden hoes called aggies to cut grass and weeds ("flatweeding"), make turnrows, clean ditches, and chop cotton. They used cane knives to harvest sugar cane, double-bladed axes to clear land and dig stumps, and bare hands to pick cotton. Furthermore, the squads walked or trotted with shouldered tools to the work site, at times as far as five miles away.

Prison rules specified that fieldwork not exceed eleven hours per day.[31] A typical workday, however, began at the first signs of sunlight and ended at sunset. During cotton-picking season, it was not unusual for the squads to return from the fields in darkness guided by truck lights. The work itself was brutal because "coffee breaks" or other rest periods, except lunch, were not allowed. The noon meal was often brought to the field on a cart called John Henry.[32] Meals in the fields were commonly called weevils and beans. This work routine went on Monday through Friday and a half-day on Saturday. It was the same routine found on slave plantations in the antebellum south.

Mounted guards barked orders, yelled, cursed, taunted, whipped, and drove the inmates. Lagging behind or working too slowly usually led to severe punishment. In the summer months, it was not uncommon for inmates in the field to be driven to the point of passing out from heat exhaustion or sunstroke. Indeed, from 1928 to 1945, 38 prisoners died this way.[33] Those who "fell out" for this reason were handcuffed, thrown in the back of a truck, returned to the prison camp, and punished later for not keeping up. The nature of the work is illustrated in the following quotes from two inmates.

A lot of times we had to come back in the building for dinner [lunch] and jump right back out there and run back our seven or eight miles to work. And you hit that road, boy, you're on the way: you don't tarry, and that was all day. You didn't let up. The weak fell out, they'd haul them back. If one was just too weak to make it walking, he'd just hang on to his buddy's shirttails or belt loop.

They [guards] think a man is a mule, don't ever get tired. But I done some days I'd sooner been dead in hell with the wicked than hear that damned big bell ring [the guards rang a bell to indicate work time]. They'd make you go ahead on from sun to sun. . . . Stand out in the field and eat your dinner. Be raining hard . . . like a cow pissing on a flat rock, wash the beans out a your plate. You keep on working. Rain didn't stop you, cold didn't stop you. There was no sick. You don't have a fever of 102, then you ain't sick. Used to work people dead in the underworld down here.[34]

To prod the inmates along, guards carried rubber hoses, brass knuckles, long wooden poles, pieces of chain attached to sticks, and bullwhips. Guards rode close to an inmate and whipped him with extralong bridle reins or actually rode their horses over him. The guards were not hesitant to fire their shotguns or pistols into the squads. Shotguns sometimes "accidentally" discharged, killing a troublesome inmate. An inmate stated: "Back in that time a man's life wasn't worth no more than a cigarette. When he'd go out he didn't know if he was comin' back in or not. He's liable to get shot down on the turnrow 'cause he left a patch of grass."[35]

Reactions to Work and Tank Life

The harsh working and living conditions regularly precipitated escapes and self-mutilations. For example, in 1922, 302 inmates escaped out of a total population of 4,868, and, between 1927 and 1947, there were 3,164 escapes.[36] It was not unusual for groups of inmates to run away from their squad or even break out of the prison camps. At the Harlem Farm in August 1945, for example, a breakout occurred "when a storm caused the lights to go out and twenty inmates escaped after window bars were cut out." Chances of actually gaining freedom in an escape, however, were only slightly better than surviving being recaptured. Texas prison folklore abounds with stories from this period of inmates who were shot down as they surrendered, killed while "resisting" capture, forcibly drowned, beaten to death in the Brazos River bottoms, or forced to fight and then mangled by the dogs.[37]

Some inmates sought escape from the horrible conditions through self-mutilation, since those with serious injuries were transferred from the farms to the main prison hospital in Huntsville. Forms of self-mutilation included amputating a foot; placing lye in razor or knife cuts to produce lingering open sores; injecting milk, saliva, or kerosene under the skin; as well as intentionally fracturing arms and legs. Severing Achilles tendons and amputating three fingers from one hand, however, seemed to be the preferred mutilations. Severing the Achilles tendon, or "heelstringing," made it impossible for an inmate to walk and, therefore, to work. Heelstringing was only temporary because the tendon could be surgically reconnected, and the inmate could then be returned to the fields. Chopping off three fingers on a hand, however, was a more permanent escape since it then became impossible to handle a hoe or other tool.[38]

The first officially recorded case of self-mutilation in Texas prisons occurred in 1932. Rupert C. Koeninger studied this phenomenon and found "a total of 411 inmates mutilated 877 times since the practice began in 1932. The number increased through each successive four-year period with 25 for 1932–1936; 174 for 1936–1940; 273 for 1940–1944; 341 for 1944–1948. . . . In a study of 100 mutilators, it was found that 58 had mutilated once, 19 twice, 1 three times, 8 four times, 2 six times, 1 eight times, 1 thirteen times, and 1 fourteen times."[39] Prison hospital records reveal that in 1940, for example, doctors treated 20 self-inflicted arm fractures and 2 foot and 1 hand amputations, while in 1942 there were 10 self-inflicted arm fractures, 65 Achilles tendon repairs, and 6 lye burns treated at the Huntsville hospital.[40] Self-abuse reached its peak in 1946 with a total of 119 reported cases.

Prisoners mutilated themselves for several reasons. Some could not endure the brutal work routine or the incessant guard taunts and injured themselves to get away from the farms. Others mutilated themselves to escape from homosexual pressures or other threats from inmates in the tanks. In some cases, groups of inmates mutilated themselves to protest the terrible living and working conditions.

The high rate of escapes and self-mutilation (as well as stabbings and murders) further documents the limited ability or inclination of Texas prison officials to control or care for inmates. Inmates virtually escaped at will and abused themselves or others with little interference from officials. These inmate responses underscore the important fact that prisoners in these times were quite powerless; there were no outside agents, certainly not the courts, to take the prisoners' side. Inside there were no grievance procedures; prisoners were essentially at the mercy of prison officials. This state of affairs was exacerbated by the often poor quality of officials charged with supervising prisoners and running the organization.

The Quality of Prison Guard Life

Living conditions for guards were little better than those for inmates. The guards worked twelve to fourteen hours a day, had few days off (sometimes one day a month), and were paid between $100 and $133 a month. Although many had little formal education (many were illiterate), the prison gave them no training. They received no uniform, and, if their job called for riding a horse, they even had to supply their own saddles. The state provided only their weapons. While the warden and a few other top-ranking staff lived in homes on the grounds, the ordinary guards lived in a room (or tank) inside the prison building. It was not unusual for the wall separating the guard and inmate quarters to have gaping holes, which promoted verbal wars and aided the contraband business. Such working and living conditions made it difficult to attract and retain qualified guards, particularly during the World War II years.

Through the early decades of the twentieth century the majority of Texas guards were often older men who could no longer work their own farms but could sit astride a horse and watch convicts. Their age helped precipitate inmate escapes and other inmate disciplinary problems. A 1948 newspaper article commented on the guards: "Last week a sixty-five year old guard dropped dead while guarding 20 of the worst Negro prisoners in the state. Seven inmates have been killed this year because of the lack of trained personnel."[41] D. W. Stakes, prison manager in 1946, characterized the prison system's employees: "In many cases, they were aged and infirm; nevertheless our need was such that we were forced to employ them and as a consequence, suffer escapes and other unnecessary reverses. Some of these men were found to be illiterate; others sadists; others so unintelligent and incapacitated that they were a distinct menace to safety or society at large."[42] Young, strong inmates easily overpowered or duped such employees. It was not uncommon for several inmates to attack a mounted guard, take his horse and shotgun, and escape. It is not surprising that greater freedom was given by prison managers to selected prisoners to keep their fellow prisoners in line.

The reasons for termination from prison employment reveal something about the quality of men hired. Table 2 lists the number of men discharged for given reasons between 1927 and 1937 according

Table 2 *Reasons for Discharging Officers, 1927–1937*

Incompetence	35
Drunk and disorderly	26
Sleeping on duty	26
No cause	24
Trafficking and trading with inmates	7
Fighting and cursing inmates	6
Whipping a convict in the woods	1
Passing guns into prison	1
Killing another guard	1

Source: Guard Record, Texas State Penitentiary, Books 6–7.

to prison personnel records. Numbers reflect guards at the farms and at the main prison in Huntsville.

These reasons for termination suggest a rather unreliable and probably transient employee population. A veteran prison officer explained: "In those days, when a train stopped nearby some guys, I mean bums and hobos, would jump off and come to work for the system. Once they got some money they just hopped another freight and they were gone."[43] Some guards worked a month, resigned, went to another unit and worked for several months and quit, then went to another unit and repeated the process.

But the very nature of guard work also accelerated employee resignations. Guards, like inmates, worked in the rain, cold weather, and blazing heat and ate poor food. On the farms, guards were expected to ride horses to and from the fields. Riding ten or fifteen miles on a horse was anything but easy. One old-time guard commented on the work: "I seen many a man get off that horse and have his legs buckle and fall flat on his face. If you wasn't used to it, that horse would wear you out. I seen men with their pants stuck to their legs. In the summer, you'd sweat and that saddle would chafe your ass so bad you'd get big blisters inside your thighs. I seen men pull their pants off and pull off them blisters at the same time. They'd ride to the field with open sores on their butts and legs."[44] Many individuals who could not adapt to such demands on the job quit. Others resigned because they simply could not accept isolation, poor pay, or life around prisoners.

Because reliable men were hard to find and harder to keep, the prison system was continuously shorthanded. Stakes described the two consequences of being short of staff in the mid-1940s: "At times, because of guard shortages, we were unable to take men to the fields

Table 3 *Official Deviance That Did Not Preclude Rehiring,*
1927–1937

Reason for Initial Termination	Number Rehired
Under the influence of liquor	17
Cursing inmates	4
Cruelty to inmates	3
Kicking prisoners in the ribs	2
Threatening inmates	2
Permitting a convict to beat a mule with a trace chain	1
Shooting another guard while on duty	1
Stealing an inmate's property	1
Carrying a state pistol while off duty, getting drunk, and being arrested for firing at a Negro	1

Source: Guard Record, Texas State Penitentiary, Books 6–7.

for work. In other cases, in order to work the men, we have had to send out squads with as many as 37 men in them. [A squad typically had from 20 to 25 men.] In one particular case, practically all the inmates in the squad broke and ran."[45] Guard shortages exacerbated the depredations in the tanks when men remained locked up instead of going to work. Limited manpower also led to escapes while the squads were in the fields.

For these reasons, the prison system regularly had to rehire some of the men it had fired, often for excellent reasons. Table 3 represents the number of guards who were discharged for some cause but later rehired between 1927 and 1937. Although some officers' transgressions were such that they were actually "blacklisted," many found their way back to state employment on the prison farms.

Social Control on the Farm

Despite poor physical conditions, inferior staff, and inmate abuse, the Texas system was not without written policies to guide the treatment of prisoners. From 1900 (and probably earlier) rule books carefully laid out prison regulations governing inmate behavior. Rules for inmates were characteristically moralistic. The 1921 prison rule book, for example, informed inmates that they were forbidden to be excused from Sunday services, to mutiny, to make unnecessary noise, to spit on the floors, to smoke indoors, to stare at visitors, to possess weapons, to gamble, or to curse.[46]

Rule violations by prisoners resulted in various official punishments stipulated by state law, such as revocation of privileges or reduction in grade.[47] The official, legal punishments were as follows:

1. Confinement in dark cell.
2. Solitary confinement.
3. Chaining or strapping up, in dark cell or other cell.
4. Deprivation of privileges, in whole or part.
5. Forfeiture of commutation, in whole or part.
6. Reduction in grade.
7. Clothing in stripes.
8. Bread and water diet.
9. Whipping.[48]

These punishments had formally defined limitations. For example, bread-and-water diets were not to exceed thirty-six hours, and confinement in a dark cell was not to exceed forty-eight hours at one time. Only the prison manager or his assistant was to punish convicts. Other, informal, sanctions were "positively forbidden." Nonetheless, these latter sanctions occurred regularly, since the rules, however elaborate, were not particularly binding on the staff. Informal sanctions were usually extensions or distortions of formal punishments.

The most infamous and highly controversial inmate punishment in Texas was whipping. Men were whipped on bare buttocks, with twenty lashes being the maximum number. A 1911 law stipulates the nature of what was called the "bat" and how it was to be used: "The strap used in administering this punishment shall be made of leather, not over 2 1/2 inches wide and 24 inches long, attached to a wooden handle. No convict shall be whipped until same has been authorized by at least two members of the Prison Commission upon their written order, and such order must be executed in the presence of the Prison Physician; utmost care must be made not to break the skin."[49]

Prison officials believed strongly that the bat was a necessary and useful tool in managing prisoners. According to Lee Simmons, "the bat to a prison warden was like spurs to a cowboy."[50] This sentiment meant that the bat was frequently used. Between 1915 and 1927, over 1,000 whipping orders were issued by the prison commission. The orders in most cases called for the punishment of two or more inmates. A typical whipping order is as follows: "Whipping Order No. 692 was issued to Captain D. J. Henderson Manager of the Blue Ridge Farm for punishment of Manuel Aguirre No. 51272; Rapeto

Trevino No. 50420; and Matias Jeminez No. 51629. Account: Mutinous conduct and refusing to obey order of Captain T. C. Rozell to get on the barrel—20 lashes each; also Andres Castenada No. 52817. Account: cursing guard Sid Fluker calling him a G—— D—— M—— F——. 20 lashes."[51] Although the prison commission was required to carefully review each whipping request, only one request was denied from 1915 to 1927. In this twelve-year period, not less than 1,500 prisoners experienced the bat. In most of these instances, the whipping was for what officials considered a serious rule violation. Table 4, which presents a sample of 100 whipping orders by offense from 1915 to 1927, indicates what offenses were considered serious. Significantly, most of these offenses reflect prisoner questioning of authority or failure to accept his place.

Though formal rules regulated whipping, abuses were common. A doctor was required to examine the prisoner before and after a bat session. But medical personnel were few, and this requirement was often waived as was the prohibition against breaking the skin. One old-time convict commented on the bat:

> You could tell all them guys what got whipped. They couldn't set down, had to lay on their stomach and other than that he

Table 4 *Prisoner Offenses That Were Sanctioned by Whipping*

Offense	Number
Fighting or cursing building tenders	12
Fighting and other assaults	12
Laziness	12
Impudence	11
Escape and attempts to	9
Refuse to work	8
Mutiny	8
Destroying crops	7
Possession of knife	4
Cursing an officer	4
Picking trashy cotton	4
Refusing to get on barrel	3
Sodomy	2
Sodomy with a mule	1
Stubbornness	1
Stealing state property	1
Writing obscene notes to a white girl	1

Source: Minutes of Texas Prison Board meetings, 1915–1927.

couldn't lay no other way. All the back part back there would be just raw blood. . . . One time Captain Powell was whipping a boy with that bat and he kept a hollerin', "oh lordy, oh lordy!" And then finally he bust him again and he say, "Oh lordy, Captain!" And captain said, "I thought you'd get around to me directly." Cause he wanted him to know that Jesus wasn't whippin' him it was him whippin' him. And Jesus couldn't help him neither. The man would step down out a his saddle and reach and get that bat, pull it across under his boot and step back over you, your britches down, then he'd rare back and bust you one. As the leather'd leave, the hide'd leave with it.[52]

It was common to have presigned whipping orders on the farms to prevent delays and ensure immediate punishment. On many occasions the guards whipped inmates first and then obtained the necessary paperwork from the prison board.

Clearly, despite the presence of formal guides for punishment, guards punished and otherwise dealt with prisoners primarily through informal means. Beatings, relentless verbal abuse, intimidations, whippings for violating unwritten rules (e.g., masturbating), and terrorization were the guards' primary means of social control. One common unofficial punishment involved forcing three or four inmates to stand on a barrel for several hours. Another consisted of handcuffing an inmate's hands over his head to the bars of the tank with just his tiptoes on the floor. The guards then clamped down the handcuffs to restrict the flow of blood to the hands. Inmates were also sentenced to "ride the pole," sit astride a six-foot-long 4" × 4" length of wood, for several hours.

Efforts at Reform

The poor conditions and harsh discipline in the Texas prisons had long made the organization and its managers suspect in the eyes of many legislators and citizens. The result was a series of investigations in the first half of this century. One of the most important of these took place in 1924. In that year the penitentiary investigating committee of the Texas Legislature conducted an exhaustive study of the prison system and made two key recommendations for reorganization. The first was the abolition of the board of commissioners and the creation, in 1927, of the Texas Prison Board (to become the Texas Board of Corrections in 1957). The second was the creation of the role of general manager for the system, whose job it would be to supervise and coordinate the work on the various prison farms. Under this new plan, the board would make policy, and the general manager would put it into operation throughout the system. Other recommendations approved included the creation of such inmate programs as Sunday schools, education, recreation, vocational training, and the monthly prisoner paper, *The Echo*.

These reforms, however, did not greatly improve the quality of inmate life or discipline. Money and general support for prison reform continued to be in short supply. The Great Depression and World War II sapped both such that prison reform was a side issue at best through the 1930s and the early 1940s. The shootings, beatings, and general abuses in the tanks continued. As World War II was drawing to a close, however, state officials rediscovered the problem of the prison system. The farms were losing money and were far from being self-sufficient. Moreover, a legislative investigation conducted by the members of the prison board in late 1943 reported the continued existence of brutal and sadistic guards, rampant escapes, inmate self-mutilation, and other abuses.

Significantly, it was citizen pressure that finally brought about the fundamental improvements that official committees had recommended for decades. For example, Judge C. V. Compton of Dallas and Mittie Waters, a San Antonio social worker, kept media attention focused on Texas prison conditions and helped get the bat abolished in 1941.

The most consequential private impetus to reform, however, came from Mrs. C. T. Schaedel and the Committee on Prison Work of the Texas State Council of Methodist Women. These church members persuaded the prison board to hire Austin MacCormick, executive director of the Osborne Association, a prison reform organization, to survey the Texas prison system. MacCormick toured the farms in February 1945, making an oral report to the prison board and the governor, and presented his findings to the legislature in 1947. MacCormick blasted the prison system, citing in great detail the lack of inmate classification, the horrible conditions in the tanks, the volume of escapes, and the presence of incompetent guards. His recommendations included hiring more and better personnel, construction of cells instead of tanks, adopting up-to-date treatment programs, relying less on farming, training guards, and hiring a rehabilitation and personnel director.

In an effort to stir public support for reform, the Texas State Council of Methodist Women mailed MacCormick's report to state legislators and interested citizens. When another legislative investigation, conducted in April 1947, echoed MacCormick's findings, the state was finally prepared to make fundamental prison reforms.[53]

Building the Texas System of Control

When Governor Beauford H. Jester took office in 1947, he was prepared to clean up the prison system, one of his most ardent campaign promises. He recognized that the prison board had to provide strong leadership, while the legislature had to provide financial support. One of his first actions was to call an emergency meeting of the prison board during which he asked for and received several resignations. Jester needed a loyal board, and with these resignations he was able to appoint supporters dedicated to reform, including Wilbur C. Windsor, the new chairman of the prison board. When, in early November 1947, Stakes resigned as prison manager, the governor and the board were ready to hire a prison manager who not only shared their commitment to reform but also had the strength and the ability to achieve it. That man was Oscar B. Ellis.

Reform under Oscar B. Ellis

Chairman Windsor, a wealthy oilman, rancher, and banker from Tyler, and board member Bert A. Stufflebeme, a prominent banker from Grand Prairie, began a nationwide search for someone to manage the Texas Prison System. Windsor paid for this search with his own money. While observing prison practices in several neighboring states, the two board members were encouraged by numerous professionals to visit Ellis' Shelby County Penal Farm operation in Memphis, Tennessee. This prison farm had gained nation-wide prestige for its livestock operation, diversified farming program, self-sufficiency, and inmate education and work program, on the one hand, and its low rates of violence, escapes, riots, and guard brutality, on the other.[54]

Close investigation by the two board members revealed that Ellis' most impressive accomplishment was in fiscal management. Ellis took over the prison farm in 1940 when it was a break-even operation, and by 1947 the farm was a revenue-making business. In 1946, for example, the farm had made a $173,000 profit.[55] Under Ellis' management the institution became a showplace that was visited by thousands each year. While touring this facility, Windsor and Stufflebeme were greatly impressed with Ellis' ability to mix prison practices and farming and to make a profit in the process. The two were convinced that Ellis was the man to do the same thing in Texas. Windsor was so impressed by Ellis that he wrote: "Sam Houston and Davey Crockett came to Texas from Tennessee and made their names immortal in Texas history. Mr. Ellis has a similar opportunity, and it is my belief that he will fulfill our greatest expectations."[56]

In late November 1947, the prison board unanimously voted to hire Ellis; he officially took over on January 1, 1948. The board also voted in favor of inspecting the Shelby County Penal Farm. In early December 1947, the nine-member board, five prison officials, and newspaper reporters from Houston, Dallas, Tyler, Fort Worth, Texarkana, Beaumont, and Grand Prairie left Texas in a rented Pullman railroad car (paid for by Windsor) bound for Memphis. Windsor arranged this two-day tour primarily as a media event to sell Ellis and his methods to the citizens of Texas.

The reporters on the trip obliged. They wired stories back to Texas about the Shelby County "model" prison. Throughout December 1947, major Texas newspapers featured articles on Ellis and his phenomenal success in Tennessee. The hiring of Ellis was hailed as a "milestone in Texas prison history." Photographs showed Ellis and board members standing next to prize bulls, observing well-kept pastures, and touring clean prison buildings. Reporters also interviewed prisoners who told of "Pappy" Ellis' "firm but fair" treatment and the absence of guard brutality. Soon after these stories appeared, editorials in Texas newspapers praised the prison board for its decision in hiring Ellis. Editorials labeling Ellis as a ray of hope and the best medicine for Texas' prison woes helped precipitate a grass roots prison reform movement.[57]

When the tour group left Memphis, they returned to Texas and immediately visited all the prison farms. Board members and reporters entered the tanks and talked with the prisoners about the poor conditions. This tour gave the reporters a firsthand look at the monumental task facing Ellis in the hope that media coverage would encourage public support. The tour and Ellis' impending arrival led to many serialized news stories throughout December 1947, documenting the brutal conditions on the farms.[58] For the first time, the public received accurate information about prison conditions not only from the press but also from board members.

During this carefully orchestrated media blitz, the Ellis Plan to revamp the prisons was unveiled:

1. Ask the legislature to finance a minimum housing and industrial expansion program, including an isolation building for incorrigibles at Huntsville.

2. Establish a merit system by which prisoners may better their own lots by doing their jobs and staying out of trouble.
3. Obtain pay raises for guards and provide better housing for them.
4. Make the prison system self-sufficient by growing more vegetables and foodstuff and increasing the industrial output to be sold to other state institutions at a slight profit. (A change in the state law would be required because the system was allowed to sell items at cost, not for profit.)
5. Modernize farm and industrial operations.[59]

In late January 1948, Governor Jester toured the prison system and afterward publicly endorsed the Ellis Plan and its $4 million price tag. Despite the governor's support and the growing public sentiment, the prison board recognized that lasting prison reform could not be accomplished without legislative support, both financial and moral. Yet, for decades, state politicos had resisted the idea of reform. How could the board convince the legislature of the need for change?

The Role of Theatrics in Prison Reform.   Throughout February and March 1948, Ellis and several prison board members stumped the state to acquire citizen support. They pled the cause of reform before Rotary clubs, chambers of commerce, and junior chambers of commerce. The most forceful and eloquent speaker was prison board member B. A. Stufflebeme. He met almost daily with various civic organizations and groups; his message was that Texas prisons were "so rotten they were beyond description" and were actually worse than the Nazi concentration camps in Europe.[60] In highly publicized "men only" speaking engagements he detailed the evils of the tank system and spoke candidly about sex perversion, guard violence, and inmate self-mutilation. At one such meeting in Dallas he said: "After my first visit to Darrington and Retrieve I went back to my room and bawled like a baby."[61] He told the same group: "You might as well sentence a man to hell as send him to the Darrington and Retrieve Farms."[62]

Stufflebeme's one-man road show received constant press coverage. Editorials demanded that the legislature "clean up the prisons now."[63] Ellis, in his speaking engagements, called for a people's lobby to support his program and to get the plan through the next legislative session. Public opinion totally supported Ellis and his plan. Then, in early March 1948, the prison board met and unanimously endorsed the Ellis Plan. The media campaign had its intended effect on the legislature because on March 7, 1948, it agreed to provide the $4 million required by the Ellis Plan. The next day Governor Jester signed the reforms into law.

Establishing Order and Control. From 1948 to his death in 1962, Ellis made many improvements in the prison system. Educational, recreational, and religious programs were reorganized and expanded. A plastic surgery program was instituted to repair inmate physical deformities. Provisions were made for civilian teachers in high school and vocational courses. He improved living conditions for inmates by putting televisions in the dormitories, segregating young from old and first offenders from repeaters, and building single cells to ensure inmate safety and to relieve overcrowding. Modern laundries, kitchens, and dining rooms were built. He introduced tractor-pulled trailers for inmates to ride to and from the fields so they would not have to walk (or run).

Ellis also made important improvements in security and control. He built the maximum security block at the Walls Unit, called the "Shamrock," to house incorrigibles. He also instituted a "no work, no eat" policy and ordered the farms to stop transferring inmate self-mutilators to Huntsville. Mutilators were kept on the farms and not rewarded with a transfer to a nicer environment. This policy, together with other improvements in conditions, dramatically reduced mutilations from 87 cases in 1947 to 0 cases in 1953.

Ellis also tried to improve the security force. In his first eighteen months, the new manager fired 50 guards for trafficking and trading with the inmates.[64] Inmate escapes dropped from 126 in 1947 to 12 in 1962. Guards were given uniforms, raises, and clean living quarters. Most important, Ellis stopped the flagrant killing of inmates by guards. In 1947 guards killed nine prisoners, while from 1948 to 1962 guards killed only seventeen. These accomplishments in control and order were achieved despite a prisoner population increase from 5,760 in 1948 to 12,129 in 1962.

Ellis was opposed to brutality and took steps to systematize discipline across the units. Some guards, even a warden, were fired for excessive use of force against inmates and for general abuse. Even though the flagrant and sensational abuses were eliminated, handcuffing inmates to bars, telling them to stand on overturned wooden Coke cartons, and other informal punishments remained routine elements of the control regimen.[65] The use of physical coercion to discipline inmates was a long-standing Texas tradition that even Ellis could not eliminate. Nor did he eliminate the building tender system as he had publicly stated he would when he became director. The traditional use of force by officers and BTs was less blatant, but it remained.

Of all Ellis' reforms, none surpassed those he accomplished in the agricultural, industrial, and construction programs. In 1949 he hired Byron W. Frierson, a Texas A&M University graduate, to manage the entire agricultural operation. Under his careful management, the prison system spent over $1 million to mechanize the farms. Mechanization and new varieties of fiber and food crops meant greater efficiency and profits. Between 1953 and 1958, for example, the prisoners' agricultural operation made an average of $3 million yearly.[66] The cattle and livestock operation was also modernized and made profitable. Better-equipped dairies were constructed to provide inmates with fresh milk and other dairy products. Prison industries, such as a textile mill and a mop and broom factory, were expanded to provide in 1958 an all-time high income of over $5 million. These measures reduced the inmate cost to the state per day from $4.00 in the 1940s to $1.24 in 1958.[67]

In 1955, over 400 inmates were sleeping on the floors of Texas prisons; Ellis engineered a media blitz that showed the extensive overcrowding and dilapidated physical plants of some farms, especially the Eastham farm. In numerous speeches to civic organizations Ellis stated that the only way out of the crisis was to construct new prisons. The legislature agreed and appropriated the money. One new unit was built—Ferguson—and Eastham and others were renovated. Labor costs for this construction work was minimal since almost all the work was done by Texas inmates.

Ellis was a charismatic administrator and a skilled politician who made sure that the prison system's progress received constant positive attention. He was sensitive to public relations and used the media to cast the organization in a good light. Ellis gave newspaper reporters virtual free rein to cover the prisons. Whenever an escape or stabbing occurred, Ellis personally called reporters about the incident. In return, reporters (such as Don Reid of the *Huntsville Item*) constantly provided updates on the prison system's remarkable progress and stated that continued financial support was necessary. These stories were then picked up by the wire services and printed across the country. Ellis also stumped the state to maintain support for his operation. He said, "You can't run a prison sitting behind a desk."[68] Ten years after his appointment, Texas prisons, once regarded as "hell holes," were being touted as prison showplaces of order and efficiency. In 1957, to reflect this transformation and to be in step with the national corrections trend toward rehabilitation, the state legislature, at Ellis' request, renamed the prison system the Texas Department of Corrections.

To further solidify the prison system's position and reputation,

Ellis periodically invited Austin MacCormick back to inspect the prisons. These inspections were carefully orchestrated media events that had a definite purpose. MacCormick wrote glowing progress reports that heaped praise on Ellis, the prison board, and the legislature for its willingness to support the prison system. Furthermore, MacCormick always attended the American Correctional Association meetings, where he "lost no opportunity to tell prison officials from other states of the remarkable progress made by the Texas Prison System."[69] Joseph Ragen, the nationally recognized warden of Stateville Prison in Illinois, toured the Texas system in 1958, and he, too, lavished praise on Ellis and all aspects of the organization.

The Ellis Plan laid the groundwork for the Texas style of prison control in several respects. First, inmate safety was enhanced and disciplinary and control procedures were systematized and made more predictable. Second, the prison system began to meet consistently its goals of near self-sufficiency. Economic success of the prison made it easier for Ellis to make state government an ally of the prison. Such a legislative relationship (including the support of three governors), in turn, eliminated legislative investigations and scrutiny while ensuring that the lawmakers approved all budgetary requests by near unanimous vote. Third, he made the press an ally of the prison system as well. Reporters constantly wrote prison progress reports which noted Ellis' achievements and maintained public support for the system. Finally, Ellis received national attention for his remarkable success and established the Texas system as a role model for other state systems. Prison practitioners from throughout the country and the world came to Texas to observe the operation. In 1959, he was elected president of the American Correctional Association, the first southerner to hold that post. He was regarded as one of the best prison managers in America.

Through his co-optation of the press and prison commentators, such as Austin MacCormick, Ellis was able to neutralize outside interference in the prison system. He was thus free to focus on internal order and control. The front stage of the Texas prison system was near perfect; the prisons appeared to be efficient, clean, and well managed. Ellis was so successful, however, that everyone forgot about the daily prison grind. The general upgrading of facilities did not transform the prisons into conflict-free institutions. A veteran convict describes in vivid detail the backstage aspects of inmate life in the Ellis era:

The lights came on at 5:30 am. The first fight would usually be over someone's locker box being burgled in the night. You prob-

ably wouldn't get the guilty party but that wasn't the issue. As
long as you knocked someone in the head, you were sticking up
for your "rights." The second fight would be over wash basins.
Sixty men and only 6 wash basins. Pecking orders and associa-
tions could get you an early shot at a basin, lack of same could
get you a punch in the eye or a dirty face for breakfast. Breakfast
in the messhall was the second arena provided you didn't wind
up with a fat lip from jostling someone in the Hall. Messhall
flunkies rarely kept their jobs over a week for they were the subject of general abuse over the food they served. While you were
eating breakfast, more burglaries transpired in your dorm area
and more confrontations would be in the making. Work time set
your teeth on edge. You had to make it out of the building in
time to get close to the front of the squad. Lead row and push
row went out first and you tried to get as close to them as possible to obtain first pick of the hoe rack and to secure a seat on
the trailer. A good hoe could make or break your morning or
afternoon work period. Since there was never enough good hoes,
there would always be fights around the hoe racks followed by
fights in the trailers over seats. When your line caught in, you
wanted to be close to the lead row or tail row since the center of
the squad moved back and forth like an accordion. If you wanted
a good position you had to fight to get it and then fight to keep
it. When the water boys brought the buckets, with the cups attached, there would be more fights. The lead row, push row, and
tail row were guaranteed a cup. All others scrambled for theirs.
Homosexuals had red cups and used them only, or else. Natu-
rally, a Boss would never leave you a long enough break for all
the inmates to water or drink their fill, that would have been the
sensible thing to do. There were many things, but never that.
Fights over jostlings in the hoe line were numerous. The width
of your cut in flatweeding was critical. If you were to keep up
with the squad, if you fell behind, you would find yourself cutting a three foot swath while everyone else was cutting one body
width. Fight time again. At noon, back on the trailers, scramble
for your seat, scramble for a basin when you got inside the building. Scramble for a seat in the messhall, more thefts while the
line was out. When you returned in the afternoon from the field,
new problems. A scramble in the laundry for clothes and then
four shower nozzles for 60 men and they were never even close
to the right temperature. If someone in the shower brushed you
with his penis it was mandatory to try to knock his brains out or
else he would show up that night trying to punk you.

You had to stand up for yourself. Cliques, groups, friends and acquaintances could make serving time easier. It did not vitiate the first rule which was and will always be, rely on yourself. Graveyards are full of convicts that relied on a friend to watch their back. Human life then had no value except to the person who was standing in the shoes. Did we fight? Indeed we did.[70]

Ellis' changes did not penetrate or drastically alter the backstage inmate living conditions on the farms. Living in the tanks and newly constructed cell blocks was as it had always been—violent, brutal, and authoritarian.

The George J. Beto Administration

In November 1961, Ellis died of a heart attack while attending a prison board meeting. Within two hours after Ellis' death, board chairman H. H. Coffield called George John Beto, who was then president of Concordia Theological Seminary in Springfield, Illinois, and asked him to become the new director of the Texas Department of Corrections. Beto initially declined, saying his first responsibility was to the Lutheran church and the seminary. Coffield, intent on hiring Beto, told the college president that if he became director he would also be chief of chaplains in the Texas system. This last sufficiently sweetened the offer, and Beto began his duties as director on March 1, 1962.

Although George Beto did not bring personal experience in correctional administration to the job, he had spent a decade working avocationally in the field. After his training in the Lutheran ministry in the 1930s, Beto was sent to Austin, Texas, as an instructor at Concordia College where he eventually became president. While in Austin, he obtained his master's degree in medieval history and his doctorate in educational administration. In 1953, Dr. Beto, at Governor Allen Shivers' request, began serving on the Texas Prison Board. For nearly seven years Beto took an active interest in the prison system, particularly inmate education and religious programs. He was an advocate of Ellis' policies and frequently spoke in public about the success of the prison system. He also regularly visited the prisons and became familiar with inmates and staff alike.

Beto's prison management philosophy was understandably influenced by Ellis. As a prison board member in Texas, Beto was able to observe Ellis' style and especially his ability to work the legislature and cultivate the press. But Beto learned as much or more from

Joseph Ragen. Beto first met Ragen in 1953 at the American Correctional Association meeting in Toronto. Through regular correspondence and visits to the Stateville complex, Beto and Ragen became close friends. Their friendship was facilitated when, in 1959, Beto was called to Springfield to become president of Concordia Theological Seminary. Shortly thereafter, Ragen persuaded Governor Otto Kerner to appoint Beto to the Illinois Parole Board. As a parole commissioner, Beto met monthly with inmates to discuss parole plans and other prison matters. In this role, he gained valuable inmate experience, and his philosophy of prison management continued to be shaped by Ragen. Whenever Beto was called to Chicago for church business, he took the train and stopped over in Joliet.[71] He stayed the night with Ragen in his apartment at Stateville, and there they discussed prison issues.

From his experience as a prison and parole board member as well as from his contacts with Ellis and, particularly, Ragen, whom he called his mentor,[72] Beto accrued a stock of knowledge about prisons and, especially, about controlling prisoners. The parallels of inmate control structures between Stateville and Huntsville are very clear. This indirect prison experience, coupled with his education, political experience, and insight, made Beto the perfect successor to Ellis.

Beto assumed directorship of an organization that was considered by many at the time to be a model prison system. Beto's stated plan was to expand the Ellis program of inmate control and treatment programs. But the transition was not smooth. Shortly after he took over, the inmates at the Harlem farm staged a work strike, or "buck." He drove to the prison and went straight to the field to talk with the prisoners, which proved unproductive. Beto wanted to avoid anything that looked like a draw. He had to win to demonstrate to the guards and inmates that he and the guards were in control. Beto tells of his decision at that critical moment and of the consequences:

> So . . . I put four or five of those wardens on horseback armed
> with wet rope, or rubber hoses, or some device of that nature;
> whatever was available, and instructed them to go out and put
> number one hoe squad to work which they did, and there was a
> flurry of excitement and number one went to work in a hurry
> and the rest of the inmates followed. The story of that buck and
> the manner in which it was solved, went out over the system
> that night by employees and by convicts. The grapevine carried it
> and someone said: "That preacher came down here with a base-
> ball bat in one hand and a Bible in the other."[73]

In this situation and others to follow, Beto made it clear that officials would control the prison and that inmates would be utterly subordinate. Beto's decision in this instance reflects the Ragen philosophy of maintaining tight disciplinary control. In specific, Beto strictly adhered to the basic Ragen maxim: "You run it [the prison] or they [prisoners] run it. It can't be both." Beto firmly established that he was running it.

Beto believed that close personal contact with inmates and staff was a critical element in prison management. He visited all the farms at least once every ten days to two weeks. He often showed up unannounced at night just to see how things were going and to talk with inmates and guards. Beto's ability to recall their names from previous visits heightened his own mystique. This penchant for checking on the farms in this manner earned him the nickname Walking George. On many occasions he walked into crowded inmate dining halls, tasted the food, and walked out. He believed in making a big show or performance in front of the inmates. It worked because the inmates knew that Beto would not tolerate poor food or other dirty prison conditions. The new director was a stickler for keeping the prisons spotless and having every tool in its place. This use of the big show and flair parallels Joe Ragen's management style of walking unarmed and unescorted in the Stateville yard every Sunday to "talk with the boys." Beto, like Ellis and Ragen, had enormous rapport with the inmates, but he kept them at arm's length; he never shook hands with an inmate.

Beto's visits ensured that TDC policies were being carried out in specific units. Equally important, these visits enabled him to develop an extensive information network. He knew what was happening on the farms. Wardens soon learned to "be on their toes" because Beto would soon be around to see if his policies were being implemented. On one occasion, while en route to Austin in the TDC airplane (Beto purchased the plane in 1962), he heard over the plane's radio that a warden was trying to find the prison veterinarian to treat a cow. Beto broke in and told the warden to hire a "free-world" veterinarian and pay for it with an emergency purchase order. Afterward the warden said: "Gentlemen, when that preacher is flying over Austin and can tell me on the radio to hire a free-world vet, there is a new day dawning." [74]

Beto's unannounced visits essentially extended the influence of the central TDC office over unit managers and operations, reminding the wardens and their staffs that they were not beyond central office control. Beto took steps to refine and further formalize the system's inmate disciplinary procedures. In 1962, the prison board approved the following punishments, listed in order of severity: counsel and reprimand, give a suspended sentence, take away points earned through good behavior, take away privileges, place overnight in solitary confinement, make inmate stand on Coke box (abolished several years later), give extra duty, take away good time, demote in class so less good time is earned, place in solitary confinement up to fifteen days, and transfer to disciplinary unit (the Shamrock, later abolished in 1962). Beto wanted wardens to employ the least severe punishment first and then escalate severity only after continued rule violations.

Initially, Beto, like Ellis, contemplated abolishing the building tender system. However, he soon realized that these inmate guards were too important to eliminate. The use of these convict elites was also in keeping with Ragen's proactive control philosophy of divide and conquer the inmate society through the active use of informers. Ragen controlled Stateville through an extensive snitch network, and Beto did the same with the building tender system.

Information and relentless supervision were the keys to control and order in the Texas system. Ellis initiated this management style in Texas, but Beto honed it. There were only seventeen inmate homicides during Beto's ten-year tenure. This emphasis on tight control and relentless supervision came to epitomize the Texas Department of Corrections.

Beto expanded the prison system's industrial program. Under Ellis, the agricultural operation flourished, but industry was limited to such operations as a textile mill, a shoe factory, and a license plate plant. Although Beto improved the livestock operation, he was more interested in industry because most inmates were from urban areas and they needed to learn useful trades. Particularly important to the industrial program's growth was the passage in 1963 of a law that mandated that prison industries sell goods to other tax-supported state agencies. Prison officials then developed numerous industries such as a dental laboratory, garment factories, a bus repair shop, a tire recapping plant, a coffee roasting plant, a wood shop, and a records conversion plant, which both employed thousands of inmates and aided other state agencies. The industrial program was also an incentive because it took the inmate out of field labor. In time, the industrial program rivaled the agriculture program in prestige and moneymaking capacity.

During Beto's ten-year directorship, the prisoner population grew from 12,000 to 16,000, a slow growth pattern. However, he took several measures to limit growth. For example, every Christmas many inmates went home early when he backdated the good time of inmates near their discharge date. He also reduced population pressure by increasing cell space at several units and by building other prisons. During his administration, he oversaw the building of the 2,000-man Ellis Unit, the Diagnostic Unit (a reception and classification prison), and the Jester Pre-Release Center and secured funding for the Coffield Unit, a 3,000-man institution.

These improvements to the physical plant, together with the industrial and agricultural operations, supported TDC's claim of being the number one prison system in the nation. Officials believed that the prison system personified Texas; it was the biggest and the best. To maintain what appeared to be a sterling reputation, one regularly underscored by prison officials, the legislature approved virtually every funding request from TDC with little or no debate.

The greatest reason, however, for the success that Ellis and Beto enjoyed with the legislature was the presence of a strong board of corrections, and, especially, of Chairman H. H. Coffield. A wealthy businessman and rancher, Coffield was shrewd, dictatorial, and powerful. When Beto needed assistance from the state or private sector and lacked the necessary personal leverage, he went to Coffield. The chairman had connections across the state and knew how and when to use them for TDC. To help maintain those connections, he hosted an annual year-end hunt on his ranch. Whiskey flowed, card games flourished, and TDC board members, political officials, and judges established and maintained relations.

Beto, like Ellis and Ragen, was skilled at public relations. He cultivated the press, who, in return for access to the prison system, wrote glowing articles about TDC. Influential reporters, such as Harry McCormick of the *Dallas Morning News*, wrote favorable articles about the prison director and the prisons. The articles praised him in 1965, for example, when he hired the first black employees and later eliminated separate units for each race and ethnicity.[75] Beto, as well as some wardens, constantly made speeches before civic and religious organizations about crime and prison programs. Austin MacCormick continued to praise TDC as he had under Ellis. Beto also opened the prisons' doors to social researchers. Bruce Jackson, for example, a folklorist from Harvard, did extensive research in the prisons and later became an advocate of the Texas system. By co-opting outside agents in this way, Beto, like Ellis, effectively neutralized interference in the prison system. Agency scandals and potentially embarrassing situations were so controlled as to seem nonexistent.

When Beto retired in 1972, inmate safety, self-sufficiency, and inmate programs, especially the Windham School District, had become hallmarks of the system. The prison system was a stable and thriving organization with few critics. In part reflecting TDC's progress, George Beto was, in 1970, elected president of the American Correctional Association.

But toward the end of Beto's administration, inmates began to succeed in calling attention to conditions of their confinement that the public view of TDC had glossed over.[76] Beto hired ten lawyers and installed law libraries at ten TDC units. The courts, though ruling in favor of TDC, were listening to inmate grievances. The inmates now had the ear of federal judges. These early challenges spelled the end of the hands off doctrine in Texas while sowing the seeds for increased writ writing. TDC's insulation from the courts and judicial scrutiny was beginning to wane. The number of inmate writ writers soon increased, and they also had the support of outside attorneys. TDC initially perceived the writ writers as troublesome inmate agitators whose legal activity was merely an annoyance. The backstage elements of the Texas prison system were slowly coming into the light.

Enter W. J. Estelle, Jr.

When George J. Beto retired in 1972, he handpicked W. J. "Jim" Estelle, Jr., to be his successor. Estelle, the son of a California Department of Corrections (CDC) employee, started his career as a prison guard in the CDC. He rose through the ranks and served as a field parole officer. His final position in that system was supervisor of a number of honor camps in northern California. He then moved to a warden's position at Deer Lodge, Montana, where he was responsible for an inmate population of less than 300.[77]

At Estelle's request, Beto visited the Deer Lodge facility in early 1971, several months before Beto announced his retirement. Beto was impressed and said afterward: "The institution was clean and fairly run, but it was also apparent that he was running it."[78] Estelle admired Beto and was well aware of the reputation that TDC enjoyed. When Beto scrutinized Estelle's management style, he believed that the Montana warden could handle the large, diversified Texas system. Beto informed the prison board about Estelle, and it voted to bring him to TDC as an assistant director in February 1971, to be prepared for when Beto stepped down six months later.

Estelle's personal style was low-key but projected a strong and complex personality. His manner was deliberate and thoughtful, indicating that his positions were firmly grounded in principles and values in which he believed strongly. With staff and visitors he was warm and even courtly, but he remained distant, to some observers private and aloof. To his staff he was always "Mr. Estelle," just as the man he followed was "Dr. Beto." Furthermore, he was extremely loyal to employees and faithfully backed their actions under almost any circumstance. A prison official from another state characterized that image and the reputation he developed in corrections nationally: "There is, I think, a fascination with the man. He comes to [professional meetings] wearing his Stetson and boots and dipping snuff, but when he starts to talk, everybody listens."[79] He was a popular figure in Texas and, like Beto and Ellis, regularly gave speeches that extolled the virtues of TDC to groups across the state. He proudly stated that TDC was unparalleled in its ability to control prisoners and keep them safe, well fed, and busy.

Estelle's intention as director was to maintain the Texas system. Characterizing his role, he later stated: "I don't think I was brought in here to revolutionize or dramatically change a system that had already some proven success in the way of efficiency and effectiveness."[80] Estelle was to preside over a mature operation with well-established agricultural and industrial programs, as well as a strong tradition of prison control, order, and safety. Estelle firmly believed in inmate discipline and work, and Texas had plenty of both. His job was to personally defend and uphold the traditions of the TDC at the state and national levels. However, the seeds of discontent and change were already sown in Beto's administration. Although Jim Estelle tried to protect TDC from criticism and outside interference, he could not weather the external pressures that slowly undermined the Texas tradition of prison management and control.

Conclusion

In its early years, the Texas prison system followed the course of most other southern state systems. Torn between the need to provide prisons and fiscal austerity, state officials turned to systems of contracting out prisoner labor. Fiscal failures and extreme abuses prompted them to develop the plantation system in earnest. Although this agricultural orientation would become the prison system's basis for self-sufficiency and its most impressive feature, it too was problematic through the 1930s and 1940s. Poor management led to continued inmate abuse and little profit.

The hiring of Ellis marked a new chapter in the prison system's history. Ellis was the first of three extremely able and successful "public entrepreneurs."[81] He, Beto, and Estelle provided the internal leadership and legislative savvy out of which grew a stable, integrated organization known for its order and control. In the next chapter we examine a major basis for that order, namely, the officer subculture and the control mechanisms that subculture defined as appropriate for prisoners.

3

Stability and Control, Texas Style

Everything here is predictable. You know what to expect. You don't have to worry about getting stabbed or raped by other inmates, or what's going to happen from one day to the next, because it's the administration that's totally in control. —TDC INMATE, 1978

Either they treat you like a child, or like an inanimate object.
—TDC INMATE, 1978[1]

BY THE late 1960s, Texas prisons had developed a national, and even international, reputation for order, efficiency, and prisoner safety.[2] Assaults on officers were extremely rare, and inmate homicide rates were low compared to those of other large state prisons. For example, in 1973, the homicide rate in Texas prisons was 0.75 per 10,000 inmates and staff, while the national average was 7.44, and the highest prison homicide rate, in Hawaii, was 49.90.[3] Escapes and riots in TDC were also rare. Visitors to Texas prisons, as well as new officers and inmates, were always struck by the dominance of the guards and the submissiveness of the inmates. There was seldom any doubt about who was in charge.

This stability and order were the result of an elaborate, and largely informal, control structure. It sanctioned and shaped the behavior of prisoners and staff alike. Emerging gradually under Ellis, maturing during the Beto years, and sustained under Estelle, this control structure had three elements. The first, and least obvious, element of the traditional TDC control structure was the officer subculture. The second was an extensive array of punishments and rewards that officials used to gain inmate compliance. The final element was the building tender system in which elite inmates were co-opted to control other inmates. These elements complemented each other and worked together to maximize continuity and control. In this chapter we will examine only the first two of these elements, deferring a discussion of the building tender system to the following chapter.

Subcultural Control of the Guards

At the heart of TDC's control continuity over the years was a strong officer subculture. Key officers carried that subculture and served as role models. Through them subcultural expectations clarified the prevailing definition of a "good officer." These officers also defined how inmates should be handled and were primarily responsible for using TDC's inmate control mechanisms.

As we have seen, TDC reforms through the 1950s and the early 1960s prompted efforts to improve the guard force. The security staff became a paramilitary organization with several layers of formal rank. In 1955, officers received uniforms provided by the state for the first time in the system's history. After Beto took over TDC in 1962, the first preservice training program for officers was established. More than a decade later, TDC's Training Academy moved into the newly completed Criminal Justice Center on the nearby campus of Sam Houston State University. These steps were intended to improve and extend administrative control over the officer corps, as well as to foster a degree of professionalism and identification with the system. While the uniforms, the academy, the salary boosts, and other administrative efforts may have influenced security personnel, the real control of officer actions and attitudes lay with the guard subculture.

Elements of the Texas Officer Subculture

The officer subculture had four fundamental elements, and the most highly respected and emulated officers in TDC reflected each one in his own way. These elements were a personal emphasis on work and the work ethic for themselves and others, strong personal loyalties to superiors and the prison system, an acceptance of paternalism in dealing with inmates and with subordinate officers, and a tough self-reliance in handling prisoners. These workplace values emerged from sources as specific as Ellis' leadership and as diffuse as the rural Texas culture from which many officers came. But they took on meaning in a prison context under a number of "old wardens" of the late 1950s reform era.

An excellent example of these old wardens is Carl L. McAdams, who was particularly instrumental in crystallizing subcultural values on the Ramsey I farm through the 1950s. McAdams personally reflected these values and impressed them on successive generations of wardens and officers. His career, which ended with retirement in 1973, spanned most of Ellis' administration and all of Beto's. During his many years as a TDC warden, he directly influenced many men who went on to become Texas wardens. Captain Mac, as he was typically addressed, was a hard man with piercing eyes and a jutting jaw; he expected his people to match his pace and to do things as he wanted them done. McAdams' drive often led him to sneak up to the prison buildings at night to check on officers and inmates through a window. Everyone knew this occurred because they regularly found the warden's footprints outside the buildings. This practice and its discovery led, according to TDC lore, to McAdams' nickname of Beartracks or the Bear. More important, it led officers to pay closer attention to the job. His obvious commitment to the prison and his strong personality motivated the people who worked for him. A recently retired warden whose twenty-three years with TDC began under him described McAdams' impact on subordinates in a statement that touches on each of the subcultural elements we will examine:

> Warden McAdams believed in convicts working . . . in the taxpayers getting their money's worth. [He] could motivate you to work. He made me want to work a lot of times when I didn't want to. He was that type of man. . . . There was never any doubt who run the farm; it was the warden. And if it took 12 hours to do it we did it. If it took 14 hours we did it. All this time we thought we was performing a service, not just for us to have a livelihood and raise our family but we thought that we were serving the state of Texas by keeping these people and working them, letting them raise their food and stuff at a cheaper [rate] than they do now . . . I respected Warden McAdams enough that I felt like that I wanted to pattern myself after him . . . We took pride in how we kept the building, how we kept the outsides, we took pride in our cotton and how much we raised. . . . We were loyal; I was loyal to Warden McAdams first and TDC second. And that's the way people were . . . [I]f there was one of us in trouble, we was all in trouble. They [the officers] were loyal, good hard-working people. And they was people that if they worked overtime two hours, they knew that [the warden] couldn't give it to them [pay overtime]. But they knew someday if they needed off [the warden would] let them off. They were good loyal people that was the backbone of TDC.

Work Ethic.   Under Ellis and Beto, TDC was able to hire and keep a number of men with leadership ability and strong personalities. These men trained and influenced subsequent supervisors to be committed to prison work. It is evident that McAdams was capable of leading and motivating subordinates to want to please him and to believe that their work was important to the state.

Another factor behind the work emphasis was probably the rural, farm background of many of the men TDC hired over the years. Most of these prison employees came from the area around the prison farms. In fact, through the early 1970s, approximately three out of four officers were raised within fifty miles of the prison that employed them.[4] This pattern suggests that many rural prison employees were familiar with hard work and long hours. For these men, working from "can to can't" was not out of the ordinary and was certainly encouraged by such supervisors as McAdams. Having been raised in the country meant that many TDC recruits brought with them a strong work ethic. As important, they were often raised to think that hard work was praiseworthy. They would expect it of themselves, of the inmates they supervised, and of any officers subordinate to them.

It is important to stress that this characterization does not describe all, or probably even most, of the men who went to work for TDC over the years. Many, despite (or perhaps because of) their farm or rural background, were adverse to work and, instead of trying to please the warden and taking pride in the job, just did enough to get by. Such employees were always peripheral to the officer subculture, seldom rising in rank.

Personal Loyalty.   Key security staff members evinced strong personal loyalties toward superiors and the prison, in addition to a general orientation toward work. Feelings of loyalty and solidarity were fostered, in part, by the relatively small size of the prisons two or three decades ago. Inmate populations on the prison farms seldom reached more than several hundred, and the security staff was proportionately small. Administration was informal and personal. Through the late 1950s, for example, the administrative structure on many farms was limited to the Big Captain (later, the warden) and the Little Captain, or the dog sergeant (later, the assistant warden or major). Below these men were the bosses. Such a structure maximized the captain's opportunity to impose his personality on the operation and on his staff. Moreover, wardens at this time often did their own hiring or at least heavily influenced whom headquarters hired and where he was assigned. Wardens could also fire guards, and the terminated men had no appeal. Such power could be, and certainly was, abused. But, when it was appropriately used, it engendered respect (and fear) among employees; being firm but fair applied to employees as well as to inmates.

The isolation of the prison units also fostered loyalty. Many of the prison units are miles from the nearest settlement and, in some cases, miles from the nearest public road. To ensure that the prison had adequate personnel on hand to meet any problems, the state early on approved the construction of staff housing on the grounds adjacent to the prison compound. Duplexes were provided, with utilities paid, for the upper ranks of officers (usually from lieutenant up) and their families. In addition, ranking officers received emoluments in the form of prison-produced meats, dairy products, and vegetables. In exchange for such subsidies, these officers were on call twenty-four hours a day.

This housing arrangement established and maintained a strong sense of community and interdependency among officers and their families. Co-workers were neighbors. Wives interacted, children played together, and the lines between work and personal relations blurred. Job-related problems and jokes could continue over a beer at a backyard picnic table only a few hundred yards from the prison where they had originated. In some cases this closed community produced interpersonal and interfamily friction, but relations seemed more often to have been positive. The result was a strong esprit de corps among key officers living on the grounds.

An illustration of how socializing fostered personal loyalty, and indirectly benefited TDC, was the regular parties that officers threw in the recreation hall found at each unit. A typical reason for the event was a ranking officer's retirement or promotion to another TDC unit. Featuring barbecue or fried fish, beer, and games of chance, these male-only parties brought together not only men from the unit hosting the party but officers and administrators from nearby units as well. It is important to note that not all officers who were off duty came to such parties. As a rule, attendees were those officers who were considered by themselves and by others to be in or near the inner core of the security force.

These parties provided a forum for reenforcing the officer subculture. Men told and retold stories about exemplary or despicable officer actions, both of which underscored appropriate officer conduct. The evening also provided an opportunity to share information about inmate characters and problems. Significantly, information about officers was also shared. For example, most officers during the Estelle administration felt that promotions hinged to a large extent on the personal approval of Dan V. "Red" McKaskle, assistant director for special services. McKaskle would attend these parties and, throughout his usually short stay, engage in discreet conversations with various unit officers. Most officers believed that McKaskle was working his snitch system, learning which officers showed the requisite loyalty and "snap" to merit the responsibility of promotion. The parties also helped to maintain ties with groups outside TDC, especially law enforcement agencies. Local police, sheriff, and state highway patrol officers were usually present. Good relations with law enforcement officials meant ready outside help for TDC in case of an escape or other emergency.

Paternalism.   The officer subculture called for TDC employees to view and treat prisoners in a very paternalistic manner. In many respects, prisoners were to officers what blacks were to whites in the antebellum south.[5] In TDC, prisoners (with a few exceptions) occupied a status below all officers, and the only approved interactions between the two groups were those that recognized and underscored the unequal status system. Accordingly, officers considered most prisoners to be lazy, immature, and certainly inferior. The prevailing paternalism encouraged officers to treat inmates much like a parent does a child, to deal with inmates in idiosyncratic ways. Ranking officers had broad discretion to settle or dismiss an inmate's claim, problem, or transgression however they saw fit. This power on the part of individual officers could, on the one hand, benefit inmates by leading to quick resolutions to problems. On the other hand, it could, and often did, result in inmate frustrations. There were no grievance procedures through which official caprice could be appealed.

The prisoners' unquestioned inferiority was apparent in the officers' style of addressing them. If they knew it, officers called inmates only by their last names. Inmates, however, always said "sir" and addressed officers as "Mr." or "boss," or simply by rank. In some cases officers used nicknames for inmates that they or other inmates had made up.[6]

Many TDC officers brought to the job the prejudices toward criminals and minorities, especially blacks, that prevailed in the rural, conservative communities from which they usually came. Accordingly, TDC officers often called inmates simply "nigger" or "meskin." Clearly, black and Mexican American prisoners were doubly subordinate. This prejudicial posture on the part of officers in TDC is not surprising since TDC's security staff was, like most other state guard forces, overwhelmingly white.

Although race and ethnicity were factors in how officers dealt with inmates, the most important status the inmate had was simply that of convicted felon. Officers regularly referred to inmates collectively as "them thieves" and to individual prisoners as "ol' thangs." To officers, inmates were morally flawed since they had actively rejected conventional values, especially the work ethic, that many officers held dear. The prevailing paternalistic attitude of officers encouraged them to see inmates in stereotypical and simplified ways. This attitude is illustrated in a Warden's Handbook described by a former inmate who served more than one term in TDC prisons in the 1960s. That guide reportedly contained the following terse suggestions on how to handle inmates by race and ethnicity: "Never give a white convict anything he doesn't ask for. Very proud, arrogant, and independent. Mexicans require close supervision, strict disciplinary procedures often necessary; cunning and rebellious. Negroes: treat like children."[7]

The subordinate posture of inmates was taken for granted by officers and generally accepted, at least overtly, by prisoners. One important consequence of the unquestioned status gap between officers and inmates was that it permitted some individuals in both groups to develop rather close personal ties. Many ranking officers enjoyed close long-range relationships with favored inmates. For example, an inmate might be widely known as the "major's boy." He hung close by, brought coffee, ran errands, provided information, and even entertained the major. And there were cases of something approaching friendships between ranking officers and elite prisoners. While such a relationship could last for years, it was always predicated on the acceptance by the inmate of his place and an understanding that liberties could not be taken lightly.

Competence, Self-reliance, and Toughness. The final subcultural element was the ability to be tough and competent in handling inmates. Specifically, these attributes were reflected in the degree to which officers had "convict sense" and the capacity to dominate inmates physically.

Convict sense was cellblock psychology, a combination of quick insight and manipulative skill. This ability reflected both an astuteness in dealing with inmates and the long experience required to hone it. At the lowest level, having convict sense would keep an officer from being tricked or duped by an inmate, "buying a hog" in TDC parlance. More generally, it meant knowing what inmates were thinking or planning and using that knowledge to control them. Some TDC officers were legendary in this regard. Their detailed memory of particular inmates and of convict propensities generally allowed them to discern which inmates to trust and when. These men could not only anticipate trouble but also make on-the-spot decisions affecting both the inmate and the prison operations. Officers with good convict sense could get inmates to comply and follow rules with the least effort or threat of punishment. Getting inmates to want to do what the officer wanted done was particularly laudable in the officer subculture.

One famous example of this ability occurred when a warden was transferred to the Retrieve Unit in the early 1960s to replace a warden who had let inmate productivity and officer morale slip drastically. Soon after his arrival, the new warden convened the field inmates and their bosses just before they went to work one morning. He announced that he was initiating an "honor squad," which would work without any supervision. The warden then asked each of the fifteen or so field bosses to pick out three of his best workers to constitute the new squad. Shortly, those inmates worked faster and picked more cotton than any other squad. Production in other squads also improved as inmates sought to join the honor squad. This honor squad, self-named the High Rollers, existed into the 1980s. It even gained some external notoriety with its precision marching in boots and berets at the annual prison rodeo.

Convict sense was also apparent in the decision to reclassify regular inmates into trusties. The chief of classification would regularly visit the units from his base in Huntsville for this purpose. In the mid-1970s, this man was a highly experienced, former warden. He was admired in TDC as a master at judging inmates. On a given day he would arrive to interview inmates that the warden had selected as possible trusties. Actually, the warden had already relied on his own convict sense and that of his staff to make this preliminary selection. Each prisoner was brought before the classification officer, who had spent a few minutes looking over the inmate's criminal, personal, and institutional records. After several questions about the man's family or the type of crime he had committed, the officer would ask the inmate: "If I put you outside (make you a trusty), will you run off?" Of course, the inmate always answered: "No, sir." This brief transaction provided enough information to the officer to make a key decision regarding an escape risk. Such transactions illustrate not only the value of convict sense but also the extent to which the system relied on it for key decisions. Information was stored in the officer's head, not in a computer.

Besides convict sense, a key role expectation was a tough, competent reputation. An officer's personal authority usually rested on a reputation developed over time through dealing with inmates in various situations. Significantly, in the background of almost all ranking officers and wardens was a reputation for being able to manage, physically as well as psychologically, inmates who balked at compliance with rules or orders.

Many officers were regularly the subject of stories about their personal characteristics or about events on which their reputations rested. For example, a very effective lieutenant at the Ferguson Unit was always seen to be open and smiling in his dealings with inmates. Yet inmates and officers alike acknowledged that, while he was highly tolerant and easy going, he was a terror if pushed too far. As a result, veteran inmates told new inmates that, while the man may appear to be a pushover, he was not to be crossed.

Successful TDC officers typically established such reputations early in their careers. Once established, those reputations preceded them and usually made actual demonstration of their physical prowess unnecessary. For example, in addition to his tough demeanor, Warden McAdams was reputed to be able to stand in front of a prisoner and kick the man under the chin with great speed and accuracy. When asked about this ability, one current warden who had worked under McAdams for years stated that he had never actually seen him perform this feat but, nonetheless, gave it credence. Inmates in McAdams' day were of the same opinion, and their compliance in his presence rested largely on an unwillingness to learn about his skills firsthand.

Officer Socialization and Acceptance

Carriers of this subculture were found on every TDC unit, usually at or above the rank of lieutenant. Having been carefully selected by their superiors, these men constituted an inner core. Membership in this inner core meant that these men reflected in their actions the attributes of a good officer as defined within the TDC security subculture. Outside this inner core was a group of men who wanted to win acceptance and the promotions that usually followed, but who had yet to demonstrate their mettle. On the periphery of the guard world was a large percentage of officers who would not or could not conform to the informal expectations of the prevailing subculture. Here, for example, were college students who wanted only to put out enough effort to get by on the job and graduate, men of slow wit with little ability or ambition, and those who were perhaps willing but too fat, too gentle, or too naïve to gain respect from anyone in this highly masculine world. These officers were really outsiders and usually had little impact on prisoners and little chance of moving up in the TDC guard hierarchy.

The officer subculture established in TDC units in the 1950s and 1960s defined the standards by which officers were judged. By reflecting those standards in his dealings with inmates and other officers, a guard could be accepted into the inner circle, included in the jokes and banter when officers gathered, and, finally, promoted. Displaying the "right stuff" on the job could move him from the periphery toward the inner core of the guard fraternity; that movement, in turn, bolstered his support of the officer subculture.

Prior to 1962, new officers went to work on a unit and learned the job however they could. There was no formal training effort. Beginning in 1962, most recruits went through a two-week training and orientation program at the Ferguson Unit before taking a unit assignment. Those two weeks in the classroom were theoretically followed by two additional weeks of hands-on training at their unit. In practice, the classroom experience usually provided little more than an adequate overview of prison work, and the on-the-job segment was often foregone altogether.[8] The only meaningful socialization occurred informally.

Becoming a TDC officer, or "boss," involved meeting two kinds of expectations. The first was learning the routine and logistics of the prison's daily rounds—when to open the doors, when to pass out mail, which inmates can go to the commissary or infirmary, and so on. The second expectation was less clear, took longer to learn, and was more consequential for the officer's advancement. This involved the occupational and workplace subculture. An officer got paid for mastering the first, but he got rewarded through co-worker acceptance and even promotion if he mastered the second.

Thirty years ago most recruits went to work on their first day supervising inmates in the field. At that time, the only focus of the prison was agriculture, and it was in the fields that employees demonstrated their skills at managing both convicts and crops. By the early 1960s, however, the focus of the prison had shifted to include industries, education, and other programs for inmates. These changes, plus some growth in the population, added significance and complexity to the building operation. Instead of being just the compound where fieldworkers were locked up at night, fed, and turned out the next day, the building also became an important center of officer duties in its own right.

This shift altered the career paths of all officers. That is, men no longer were hired and placed directly in the field, nor did they have to work as a field boss to be promoted. All recruits began their service in the cellblocks and moved up from there. For the vast majority of TDC officers, assignments and promotions over the years never involved the field. Others, after some period in the building, sought a field assignment. Some of these men found they preferred field work; they neither sought nor received another assignment, though they may have been promoted within that setting. Finally, some men cycled through the field, then moved back, usually via a promotion, to an administrative post in the building.

The critical point is that to advance in the TDC security hierarchy, whether in the building or in the field, officers had to demonstrate the elements of the subculture described above. Because the building and the field were quite different work settings, we will examine them separately, beginning with the building where, by the 1960s, almost all officers started.

Guard Work in the Building

When new officers arrived at their unit, they often found that veterans and ranking staff generally ignored them. Given the rapid turnover among recruits, veterans did not want to waste time and advice on a recruit who might be gone in a month. It was not uncommon for a recruit to feel that he was treated little better than an inmate. The recruit had to rely largely on his own observations to learn routines and how to handle himself. The specific instructions he got on the cellblock routines usually came from the elites of that tank, the building tenders. Inmates would test him,[9] and officers would be as interested in his reactions as were the inmates since his responses revealed much about his potential for handling himself according to subcultural standards. In a sense, new officers were "thrown to the wolves," tossed into the cellblocks to see if they could demonstrate potential for meeting those standards. To officers in the inner core, only those men who passed the test were worth much attention.

A cellblock officer who showed potential was typically made a "hall boss." This was a man who "ran a good tank" (kept the noise level down, stayed awake, kept accurate inmate counts) and generally displayed a degree of strength and convict sense. A hall boss, as the name implies, worked in the long halls characteristic of TDC's typical telephone-pole design. In this less-structured setting he supervised the movement of inmates. Shift supervisors often groomed three or four promising cellblock officers to be hall bosses. Being tapped to work in the hall was considered a reward because it freed the officer from counting, opening doors, and delivering mail to cells and made his interactions with inmates more visible to supervisors. Indeed, his selection rested on the presumption that he could competently handle prisoners. As one supervisor stated, "I don't want him out there [in the hall] if he doesn't have nuts." A new hall boss had to prove that he could handle himself in the new assignment, and, until he did, he was not fully accepted by the other officers.

One of the authors, while working as a new hall officer at the East-ham Unit, had a confrontation with an inmate that very much transformed his relations with other officers. When an inmate at-tacked him, this officer first defended himself, then forcibly subdued the inmate. After that incident, his co-workers saw him in a new light. Veteran officers on the same shift who had not even deigned to speak to him sought him out for details of the fight. One previous stranger loudly asked the whereabouts of "Joe Palooka." Clearly, the incident moved this new hall boss from the subcultural periphery toward the core. His behavior adequately approximated the informal standard of a "good officer."

When officers demonstrated the potential for being a good convict man and the toughness required to handle noncompliance, they were admitted not only to participate in the locker room banter of the masculine workplace but also to learn important job-related knowledge. Because ranking officers did not trust cellblock officers (thought to be incompetent until they themselves proved other-wise), little information was shared with them. If, for example, an investigation of drug trafficking was underway, it was kept from the bosses in the blocks for fear they would compromise it. Those lower-ranking officers and hall bosses who did show promise, who had demonstrated they were OK, in time became privy to such guarded information. They also had access to the major's office, where they learned how and when physical force was used as a con-trol device.

The typical promotion route for a TDC officer then was from the cellblocks, where everyone started (and to which they were some-times reassigned as punishment), to the hall. Moving to duty in the hall was usually not a rise in rank. It was instead a test that, if passed, would lead to a shift sergeant's or lieutenant's job. This pro-cess could take a period of years because, although turnover was and remains high for the lowest-ranking cellblock officers, turnover in the ranks was usually quite low. Low ranking-officer turnover was due in part to the feelings of interdependence and esprit de corps. It was also due to rather careful selection by supervisors over time of men who approximated the TDC ideal officer—men able to generate inmate compliance on their own.

Guard Work in the Field

The field was also an important training ground for some officers, providing experience important to advancement. Being transferred to supervise inmates in a fieldwork squad often followed becoming a hall boss. But getting a field assignment was sometimes not easy. If a man wanted to move to the field, he had to first prove his mettle in handling prisoners in the building and then wait for an opening. Usually there were more men wanting to move than there were field officer vacancies.

Men sought field experience for reasons beyond the fact that it familiarized them with the agricultural operation and was thus useful in subsequent management posts. Another obvious attraction was that fieldwork was not shift work. It demanded only five days per week from about 7:00 A.M. until about 5:00 P.M. each day, although in earlier years it was from sunup to sundown.

A more subtle, but equally important, attraction to fieldwork was that the field force enjoyed, and to some extent cultivated, a special reputation. When the field bosses were in the building, either because the squads were in at day's end or because weather prohibited the squads from going out, they made quite an impression with their tanned, rugged faces and hands, boots and spurs, hats, and gunless holsters.[10] These men epitomized the officer subculture, especially the element of toughness and self-reliance; indeed, it was for these characteristics that they were often assigned to the field in the first place. Their reputation for force, their horses, their guns, and their rough demeanor made them a separate breed.

A field boss "carried," or was responsible for, a squad of between twenty and thirty inmates while they worked at such tasks as picking cotton, pulling corn, weeding, and digging irrigation trenches. In one sense, the field boss' job was more difficult than a building assignment. Without walls and routine to help control his prisoners, a field officer was more in charge of a specific group of inmates working at a specific task and thus was more directly accountable. Yet, field tasks were more straightforward. There was no paperwork and few visitors since his work was typically done some distance, even miles, from the building compound. Essentially, the job consisted of security (allowing no escapes) and work productivity.

The field boss had considerable help with security (other armed guards, dogs at the ready, and a high rider), but in getting the inmates in his squad to work satisfactorily he was largely on his own; how he achieved that end was his own affair. Some officers sought to frighten inmates into compliant production. Officers referred to this method as "acting crazy," leaving inmates uncertain as to their safety should they fail to work or obey their boss' orders. How extreme this posturing got in the past is suggested in the following former convict's account of the day his squad got a new field boss:

"When he raised his head enough so the brim no longer hid his sinister-looking face, I quickly squinted a peek at his eyes. Their icy-blue color contrasted his heavily tanned weathered skin. He seldom blinked, roving his eyes over us. 'I'm gonna tell ya'll one time, an one time alone how I'm gonna deal. First off, if airy one uv you tries to run off, I'm gonna kill ya. If airy one uv you 'sputes my word, I'm gonna kill ya. If airy one uv you don' do lak I tell ya, I'm gonna kill ya. If you lay th' hammer down under me [refuse to work], I'm gonna kill ya. And if I jes take a notion to, I'm gonna kill ya.'"[11] Though extreme, this officer's threats illustrate the dominance and tough persona that the officer subculture encouraged. It also suggests something about many of the men who became field bosses and who remained at this job for years. Often these men were rough and direct and lacked both finesse and management skills. They preferred supervising inmates in the field because of the straightforward nature of the job and relied on intimidation and fear to motivate their squads.

Other field officers, however, could temper their tough demeanor and paternalism with some humanity, even respect, for their squad. The following introduction by a field officer illustrates this more moderate approach and contrasts sharply with the fearful tirade above: "My name is Robles. Ya'll kin call me Mr. Robles or Boss Robles. I'm gonna call ya'll by yore names afta I learn 'em all. So don' gitcha dandruff up if I say 'hey, you' til I git a handle on 'em. Okay? Anutha thang, I ain' gonna be cussin' ya'll out. I don' feel lak thas gonna be necessary. Do ya'll?"[12] This statement conveys a willingness to establish a relationship with the squad based on something besides fear. By treating the inmates as men even though they are prisoners and are compelled to work, the officer could expect some reciprocity in the form of labor. Many officers approached field supervision in this manner. They could foster that reciprocity in many ways. They could, for example, help an inmate get a job (work in the building, which generated more good time than did field-work), attend to whether their squad had appropriate or adequate tools, or even surreptitiously provide tobacco and paper for those inmates who could not provide their own.[13] Indeed, it was not uncommon for some squads to work very hard for one officer but to lag for a substitute.

For the most part, TDC seemed to have been relatively successful in promoting men who understood that inmate compliance could be achieved by "out thinkin' 'em" or "trickin' 'em" (convict sense), men who had also established that they could and would "put their hands on one" (physically enforce their orders). To the extent that fieldwork showed that an officer had the "right stuff," it helped in promotion.

Promotion and other rewards that stemmed from the manifestation of subcultural values served to standardize the behavior and attitudes of TDC's middle managers (lieutenant through warden). Supervisors selected those subordinates who demonstrated the traits for which they themselves had been promoted for exhibiting. In this way, the prison organization achieved some measure of control over officer attitudes and behavior. The officer subculture also standardized the prison's strategies for controlling inmates.

Controlling Inmates, Texas Style

Texas prison officials enjoyed great autonomy when it came to controlling inmates. This autonomy was due to the prison system's geographic, political, and legal isolation. For example, inmate contacts with the outside were limited by strict controls on mail and on telephone calls. Moreover, the physical isolation of most TDC units limited visits from inmates' families and from state officials as well. These conditions only enhanced the authority of prison officials.

That authority was bolstered by prisoners' expectations. In jail, men destined for the prison learned from TDC veterans about the killings, the beatings, and the generally tough treatment they could expect in prison. On arrival, the "drive up," or new inmate, usually found his expectations confirmed. The immediate effect of a Texas prison on a new inmate was simply overwhelming. Order prevailed, and everything and everybody seemed to have a place; regimentation crushed individuality. "Making it," or surviving as a prisoner, meant accepting your place and the paternalistic relations to officials that defined that place.

Social control in the pre-Ruiz era was so pervasive that the individual units reflected many elements of totalitarian societies.[14] Regimentation, for example, called for uniform dress. Prisoners were required to wear standard white uniforms, to be clean shaven, and to have a neatly trimmed head of hair. Clothing could not be altered. If, for example, a man scraped off the first layer of leather on his state-issued brogans to obtain a "stylish" brushed look, he would receive disciplinary action for "damaging or destroying state property."

Inmate movement was also strictly regimented. In the field, inmate squads usually moved two abreast, a formation they quickly learned to assume when they heard the order "Deuce it up!" Inside, prisoners lived and moved by specific rules. At the Eastham Unit, for example, a sign in English and Spanish above the barricade doors in the main hallway read: No Smoking; No Talking; No loitering; Single file. When walking the hall single file, prisoners had to stay between the wall and a conspicuous green line painted on the floor about four feet from the wall. Outside their cellblocks, men had to have their shirts buttoned, their shirttails tucked in, and their pants buttoned and belted. Even an expressive way of walking by an inmate could draw an admonition from a boss: "Get off that south Dallas shuffle in my hall!" Finally, interaction among inmates outside the cellblocks was limited. Only with special permission could a prisoner go to see a friend or relative in another part of the prison compound. And in the dining area, once they had been through the hot food line, inmates had to take the first available seat, regardless of who was already at that table. Talking was limited at the meal, and leisurely eating, reading, and smoking were not permitted.

A second element of the authoritarian system of the prison was the specter of fear. Inmates feared those staff members who had earned reputations for toughness. They also feared the building tenders. These elite inmates were to the correctional staff in TDC what secret police are to a totalitarian society; the BTs were capable of unbridled abuse. Physical coercion and retaliation from either source was an ever-present reality. Although physical punishment did not follow most misdeeds, inmates knew that it was used with some frequency. This knowledge added weight to the more common tongue-lashings and verbal threats.

The third authoritarian element was the staff's strategy of penetrating the prisoners' world. Ranking officers constantly worked at securing information on inmates and their activities. Skill at gaining and retaining information personally or through carefully curried snitches demonstrated a good "convict man" and was central to the officer subculture. By being able to anticipate inmate plans, officers kept inmates off-balance and uncertain while intensifying inmate fear of the staff and of each other.

The final element of the Texas control regime was work. Again analogous to totalitarian societies, TDC used work by the subject population both to benefit the system and to control that population. Prison officials used fieldwork in particular to punish individual inmates and to communicate their dominance over prisoners.

Together with the socialization of the bosses, these elements—regimentation, fear, penetration of the inmate's world, and work—

were the fundamental bases for controlling inmates in TDC. From these elements flowed an array of formal and informal techniques that officers used to keep prisoners in line.

Formal Control Mechanisms

On arrival at the Diagnostic Unit in Huntsville, all prisoners received a copy of the department's rules and regulations. Once at the unit, they were again told about the rules and about what official action would be taken for transgressions. The formal (i.e., recorded) response by the officials typically involved a write-up, a disciplinary, or "court," hearing, and some type of punishment.

Official Discipline through Unit Court.   Until the early 1980s, TDC's rule book listed nearly one hundred inmate offenses. Some, such as laziness and disrespectful attitude, were quite vague and gave staff great discretion in judging a violation. When a cellblock officer saw an inmate violating a rule, he would typically notify his supervisor (sergeant or lieutenant) and describe the infraction. If the supervisor believed the officer was reliable and the case clear-cut, he told the officer to write him up.

Once written, the charge was given to an inmate bookkeeper in the major's office. These bookkeepers were responsible for, among other things, typing formal disciplinary reports based on the officer's written statement. Actually, bookkeepers routinely tailored the offense reports to vindicate officials and even assisted supervisors in selecting the proper rule violation to cite.

Until the late 1970s, a disciplinary panel ("court") composed of a major or captain, a lieutenant, and a representative from treatment (drug counselor, school administrator, etc.) heard cases involving the full range of prison violations. Court was held on an as-needed basis, usually several times a week. Before each session, accused inmates lined up in the hall outside the major's office where court was usually held.

Inmates were brought in one at a time, told the charge, questioned, and then told to state their plea. A plea other than guilty was usually greeted with howls and glares. (Sometimes, before the first rule violator was brought before the court, one of the officers placed on the desk a sheet of paper with *guilty* written on it in large letters so that inmates could correctly spell their plea when they were told to write it down on the disciplinary hearing form.) No witnesses were brought, the charging officer was almost never present, and no notes or tape recordings were ever made. Sometimes the field major held his own rump hearings after the inmates had returned from the field. In one case, when the field major asked what the offender had done wrong, the answer was "fucking off" (i.e., not working hard enough).[15] The inmate received a minor restriction on the spot, although the record of the discipline was not made until the next day.

Responding to Supreme Court decisions regarding prison disciplinary actions[16] and the impending Ruiz litigation, TDC began in the late 1970s to differentiate between minor and major cases, with the decision depending on both the severity of the offense and the inmate's reputation. For example, "failure to work," "fighting without a weapon," and "being in an unauthorized area" were almost always minor cases. At the same time, such offenses as "fighting with a weapon," "possession of drugs," "escape attempts," "mutiny," and "striking an officer" were all major cases, regardless of the offender's circumstances and institutional reputation. Some offenses, however, could be classified either way depending on the inmate's reputation. Thus, subjective decisions determined how some cases were defined and tried. The significance of this determination for the inmate was simply that the possible sanctions were quite different; major cases drew more severe punishments.

Minor cases were in the province of a hearing officer rather than of a tribunal. After the inevitable guilty plea, the case had several outcomes. In some instances, the officer weighed the circumstances and just let the man off with a warning or a kind of probation. "You've got a pretty good record, and I'm going to let you 'make it' this time; don't do it again." The most common punishment for minor offenses was cell restriction for between seven and thirty days. Inmates on cell restriction could only leave their cells to eat and to work. This meant no television or evening fraternizing in the cellblock dayroom. During football season, this was not an insignificant punishment. Other minor-case sanctions included having to do extra work at one's job (field, kitchen, or laundry) and shelling peas or peanuts.

Major court involved more formal procedures and harsher penalties. For example, if one inmate was seen hitting another with a metal tray in the dining hall, the aggressor was written up for fighting with a weapon. The officer who observed the altercation then wrote an offense report just as he would do with a minor case. If the victim required medical attention, the offender would usually be confined in administrative segregation. Segregation was used to detain most inmates for seventy-two hours prior to a hearing, a move that required the order of a captain, major, or warden. Inmates facing

a major case received a written notice of charges and were supposed
to appear before the disciplinary committee within three days. During this time, the inmate could prepare a defense, solicit witnesses,
and secure substitute counsel or someone to speak for him during
the hearing. Officers collected statements from the accused witnesses, and these were entered as evidence at the proper time. Ranking officers composed the committee, and, by the late 1970s, all proceedings were tape recorded. After being found guilty, and almost all
were, the prisoner faced one or some combination of several major
sanctions.

Officers considered putting offenders in solitary confinement (the
"shitter") to be the least damaging to the inmate and thus the least
severe sanction. Until TDC revised its policy for the use of solitary
in the late 1970s, inmates sent there usually received a pair of over-
alls and a blanket, no reading material except a Bible (if that), and a
limited diet. Prior to the 1970s, that diet was a kind of gruel, a com-
posite of food off the line, slopped together and recooked. By the
mid-1970s, inmates were receiving at each mealtime a vegetable
tray for two days in a row and then a complete tray for each meal on
the third day; this cycle was then repeated for as long as the inmate
was in lockup. That period was typically far short of the fifteen
straight days inmates could be kept in solitary, according to TDC
policy. The experience was not pleasant, and when the warden or assistant warden made his daily rounds of solitary and asked, "Are you
ready to go to work and straighten up your business," the answer
was usually a hardy "Yes, sir." The warden could, and often did, decide that a man was sufficiently sanctioned after only a few days or
even hours and let him out. This decision was always based on his
convict sense, his judgment of that particular inmate.

As TDC was forced in the late 1970s to be more attuned to inmate
rights, officials altered the conditions of solitary accordingly. In addition to the Bible, inmates were allowed any legal materials (writs,
books, briefs, trial records) and such personal items as writing paper
and pens. They also began receiving three meals a day exactly as did
those in the general population. At the same time, however, almost
all inmates began staying in solitary the full fifteen days.

Considered more severe than solitary and often used in addition to
it following a major case was the taking away of accrued good time
and possible reduction in classification so that prisoners earned less
good time. Texas prison officials have always argued that the state
has a generous good time law and that this law is one of their most
effective tools for controlling inmates. A trusty, for example, could
gain up to thirty days of good time for every thirty days he actually

served on his sentence. For a serious infraction a man could lose good time already accrued plus his opportunity to continue earning good time at that rate. Punishments of this type might also mean the loss of a good job (garment factory, bus repair shop) and a return to the field. Another consequence might be the loss of a dormitory bed and a return to a cellblock. Thus, a major case could cost a TDC prisoner dearly.

For a particularly serious offense a prisoner could, in addition to losing good time, be sent to a tougher prison. For example, troublesome inmates at the Ferguson Unit, which was for eighteen- to twenty-one-year-old "first timers," were regularly sent to the Ellis or Eastham units, both of which were for older and much tougher convicts. Such moves were both a punishment of the young offender and a warning for others.

At the same time, transfers, especially from one cell or block to another, could be used as informal rewards. Officers maintained co-operative relationships with elite inmates by moving them to more desirable locations or by having "desirable" prisoners moved to their cells or blocks.

Surveillance as Official Control. The prison staff also relied on surveillance, an official, though less formal, control strategy. Through surveillance, officers sought to anticipate rule violations and to communicate to the inmate population that the officials were constantly watching.[17] Types of official surveillance included observation, shakedowns, and counts.

When an officer saw illicit activity, his reaction had important implications for control, as well as for the officer's reputation. Inmates holding hands or surreptitiously nuzzling each other in the dayroom meant homosexual activity, which often led to trouble. Similarly, officers watched the dayroom for gambling. Although cards have always been proscribed, prisoners had dominoes, and what can be done with cards can be done with dominoes. Officers watched constantly to keep inmates from playing such games as "tonk," a form of poker playing using dominoes. Inmates trying to enter the dayroom with a sack containing bags of coffee, ice cream, envelopes, or other negotiable items were tagged as gamblers and turned back. Similar surveillance took place in the dining hall to keep inmates from cutting in line or trying to eat more than one time on those days when a particularly good meal was being served. One officer noted that "today we [i.e., the inmates] had roast beef, corn on the cob, and mashed potatoes, and I got ready for the games because they are going to try to double back on you and eat twice. I caught eight today. I missed a whole bunch of them but you're never going to get them all. But you can spot the ones who are trying to eat twice. See, they'll come up and then look at the menu real sneakily or they'll turn their heads away. It's kind of funny really, but they give themselves away."

Shakedowns were another type of surveillance. Inmates were at all times subject to personal searches. Officers searched them routinely as they went to and from meals and work. Since all eating utensils were metal, the possibility of an inmate trying to sneak weapon material out of the dining area was the major concern, though searches more often produced boxes of cereal in shirts or sandwiches in pockets. Personal searches were so routine and accepted that inmates approaching an officer would take comb, cigarettes, and lighter from their pockets and hold them in outstretched hands so that the pat-down for contraband would be easier for the officer.

Officers also frequently, though irregularly, shook down living quarters. Such searches were not done at random, however. Limited manpower meant that supervisors had to be reasonably sure contraband was present in a dormitory or cellblock before initiating the shakedown. Information about weapons, tattooing equipment, drugs, or other proscribed items usually came either from officer observations or from a tip. Inmates did not have to be present during the search, and officers were seldom careful with the inmate's belongings whether they found anything incriminating or not. Consequently, inmates often returned to their "houses" to find their personal belongings strewn across the cell floor and their bedding in a heap.

Finally, officers counted inmates four and five times a shift. This practice obviously limited the chances of escape, while its latent effect sustained the feeling of constant surveillance. During counts, all inmate movement stopped; inmates had to wait in one place until the count was complete. Most of the time the count "cleared" (i.e., the body count matched the official total) on the first try. Often, however, counting errors were made, and the count had to be repeated time and time again. When the count failed to clear, inmates were often rousted from their cells, even if they were asleep, and placed in the dayroom for a more careful count. Such actions certainly communicated to inmates the relative importance of their rest vis-à-vis unit security.

Formal Rewards.   Texas prison officials did not rely solely on punishments to achieve control; they also recognized the significance of rewards. Some of the formal rewards extended to inmates were tied to rehabilitation goals, as in the case of certain jobs, academic and vocational education, and furloughs. Other rewards offered diversion (access to the craft shop), comfort (better housing), or an earlier release date (good time).

In TDC, all medically able inmates worked, and, almost without exception, an inmate's first job would be in the field, where he picked cotton, pulled corn, or harvested vegetables by hand. After many months of such labor the inmate could be moved into the building to a laundry or a kitchen slot, a move the prisoner was meant to see as a reprieve. Such a move hinged on an opening in the building and, most important, on his field boss' assessment of his attitude and willingness to work and comply with prison rules. Even if the inmate was not keen on working in the kitchen, the garment factory, the cannery, or wherever else officials needed another pair of hands, he usually went along. After all, it got him out of the field. The new inmate could not forget that the job change was not a right; it was a reward for his good conduct and attitude. If an inmate acted hesitant about his newly assigned job in the presence of a supervisor, the officer simply revoked the job and reassigned him to the field. With an exceptional record (few or no disciplinary cases), an inmate, with the warden's approval, could be considered for a state-approved trusty job. The highest-level trusties could be left unsupervised for hours at a time and some even made trips into town in prison vehicles to pick up or deliver parts and equipment for the unit.

Often correlated with a job change was a change in living quarters, a very significant reward in itself. When an inmate received a job, officials tried to move him in with others similarly employed; this sometimes meant moving from a cellblock to a dormitory, where supervision was more lax and there was more freedom and less danger.

A second reward was access to basic or vocational school. Under George Beto, TDC had established the Windham School District, an ungraded system of education using free-world teachers, which could take inmates from illiteracy through high school. To be eligible, inmates had to have a clean disciplinary record for the previous six months and the warden's approval. College classes were also available through area junior colleges. Vocational-technical classes included, among other subjects, auto mechanics, auto body repair, air conditioning, upholstery, wood finishing, meat cutting, and welding. Here, too, the instructors were state employees rather than inmates.

The school program was a reward, especially to inmates who worked in the field. If one of these inmates was selected for a vocational class, for example, he was assigned to the class for its duration, usually six months. Inmates with key jobs in the building, however, had to go to school on their free time. Whether the motivation was to escape the field or to improve himself, the prisoner usually viewed the chance to participate in school as an attractive alternative, making the school program a significant element in the official reward system.

A much more restricted and, among prisoners, prestigious reward was access to the craft, or "piddlin'," shop. Here inmates tooled leather belts, wallets, bullwhips, saddles, boots, and holsters; worked silver or stainless steel into buckles, spurs, and jewelry; painted pictures; and carved toys. These goods were displayed for sale at the unit, and the system maintained behind the central headquarters in Huntsville a separate building devoted to the sale of these items to the public. Business was always brisk during the four Sundays of October when TDC put on its annual rodeo. Clearly, access to the craft shop to make such goods could be an economic benefit for the talented inmate, since inmates received money from the sale of their crafts, as well as a break in the tedium of doing time. But to get to go to the craft shop, a man had to have a craft card, or ticket, a pass available only from the warden or the major.

A craft card was available only to special inmates, perhaps less than 10 percent of the population of each unit. Evidence suggests that only those inmates closely allied with staff received a card. One long-time prisoner indicated that he had been trying to get a card for two years, but top-ranking officers had refused him; he felt that the major's attitude was one of "well, what have you done for me?" Perhaps most important in getting a card was the recommendation of a politically powerful inmate who already possessed a card.

A particularly important reward was a five-day furlough, a program begun in the mid-1970s. Inmates not only got a chance to be with family and friends but also had a chance to investigate jobs and other situations in anticipation of parole. To be eligible, inmates had to have a clean record, the recommendation of the warden, and an approval from TDC's central administration. Criminal records were an important consideration, but it was not uncommon for murderers and armed robbers to go on furloughs; sex offenders, however, had little chance of being selected.

Much less tangible, but by far the most important reward available to inmates has already been mentioned—good time. An inmate's "line class" indicated the amount of good time he drew; for every thirty calendar days they served, new inmates got twenty extra days (Line Class I), miscreants could be reduced to no extra days (Line Class III), and state-approved trusties (SATs) got thirty extra days. Prison officials frequently stated that they had nothing to do

Table 5 *Good Time Classification of Inmates by Race (in Percent)*

	Whites	Blacks	Mexican Americans
State-approved trusties	55	54	38
Line Class I	35	35	52
Line Class II and III	10	11	5

Source: James W. Marquart, "Cooptation of the Kept: Maintaining Control in a Southern Penitentiary."
Note: N = 310.

with parole when, in fact, they had a direct hand in deciding when an inmate would become eligible for release. That is, their assessments of an inmate's behavior determined his line class and, if he was demoted, the length of time he stayed in a disadvantageous class receiving less good time.

Because good time was such an important control device, its distribution is instructive. Data collected on a random sample of inmates at the Eastham Unit in the early 1980s revealed the distribution across good time classifications shown in Table 5. These data make two important points. First, officials appeared to have dispensed class/good time rewards without regard to race. Second, few inmates were in Line Class II and III, drawing either ten or no extra days per month, respectively. At the same time, over half of the black and the white inmates and nearly 40 percent of the Hispanics were drawing thirty extra days per month. These figures suggest that even in the tough Eastham Unit officials recognized the value of good time as a positive control tool and used it extensively.

These punishments and rewards were official in that they were usually reflected in rule books; could, for the most part, be applied by the staff in front of outsiders (though they seldom were); and were recorded in an inmate's file, or "travel card." But they certainly did not exhaust the control regimen in TDC. There were other, more informal means of keeping institutional order, believed by many officers to be the real basis for TDC's reputation for tight control.

Informal Control Mechanisms

We treated the convict just like he wanted to be treated. [I]f he wanted to come in and go to work and do his time, we'd leave him alone. Now if he come in and wanted to be a horse's butt, we were a horse's butt. If he wanted to fight, we'd fight. And we expected them to go to work. Back then, in my way of thinking, there's two ways you handle people. They either fear you or they respect you enough to do what you ask them to do. And back then we had some fear, but we had some respect, too. If a man wanted to get out and show his back end [work hard], then we would help him.

This statement from a retired warden reflects the official attitude toward inmates and their control prior to the 1980s in Texas prisons. That is, inmates themselves were responsible for how they fared inside. The warden also points out two of the most important traditional control devices used by TDC officers, namely, work and fear. Well-socialized officers knew how to remind inmates that crossing them or failing to obey orders would be dreadful. For example, many learned to glare at inmates in an accusatory manner to make the inmate feel very uncomfortable. Some officers chose to act crazy, to bluster and use extensive profanity to intimidate prisoners. Others walked and talked more softly but carried a fearsome reputation.

There were more institutionalized, informal control devices officers used to dominate and control inmates. These included fieldwork, gaining information, a range of sanctions for minor offenses, and the use of force.

Fieldwork.   Consistent with TDC's traditional emphasis on inmate work and the work ethic, all inmates had a job. Though inmate work ostensibly promoted the work ethic and maximized prison self-sufficiency, it also promoted control, especially in the field. The harshness of fieldwork made prisoners compliant just to avoid it, and it communicated to prisoners precisely who was in charge.

The field major assigned new inmates to squads differentiated by size and race. Since squads not only worked together but also lived together, this "equalizing" strategy in field assignments was intended to both match work speed and minimize exploitation, or "hogging," in the tanks. The hoe squads were numbered, with "one hoe" being the squad with the biggest white inmates, "two hoe" having the biggest black inmates, "three hoe" having the biggest Mexican American inmates, and so on, up to perhaps fifteen squads. Garden squads involved lighter work and were usually reserved for small, weak, or homosexual inmates. Because they were reserved for bigger and stronger inmates, the lower numbered, or "bull," squads were expected to work harder and faster than other squads. The significance to inmates of hoe squad assignment is evident in the following account by Albert Sample, who found himself back in TDC in the 1960s:

I had learned on Clemens [during a prior TDC term] that the higher the squad number, the better off you were. Judging my size against [two other men], I figured I'd probably be put in Number 7 or 6 at least . . .

I was next, "You ain't all that big," [the boss said] "but you wuz big enuff to rob them folks. Got sum big time this time didn't ya?"

"Yes, suh."

"Well, I'm gonna put yore yeller ass where you kin start doin' sum of it. When that Number 1 hoe cums out, you ketch it.". . .

Back on the tank one of the cons said, "Man, Cap'n Smooth put you in a bad-d-d muthafucka! All them niggahs is wild. An' the lead row niggah they got, Ol' Road Runner, runs wide-open all day long. An' Boss Deadeye is a sho' nuff number one driver. You betta be ready to hit the door runnin'!"[18]

Not just the number one squad, but all squads, had to "hit the door runnin'." After rising early and eating breakfast, the line (all field squads) would move to the area behind the building just inside the back gate. Each man knew his squad, and each squad knew to deuce it up so that they could quickly be counted into the charge of the appropriate field boss.

The new inmate's first days in the field were always painful. Usually, the field force rode to the field on trailers pulled by tractors. Prior to 1950, however, the trip to the work site was on foot, and the pace was often a rapid walk or even a trot. Work patterns remained the same for decades. If the work involved row crops, the "lead-row" man (Ol' Road Runner in the above quote) would take the first row, and each member of the squad would quickly take a row counting from where the lead-row stopped. Each man would then begin to work, trying to keep up with the lead-row, whose job it was to set the pace. Since the lead-row was selected by the boss for his working stamina, the pace was usually rapid. At the other end of the line was the "tail-row," an equally good worker who matched the lead-row's pace. The idea was for the line of prisoners between these two to remain straight. Laggers, new or less-skilled workers, would cause the line to bow in the middle, which would result, at the very least, in verbal reprimands from the boss and sometimes physical abuse from the lead- or tail-row.

Although the oppressive nature of fieldwork itself certainly encouraged prisoners to "keep their business straight" and get a job in the building, there was a more fundamental sense in which fieldwork fostered control in earlier years. That is, labor under the sun and under the gun conveyed to the inmate in the most graphic terms that he occupied a powerless and subservient role in the organization. By passing through the back gate from the building to the fields, inmates moved from one world into another. While life in the building could be, at times, painful, it was nonetheless the place of sleep, television, food, periodic visits, and opportunities to engage in the myriad scams that make prison life more bearable.

The field, however, offered no such amenities. There inmate behavior could be easily observed and, in the isolation of that setting, often "corrected" by officers with a rather single-minded concern for work and obedience. As the squads lined up inside the gate to be counted out each morning, they could see their mounted bosses sitting stirrup to stirrup, waiting for their squads to be "turned out." The image these officers presented was one of power and dominance. Mounted officers always towered over inmates, regardless of the inmate's size; all inmates were always below all officers. This physical relationship constantly reminded the inmate of his subordinate relationship to his keepers.

The individual and collective persona projected by field bosses reinforced this message of official power. In varying degrees, they tapped the powerful cultural imagery of the cold-eyed gunslinger, the tough cowboy, or the Texas Ranger. The horse, revolver, hat, spurs, weathered visage, and no-nonsense demeanor of these men suggested that, like these western archetypes, they were tough, competent, and probably little concerned with legal or personal niceties.

Inmates who did not meet the boss' expectations in the field sometimes got a more concrete reminder of his power. Sample recalls what happened to him after being singled out for working too slowly during his first day in a hoe squad. "Cap'n Smooth took my right wrist and clamped the cuff on tight-tight. Then he backed me up against the iron bars that separated the messhall from the inner hall. With one cuff clamped on my right wrist and my back against the bars, he took the unclosed cuff and looped it through the bars above my head. Then he told me to fold my left arm above my head while he clamped on the other cuff. When he finished, I was left hanging with my toes barely touching the floor."[19] This treatment, known as "puttin' 'em on the bars," was applied with no hearing and little explanation because Boss Deadeye did not think Sample had the right attitude toward work. Usually, officers let the prisoner or prisoners hang there all night, then took them down just in time to turn out for another day. Such treatment of inmates by field officers became less frequent in the 1970s compared to earlier decades. It was not uncommon in these later years, however, for a field boss to discipline a man he believed to be "slow bucking" by denying him the evening meal and/or making him stand in the hall all night.

Such treatment underscored the relative dominance of prison officials. That dominance gave officers the power even to redefine a prisoner's identity. Field officers, in particular, regularly gave new names to some or all of the prisoners in their squad. Those names were typically inspired by physical features (e.g., Eggplant for a black man with shiny skin or Carrottop for a red-haired man) or work ability (e.g., Ol' Racehorse or Ol' Roadrunner). Reflecting racial and ethnic perceptions by officials, this renaming was almost universal for blacks, occasional for whites, and rare for Hispanics.

For their part, prisoners in the field adhered to an elaborate etiquette contrived to underscore their subordinate status. Besides answering to a new name, field inmates usually took off their hats when they addressed a boss, especially the major or the captain. On one occasion in the mid-1970s, a squad of inmates on the Ferguson farm was moving from a field they had finished to another a short distance away. Trotting in pairs, they crossed in front of the field captain. When they drew even with him, the lead-row man shouted, "Hats off," at which each man in the squad snatched off his hat as he passed. In so doing, they complied with one of the rules of the field.

The clearest illustration of how etiquette designates authority was the traditional practice of asking permission of the bosses to do anything other than work. Indeed, the mode of asking was itself highly stylized and found on all TDC farms. If an inmate wanted to stop for a cigarette, he said, "Lightin' it up, Boss?" and to urinate, he said, "Pourin' it out, Boss?" The boss' permission would come as "Light it" and "Pour it out."

Fear and intimidation as control devices were generally more pronounced in the field than in the building. The possibility that a recalcitrant inmate could be shot, purposely knocked over by a horse, hit with knotted reins, beaten by an officer or by another inmate at a boss' bidding, or "put on the bars," together with the hard work, sparked considerable fear. That fear usually translated into compliance.

Yet, as suggested earlier, there was sometimes a kind of grudging respect between the field boss and his squad. It, too, could foster compliance. Although many officers rotated among hoe squads, some officers carried the same squad each day. When this was the case, the supervision became more personalized, though still highly paternalistic. Officers came to know the characteristics of the men in their squad and, as we have mentioned, were capable of taking care of "their mistakes" in various ways.

At the same time, individual inmates in such a squad often thought of and referred to their supervisor as "my boss" and thereby bolstered paternalism. The nicknames he gave them were often accepted; they were theirs under his supervision in the field. If others in the building used the nicknames, however, the inmates might take offense. They would work for him and loaf for another boss. Indeed, his orders might mean more to them than those of others. For example, on one occasion a squad was counted back into the building and was in the shower. The building officer was telling them to hurry, but they were moving very slowly. Their field boss happened to come by the shower, noticed their lagging, and simply shouted, "Ya'll get yer asses outa that shower" (almost exactly what the building officer had said), and the inmates immediately got out, some even trailing soap. This example is not meant to suggest that building officers had little personal authority; many had a great deal. Rather, in this case, the field boss' order meant more partly because he was their boss and partly because he reflected the authority of that other world, the field.

Information.   Although fieldwork introduced inmates to their subordinate position in TDC, by the 1960s no more than 40 to 50 percent of a farm's inmate population was assigned to the field at one time. The rest had a job in the building. To maintain control over this population, as well as the line at night and on weekends, officers relied heavily on gathering information about inmates and about possible rule-breaking activities.

Perhaps the most universal element of the "convict code" is that prisoners will not give information to the authorities about other prisoners.[20] Violators are "snitches" or "rats" who, at best, suffer ostracism and, at worst, death at the hands of other inmates. Yet, just as in other large prison systems, inmates in TDC passed a great deal of information to officials.

They did so for many reasons, in many cases because it was their job. Building tenders and turnkeys supplied TDC officials with much of the information they received. As we will see, BTs were, among other things, institutional snitches. Because they were often dominant inmates and had the support of the staff, they were unlikely to suffer for carrying information to "the man." Other inmates passed along information to protect themselves or to remove a troublesome element from the living area.

Developing information was for officials critical both for prison stability and for their own careers. A traditional TDC control strategy was to penetrate as deeply as possible into the inmate's world. By constantly collecting information on inmate activities, officers could avoid being surprised by anything. At the same time, skill in developing information indicated a good officer. It could gain him promotions, better duty assignments, or, on another plane, simply satisfaction.

Inmates did not give sensitive information to just anyone and almost never to cellblock officers. Because of their low rank, inexperience, or youth (and frequently all three), these officers were not trusted. But rank did not guarantee that an officer would receive information. Only if he was trusted would prisoners bring him information.

An officer who was trusted had demonstrated that he could be reasonable toward inmates. Specifically, he had demonstrated that he could be discreet with information that might be sensitive enough to get someone injured or even killed. A former TDC warden described his approach to garnering information:

> If I wanted to talk to [an inmate] about something serious, I didn't call him down and leave him standing in that hall. I didn't do that. I'd get up tonight after everybody went to bed and I would tell the captain that at a certain time [that inmate's] due up in the visiting room or whatever. I don't care; I'd be sitting outside. Or if he was working in the field and I knew he wanted to see me I'd get on the radio and I'd call the foreman and I'd tell them to bring [the inmate] because he's got an "attorney visit." You covered them.

By providing a cover story for the encounter with the inmate, the officer protected him and ensured that the inmate would provide other useful information.

Most inmates complied with official expectations either because the overwhelming dominance of the system first experienced in the field broke their spirit or because the official information network made deviance too risky. But inmate deviance certainly occurred. Though officials regularly relied on the formal sanctions we have already considered, they more frequently relied on an array of informal, unofficial sanctions. These informal control devices bolstered the formal sanctions and underscored the power of TDC personnel.

Informal Sanctions for Minor Offenses.   Many inmate transgressions were considered too minor to warrant the trouble of formal proceedings. Such offenses usually involved an inmate's failing to see a situation as the boss did or an inmate's giving the officer a hard time. Examples of such offenses include repeatedly moving slowly on the job, glaring back at an officer, or just being in the wrong place at the wrong time. Punishment in such cases was usually some form of humiliation, an experience calculated to cause the inmate to lose face.[21]

For some infractions officers made inmates stand against the wall in the long central hall of the building in full view of other inmates. One version of this punishment used at the Ferguson Unit was called Texas TV. To "watch," inmates had to stand with their toes and nose against the wall, usually across from the major's office in the main compound hallway. They stood there until the officer who put them there sent them back to their cellblock. A variant of this practice was common at the Eastham Unit. Inmates were told to "catch the wall." The wall at Eastham referred to the area adjacent to the major's office in the long hall. When so ordered, the inmate had to go directly to this area and wait for some further action. In fact, when inmates faced formal sanctions for a serious offense, officers often put them on the wall, sometimes for hours, until the proper paper work was completed. The wall was most often a holding area for inmates who had minor confrontations with officers. The following illustrates such a confrontation and the minor punishment it prompted. "See, I was watching this inmate and all he was doing was talking, talking, talking. So I finally went over to him [in the dining hall] and said, 'I've been watching you for the past five minutes and all you've been doing is bullshitting; you haven't been eating.' He said 'Well, I just wanted to finish my cake.' I said, 'Man, get your goddamn ass on the wall.' He left the dining hall and stood on the wall alright. [The lieutenant] had a few words with him and then cut him loose." Putting an inmate on the wall singled him out and discredited him while he waited on the staff's "turf" for something to happen. Those inmates standing on the wall who attempted to interact with staff were ignored or told to be quiet. Moreover, inmates passing by these areas always looked to see who was on the wall and then gossiped about the likely reason for the punishment.

Another minor punishment, also aimed at humiliation, was the verbal assault, or tongue-lashing. During or following court, when a formal punishment had been pronounced, the major or ranking officer on the tribunal would often upbraid the inmate. This punitive tirade was usually the province of the higher-ranking officers, although it was sometimes done by hall bosses. The harangue involved almost always profanity and frequently racial or ethnic epithets. The purpose of verbal assaults was to terrorize and intimidate the inmate. Indeed, these verbal assaults sometimes involved force threats. Although these threats were seldom carried out, physical punishment occurred often enough that the threats had the desired impact. The following examples were recorded in 1982 at the East-ham Unit of TDC:

> You stupid nigger, if you ever lie to me or to any other officer about what you're doing, I'll knock your teeth in.
>
> You know something, you [the inmate] get along with us pretty good and you even do us some favors [snitching] once in a while. But if you ever give my officers a hard time out there [in the hall] again, we'll stomp you into the concrete.[22]

Verbal control of inmates by officers did not always involve force threats. At times officers simply "messed with their minds," keeping inmates off-balance and unsure of themselves and their limits. As one officer put it, "You got to make them think you are crazy." Intended to intimidate, such mind games communicated contempt for the inmate's status and kept him off-balance. For example, a warden might tell a slow and probably superstitious inmate, "I had a dream about you last night," and then proceed to tell a fabricated tale intended to frighten the inmate and to impress him with the warden's clairvoyance. Another example is that of an inmate who approached the "searcher's" desk, a central control point in the hall, and placed his hands on the counter waiting for a chance to speak. The lieutenant, surrounded by several other officers, suddenly whipped around to the inmate and said, "Get your goddamn hands off my desk!" The startled and immediately cowed inmate jumped back and apologized. On another occasion, an inmate approached a hall boss and asked to see the chaplain. The officer replied, "Go on back to your cell, he's taking inventory today."

A final example illustrates how an officer sometimes acquired information from inmates by playing on their fears.

> OFFICER (in front of the inmate's cell): Get that booster [radio antennae] and let's go.
>
> INMATE: Well, I was just using it.
>
> OFFICER: I don't care, just get it and let's go.
>
> INMATE: Am I in trouble?
>
> OFFICER: That's right, you're in big trouble.
>
> INMATE (starts crying): What's going to happen to me?
>
> OFFICER: We're going to try to lock you up [in solitary] for about a year.
>
> INMATE (trembling): Oh, no!

OFFICER (jokingly): Actually, they are probably going to slap you around a bit in the major's office.

INMATE: Oh, no!

OFFICER: Well, if you tell me where you got that booster from, I'll tell the supervisor and we'll put in a good word for you to see that it goes easier on you.

INMATE: I bought it from . . . [another inmate] for two bags of punch.[23]

These tactics clearly put inmates on the defensive and reiterated their subordinate status. Humiliation and keeping inmates off-balance were powerful means of control. Part of the reason they were effective, however, was that behind official power displays was the very real possibility of punishment involving overt, physical force.

Use of Force

Within TDC, physical force as punishment and deterrence was an important element of the overall control strategy. Coercion was deeply entrenched in the guard subculture and institutionalized to the extent that a gradation of force levels was apparent. Specifically, Texas officers relied on three increasingly harsh types of physical coercion: "tune-ups," or "attitude adjustments"; "ass whippings"; and severe beatings.[24]

Tune-ups were directed at inmates who openly challenged an officer's authority by cursing him or being flippant, insubordinate, or belligerent and did not ordinarily involve serious injury. This sanction involved verbal humiliation, profanity, shoves, kicks, and head and body slaps and was intended as an "attention getter," to scare the inmate into compliant behavior. The following account illustrates the circumstances leading to most tune-ups.

I [hall officer] had a hard time in the north dining hall with an inmate who budged in line to eat with his friend. Man, we had a huge argument right there in the food line after I told him to get to the back of the line. I finally got him out [of the dining hall] and put him on the wall. I told my supervisor about the guy right away. Then the inmate yelled, "Yeah, you can go ahead and lock me up [in solitary] or beat me if that's how you get your kicks." Me and the supervisor brought the guy into the major's office. Once in the office, this idiot [inmate] threw his chewing gum in a garbage can and tried to look tough. One officer jumped up and slapped him across the face and I tackled him. A third officer joined us and we punched and kicked the shit out of him. I picked him up and pulled his head back by the hair while one officer pulled out his knife and said, "You know, I ought to just go ahead and cut your lousy head off."

This experience certainly got the inmate's attention, especially since he had believed that the officers would not hit him. He said, "Man, I didn't think you got fucked up for smarting off." Although the inmate had been at the unit for over six months and knew the guards used force, he mistakenly thought they would not hit him for such a "petty ass" violation.

Many tune-ups took place during and after disciplinary court. One informant provided this account of two tune-ups in court. The first inmate was tried for refusing to work.

A supervisor said, "You're going to work from now on, you understand?" After this, the supervisor slapped him [inmate] on the head, kicked him in the ass, and literally threw him out the door. The next inmate was brought in, tried, and found guilty of self-mutilation. He had ingested numerous razor blades. One supervisor yelled at him, "It's hard enough for me to keep the rest of these inmates in razor blades to shave with around here, let alone having you eat them all the time." The inmate stuttered and a supervisor slapped him twice across the face.

Obviously, inmates handled this way in court received both formal (loss of privileges, solitary, etc.) and informal punishment.

The second type of physical coercion was commonly called an ass whipping and regularly involved such weapons as blackjacks, riot batons, or aluminum-cased flashlights. Such a whipping occurred when an officer instructed several inmates in a cellblock dayroom (TV room) to "hold the noise down." An inmate yelled back, "Shut up yourself and stay the hell out of the dayroom." He was ordered to the major's office where he was punched, kicked, and blackjacked by several officers.

These more punitive episodes occurred most often when an inmate decided to really fight back during a tune-up. On one such occasion, the inmate was thrown to the floor by several officers. One literally stood on the inmate's head (called a tap dance) while another "spanked" him on the buttocks and thighs with a riot baton. During this event, a supervisor was heard yelling, "Hurt him, hurt him," and even encouraging the other officers by saying, "Go on, get you some of that ass."

The third type of force used in TDC was the severe beating. These occurred infrequently and were reserved for inmates who violated serious rules, such as attacking staff members. Beatings differed from ass whippings only in degree; they were intended to inflict serious injury on the inmate. For example, one inmate was dragged from the hall into the major's office and beaten, then beaten again while being locked up in solitary.

Like other force situations, beatings were usually covert events. Sometimes, however, they were carried out in full view of other inmates. An officer related the following account, which reveals the provocation and the spontaneity with which officers resorted to extreme force.

I was sitting at the searcher's desk and Rick [inmate] and I were talking, and here come Joe [inmate] from 8-block. Joe thinks he knows kung fu; hell, he got his ass beat four months ago. He comes down the hall and he had on a tank top, his pants were tied up with a shoelace, gym shoes on, and he had his property in a large sack. As he neared us, Rick said, "Well, Joe's fixing to go crazy again today." He came up to us, and Rick asked him what was going on, and Joe said they [staff] were fucking with him by not letting him have a recreation card. I told him, "Well, take your stuff and go over there to the major's office," and there he went. Officer A went over and stood in front of Joe, so did Officer B who was next to Officer A. Inmate James, an inmate who we tuned up in the hospital several days before, stood about ten feet away. All of a sudden, Joe took a swing at Officer A. A and B tackled Joe. I ran over there and began kicking his legs and genitals. Hell, I tried to break his leg. At the same time B was using his security keys, four large bronze keys, like a knife. The security keys have these points on their ends where they fit in the locks. Well, B was jamming these keys into Joe's head. Joe was bleeding all over the place. Inmate James threw a punch at Officer D as he came out of the major's office to see what was going on. James saw Joe getting beat, and he decided to help Joe out. I left Joe to help Officer D. By the time I got there [about two seconds] Officer D and about six convicts were beating the shit out of James. Officer D was beating James with a blackjack. Man, you could hear that crunch noise every time he hit him. At the same time a convict was hitting him in the stomach, chest, and face. These other inmates were kicking him and stomping him at the same time. It was a wild melee, just like being in a war. I got in there and grabbed James by the hair, and Officer D was hitting [him] on the face and head with the blackjack. I mean he was hitting him, no love taps. He was trying to beat his brains out and yelling, "You motherfucker, you think you're bad, you ain't bad, you motherfucker, son-of-a-bitch, you hit me and I'll bust your fucking skull." I think we beat on him alone for ten minutes. I punched him in the face and head. Then Officer D said to take him to the hospital. Officer C and me had to literally drag him all the way to the hospital. Plus, we punched and stomped him at the same time. At the hospital, Officer D began punching James in the face. I held his head so D could hit him. Then D worked James over with a blackjack. We stripped James and threw him on the bed. D yelled at James, "I'm going to kill you by the time you get off this unit." Then D began hitting him in the shins and genitals with a nightstick. Finally we stopped and let the medics take over. James had to leave via the ambulance. Joe required some stitches and was subsequently put in solitary.

This beating was the talk of the prison, and many officers used the incident as a threat, suggesting that inmates should think twice before they tried to strike an officer.

Force was considered by officers to be a legitimate response to blatant inmate transgressions. It was legitimated first by tradition. Prison is a violent world, and physical coercion had always been employed to control inmates in Texas. Moreover, because of this tradition, officers found ready justifications for such actions as illustrated in "all some of these thieves understand is force; you've got to dust some just to set an example."

Nonetheless, officers recognized that many, if not most, force episodes would be viewed by outsiders, especially the courts, as inappropriate, illegal, or both. As a result, in almost every situation where guards struck an inmate, post facto explanations were manufactured.[25] To avoid possible civil liability or even criminal prosecution, officers regularly got together after an episode and wrote statements to the effect that the inmate assaulted an officer and that force was required to subdue him. The more force the officers used, the more the inmate was said to have "fought back." For most tune-ups, cover charges were not created. However, ass whippings and beatings quickly prompted disciplinary report-writing sessions. Because the use of force against inmates usually took place in such closed settings as the major's office, the solitary wing, or the hospital, officers were further able to minimize legal consequences of their actions.

Functions of Force Episodes

The most obvious function of force in TDC was to effect control and order. By physically punishing prisoners, in some cases severely, officers believed (with some justification) that these sanctions provided both general and specific deterrence.

This belief prompted the instrumental use of force. That is, it was not used randomly. Minor inmate-inmate infractions (gambling, tattooing, stealing) did not bring on physical reprisals since officers did not consider these acts to be threats to either their authority or prison order. Force was reserved for certain inmates and for serious infractions. These infractions included sexual attacks, threatening another prisoner, and fighting with a weapon.

A second function of force in TDC was the perpetuation of staff dominance over inmates.[26] Failure of an inmate to respond in the appropriate manner frequently led to a force encounter. After being confronted with a rule infraction, those inmates who responded in an antagonistic or nondeferential manner were much more apt to evoke a physical response from the bosses.

Detailed analysis of thirty force episodes at the Eastham prison unit underscores how force supported the status quo. Specifically, only nine of these episodes involved serious inmate-inmate infractions; the remaining twenty-one cases, over two-thirds of the total, involved direct challenges to official authority. The nine cases consisted of three homosexual threats, four physical threats, and two cases of continuous fighting (no weapons were used, but the participants had had several fistfights at work and in the cellblocks). The sanction in each case involved little more than a tune-up.

The remaining twenty-one force episodes were considered much more serious by staff since they called staff dominance into question. Minor inmate offenses of this type (refusing to obey an order, swearing at or threatening officers) brought about a tune-up as a matter of course. On one occasion, a guard ordered an inmate to quit talking while standing in line to receive medicine; the inmate replied, "I can talk to anybody I please, and I sure as hell can talk as loud as I want." This inmate wound up in the major's office where he was slapped across the face and kicked in the buttocks by several officers.

The consequences for striking or even trying to strike an officer, however, were much more severe. As the above account of the beating of James clearly reveals, such an offense typically led not to a tune-up but to an overhaul. The attitude of most officers about such challenges to authority always called for a beating. As a veteran guard put it: "We don't tolerate officers getting jumped on or talked crazy to around here. They'll [inmates] ride the ambulance if they try it."

Given the prevailing racial attitudes among the overwhelmingly white security force, black inmates on all TDC units were more subject to force than other prisoners. White officers viewed black inmates as basically antiauthority, inferior, aggressive, and generally disrespectful. Such attitudes help explain why twenty-four of the thirty force episodes examined involved black prisoners. Only one Hispanic and five white prisoners were physically punished. Many staff members subscribed to the notion that black prisoners occasionally needed physical coercion to "keep them in their place."

A third function of physical coercion was validation of the "right stuff" among officers. Indeed, an officer's willingness to control inmates physically when necessary reflected a key subcultural value and fostered acceptance by his peers. Fighting was a measure of both the officer's manhood and his potential. At many TDC units, especially those for tougher prisoners, a cult of male honor prevailed in which personal violence was obligatory to establish the officer's reputation and status.[27] As one ranking officer put it, "You have to make a convict fear you or respect you, or you won't make it here."

Finally, using force strengthened solidarity among the inner core of officers. While most TDC officers supported the value of force, its actual application was restricted to ranking and hall officers. Cellblock officers simply did not raise a hand except in rare cases of self-defense. Force episodes were initiated by a ranking officer, and other officers then joined the fray. It was not uncommon for five or six officers to be involved. These officers interacted daily on and off the job, and they accepted other officers whose control orientation paralleled their own. Predictably, this acceptance translated into low turnover and high morale. Once accepted into the inner group of officers at a unit, officers learned about the code of secrecy.[28] As a rule, hall and ranking officers refrained from talking about force episodes with outsiders and even lower-ranking officers. Keeping one's mouth shut was an important norm. It was common for low-ranking guards to ask hall officers about force situations they had heard about only to have their inquiries closed off by replies of "I don't know what you're talking about" or "I wasn't here that day."

Conclusion

A "good" officer in TDC through the 1970s reflected the officer sub-culture. Ideally, he was loyal, hard-working, and paternalistic. He could also, largely on his own, ensure that inmates deported themselves in the acceptable, subordinate manner. These were the officers most often promoted in the "old days"; they constituted an inner core and evinced a high degree of comradery and cohesion.[29] That solidarity, plus a widely shared definition of how guard work should be done, served to shape and control officer behavior.

Since officers felt that failure to subordinate inmates undermined both personal authority and unit security, they developed a wide assortment of devices to control inmates. Though formal procedures were available and used daily, they rested on, and were to some extent overshadowed by, the more subtle, informal control system employed by the staff. Force was certainly not the most commonly used control tactic, but it was a fundamental one.

Besides those discussed above, there was another, very important, control device that officials through the early 1980s relied upon to subdue inmates. This device was the use of elite inmates as guards. Though inmate guards were certainly not unique to Texas, TDC's building tenders represented perhaps the most extensive and institutionalized system of inmate guards in American corrections. That system is the subject of the next chapter.

4

Co-optation of the Kept

The inmates invented the building tender system. The "Man"
only refined it and twisted it into parameters that would be bene-
ficial to the prison system. There was no great architect of the
building tender system. It evolved over time and guys like the
Bear and Billy "G" refined it. —TDC INMATE[1]

FOR NEARLY 100 years, Texas prison officials relied on a system through which elite prisoners—building tenders, turnkeys, and bookkeepers—directly controlled other prisoners in the living areas.[2] Drawing authority from the officials they worked for, these inmates were an extremely powerful feature and a key element in the control of Texas prisoners. In many ways the use of inmate elites was a legacy of slavery. Texas prisons were (and still are) located primarily in East Texas, an area with a long history of cotton plantations and slavery during the antebellum era. In that era, selected slaves were used as drivers or foremen to manage, lead, work, and discipline other slaves.[3] The transference of this practice from slavery to an analogous coercive institution, the plantation prison, is evident.[4]

In this chapter we explore the history of the building tender system, examining its structure and role in the years just prior to the court's intervention. Although this system existed in some form on almost all TDC units, our analysis will be limited to only one, the Eastham unit. The building tender system at Eastham, according to court and prison officials and our own observations, is generally representative of how elites were co-opted for control at other units, especially at units for tough prisoners.

Building Tenders in Historical Context

The use of dominant inmates to enforce order and maintain control in Texas prisons began sometime in the late 1800s, although the exact date is unknown. Prison records from 1880, however, indicate that building tenders, turnkeys, and bookkeepers were used at the main prison in Huntsville, the Walls Unit.[5] These records list all inmate prison job assignments. Building tenders, gatekeepers or turn-keys, and clerks or bookkeepers were classified in 1884 under the category of Indispensables. The records indicate that in that year at the Huntsville Unit there were eleven BTs, eight clerks, and four gatekeepers. Records in the same year for the Rusk penitentiary, built in 1876, list ten BTs, six clerks, and six gatekeepers under the category of Indispensables.[6] By 1920 the use of inmates as extensions of the guard force was well institutionalized throughout the prison system.

Early and Unquestioned Authority of Elites

It is unclear as to how the guards selected their inmate agents during the nineteenth century. Probably, the wardens at the Huntsville and Rusk institutions simply selected inmates who showed some intelligence, loyalty, and knowledge of convicts. By the early 1900s, however, BTs, bookkeepers, and gatekeepers had come to be classified as trusties and thus had to be approved by the Board of Prison Commissioners. Individual farm managers recommended inmates to the board for BT positions, and when this body met it decided which inmates would be approved. The following excerpt is from a November 4, 1915, board of commissioners meeting: "In accordance with the recommendation of Manager T. G. Walker convict No. 36838 H. M. Collins was approved as trusty to be used as a building tender at the Wynne State Farm."[7] These early records also indicate that the ultimate authority to "hire" inmate control agents rested with the board and not with the individual farm managers. This formal approval process suggests that the penitentiaries were not private fiefdoms of the wardens. The board of commissioners exerted at least some control over the wardens.

Once selected, the building tenders and other elites enjoyed great authority over prison operations, as well as other prisoners. Though their work for prison officials regularly made them a focus of hatred among their fellows, their authority was so great that they were able to live in the same tanks with those they supervised.[8]

Elites performed many vital logistic and administrative roles for the prison through the late nineteenth and early twentieth century. For example, turnkeys possessed the keys to various doors within the institutions, while bookkeepers maintained the prison records. Inmate bookkeepers were especially important as they served as secretaries and handled numerous official transactions, records, and documents. In fact, the prison system was so dependent on skilled inmate help that from 1900 to 1907 an inmate bookkeeper at the Huntsville Unit maintained the prison system's bank account and worked in the general accounting office.[9]

Those elites designated as building tenders, however, enforced order in the tanks and, for that reason, were, and remained for nearly a century, at the top of the prisoner hierarchy. Officially, the several BTs assigned to each tank were janitors who cleaned or tended the prison building and the inmate living quarters. For example, they mopped and swept floors, dispensed laundry, washed windows, cleaned spittoons and commodes, and in the spring and summer months aired and fumigated the mattresses.

Unofficially, however, they were the acknowledged rulers of "their tanks" and worked directly with officials to maintain control. For example, building tenders primarily served as conduits of information. The following inmate account from the Clemens farm in 1910 vividly describes the punishment of two inmates who were "snitched off" by a BT: "I got whipped 45 licks because the building tender told him [the captain] I was squabbling in the building. He [the captain] made me kiss Drummon's tail. He would whip me and make Drummon kiss my behind and then whip him and make me kiss him. He [the captain] made me kiss the other fellow's tail, right in the hole, and made him do me the same way. He would make the other fellow get down on his knees and hands and make me drag my tongue right through the hole, and say 'Now, don't that taste good, you G—— d—— m—— f—— s—— of a b——;' and I would say, 'Yes sir.' . . ."[10] In this instance the captain apparently never questioned the BT's story. Evidence suggests that inmates were regularly punished solely on the basis of a BT's word.

These elite inmates also assisted the guards in dispensing formal punishments. Inmate testimony from various penitentiary investigation committee reports in the early 1900s detail instances in which BTs, for example, held inmates down while guards whipped the offenders with the bat. In other cases, BTs forced inmates who fought or talked too loudly in the tanks to climb and suspend themselves for hours on the bars separating the tanks. Building tenders also helped guards handcuff inmates to the bars so that their toes barely reached the floor.[11]

Finally, building tenders maintained discipline in the inmate living areas. In the decades prior to 1950, the prisons were chronically understaffed; available employees were often older, and even infirm, men who were no match for the younger, aggressive inmates. Moreover, because of overcrowding, even fit officers found it difficult to impose their will in the tanks. Thus, prison officials necessarily relied on inmate-guards to maintain some order there. The following account from an inmate in the 1920s summarizes the control role of BTs:

> The men who showed us to our bunks were called building tenders. There were two of them and they acted as a kind of police. They kept down fights and loud talking in the building. They carried dirk knives and clubs similar to a policeman's billy and believe me they would certainly use them if the occasion arose. You see in a prison camp there is always a bunch of rowdies who have to be disciplined by drastic measures. You can see also that the building tender's job was not an easy one, so naturally the authorities had a hard time finding men nervy enough for the job. Also you may realize there were lots of tenders killed. Of course the picket boss [cellblock guard] backed any play the tenders made, as long as they were fulfilling their duties. Under those conditions naturally the tenders had considerable authority. I have seen them make all the men, except a chosen few, get on their bunks and stay there during a rainy day when we couldn't work. If you wanted to get off of your bunk for anything you had to get permission from the tender. . . . It is the building tender's job to keep order in the building and help prevent anyone from getting out of the building.[12]

Building tenders enjoyed near limitless authority to maintain control. Keeping peace in the tanks often involved "set ups," contrived evidence to injure another for some gain, and terrorism. They openly carried, with staff approval, clubs and knives to protect themselves as well as to threaten and intimidate other inmates. The following describes BT violence during an escape attempt that occurred on the Eastham farm in 1922.

> Well they [three inmates] cut a hole in the loft and were making one in the roof when the building tender went and told the night guard, or picket boss. The boss told the building tender to go up and bring the boys down. He went up on top of the bunk rack, about seven feet below the loft, and told the boys the jig was up, that the boss had heard them, and they must come down. They started down, feet first, through the hole they had made. It was barely big enough to squeeze their bodies through, and when they got all but their arms and head through, he [the building tender] stabbed two of them. But the third man saw what was

taking place so he dived through head first. The building tenders [there were two of them] followed him and like to beat him to death. Then when they finished with him they went back up there and pitched the corpses off the top bunk, which was about ten feet high. They dragged them up to the picket. One of the boys still had a little life, and he tried to raise up. When he did, the least one of the building tenders hit him back to the floor. Then the boy they had beaten was made to go down there where the boys had bled and wash up the blood. While he did that the building tender—the one who had done the stabbing—walked up and down the aisle raving like a maniac. He licked the blood off his knife and asked us if any of the rest of us wanted to [escape].[13]

Rewards for Inmate-Guards

Building tenders, bookkeepers, and turnkeys were essentially foremen, usually possessed of practical knowledge of prison life and able to manage men one way or another. The guards knew their worth and rewarded them accordingly. One reward was good time. The inmate-guards obtained certain good time credits per month in 1929, as listed in Table 6.

These inmate control agents were also exempt from fieldwork, and this alone often made the dangerous job attractive. Other informal perquisites of the job included free movement within the prison building, access to ranking staff, extra food and clothing, and ability to possess and carry weapons. Considering the terrible living conditions that prevailed in Texas prisons, the availability of these privileges ensured that the guards had a constant pool of candidates for these jobs.

Perhaps the most important reward the inmate-guards received was the unswerving support and protection of the guard staff. The guard force stood behind "their" inmates. This is evidenced in the

Table 6 *Monthly Flat-Rate Overtime Schedule, 1929 (in Hours)*

Head bookkeepers	300
All other clerks	250
Head building tenders	300
Assistant building tenders	250
Head turnkeys	300
Assistant turnkeys	250

Source: Minutes of Texas Prison Board meetings, 2:282–283, 1916–1927.

whipping orders that were presented in Chapter 2. Between 1916 and 1927, a total of 949 whipping orders were issued, and 1,816 inmates were whipped for some rule violation. Close examination of these orders reveals that inmates were often whipped for fighting with or attacking building tenders. In this eleven-year period, 40 orders (4 percent of all orders) were issued, and 69 inmates (4 percent of all inmates whipped) were formally punished for disobeying, attacking, or fighting with building tenders.[14] The following examples typify the circumstances surrounding these whipping orders:

> Whipping Order No. 257 issued on January 22, 1923 for inmate Rubio Thomas for slipping up on Building Tender while Building Tender was asleep and hitting him in the head, 20 lashes. (Ramsey state farm)

> Whipping Order No. 314 issued on September 4, 1923 for inmate David Garrison for possessing dirk and making threat to kill Building Tender and actually attacking him, 20 lashes. (Retrieve state farm)[15]

Clearly, officials went to great lengths to reward and protect their inmates.

Early Lessons of the Building Tender System

Using elite prisoners in this manner was generally effective in terms of cost and control of prisoners. And as long as the prisoner population remained relatively small and stable, the few prison employees were able to oversee the actions of their surrogates in the tanks. In the first three decades of this century, however, Texas prison populations began to expand rapidly. For example, at the Eastham Unit in 1927 there were 337 inmates confined in four tanks, or 87 per tank. By 1939, the prisoner population was 981, with 245 inmates housed in each tank.[16] Despite the fact that the inmate population nearly tripled by 1939, no additional guards were hired and no new prisons were built.

Population growth and attendant control problems forced officials to rely even more heavily on the inmate-guards. This dependence was so extreme that by 1947 the system was out of control. Building tenders had become nearly autonomous control agents. Most were corrupted by their power and used their influence to exploit other prisoners materially and sexually or to sell illicit goods and services.

Contemporary Co-optation of Elites, 1950–1980

It was this turmoil and abuse that O. B. Ellis found when he became prison director in 1947. Recognizing that this type of convict rule was a dangerous and violent method of prisoner management, he publicly stated that he would abolish the system. Yet, after viewing the system in operation, Ellis decided that it had merit as long as it had strict staff supervision. In the next five years, he took several major steps to bridle the BTs. First, he demoted or transferred several lax wardens and encouraged several wardens to retire. Ellis felt these old-timers simply let the convict-guards run the prisons. He held their replacements more accountable for the actions of building tenders. Second, Ellis demoted such particularly notorious building tenders as Jack Rudisell and Ed "Moon" Mullins of the Eastham farm. Third, Ellis insisted on closer selection procedures and assigned this task to the newly formed classification division.[17] Fourth, he changed their names from building tenders to "floor boys," but, by whatever name, they remained a pivotal element in the control system.

When George Beto became director in 1962, he, too, had reservations about the building tender system. He concluded, however, like his predecessor, that these inmate intermediaries were a crucial source of intelligence and helped to maintain control. At the same time, he believed that they must be closely selected and restrained.

As noted in Chapter 2, Beto made it a practice to visit the units frequently and unexpectedly. He used these visits to observe operations and collect information on the BTs. On one occasion, Beto was at the Ellis Unit and observed an inmate standing in the hall. He asked the inmate (whom he knew) why he was not at work. The inmate replied, "I'm a building tender now." Beto immediately chastised the warden for using this inmate as a tender. According to Beto, he was dangerous and "would rape a snake through a brick wall if he had the chance." The inmate was removed from the tender role.

Beto also routinely conversed with inmates being paroled or discharged. He randomly asked these inmates whether building tenders were abusing other prisoners. If he decided abuses of power were occurring, tenders were removed or reassigned. Through these "exit interviews" and unit visits, Beto attempted to keep his inmate-guards in line.

The use of inmate-elites to control and run the prison was well institutionalized under Beto and continued relatively unchanged under W. J. Estelle, Jr., through the 1970s. The following detailed examination of how elites controlled regular prisoners and how TDC officials controlled (or failed to control) those elites is based on research conducted primarily at the Eastham prison unit, which epitomized the intrusive, but effective, control for which the entire organization was known. The inmate-guard system at Eastham involved three elements: the building tenders, the turnkeys, and the book-keepers, each of which played an important role in the unit's control machinery.[18]

The Building Tenders

Since its inception in 1913, the Eastham Unit housed older, violent, hard-core, and escape-prone multiple recidivists. This population required strict control, and BTs were believed to be critical to that control. This belief produced not only a long history of using the BT system at Eastham but also some of the most notorious BTs. While BTs were assigned to all living areas, it was in the cellblocks that their presence was most significant for control. Our discussion, therefore, is aimed at the structure and operation of this system as it was found in the blocks.

Stratification. The building tender system at Eastham involved three levels of inmates.[19] At the top of the hierarchy were the "head" building tenders. Each of the eighteen cellblocks had one building tender designated by the staff as head BT. They were the blocks' representatives to the prison staff. These BTs were responsible and accountable for all inmate behavior in their particular block. Block "ownership" was well recognized: inmates and officers alike referred informally, but meaningfully, to, for example, "Jackson's tank" or "Brown's tank." Because of their prestige and role, head BTs were the most powerful inmates in the prisoner society.

On the second level of the hierarchy in the blocks were the rank-and-file building tenders, the turnkeys, and the bookkeepers. In each block, there were usually three to five inmates assigned as building tenders, for a total of nearly 150 BTs within the institution. These inmates "worked the tank" in five- to seven-hour shifts, either assigned by the head BT or through self-selection. Building tenders were officially on duty from 2:30 A.M. until 10:30 P.M. on the weekdays and until 1:30 A.M. on the weekends. However, BTs were actually on call twenty-four hours and formally charged with the day-to-day task of managing the cellblocks.

These inmate control agents also socialized new inmates into the system. Typical guidelines might be "keep the noise down, go to work when you are called, mind your own business, no grab assing around, and tell us [the BTs] when you have a problem." BTs also broke up fights, issued orders to other inmates, protected officers, protected weak inmates, and passed on information to the head BTs and staff members.

The third rank among building tenders consisted of runners, strikers, or hit men. These inmates primarily performed the janitorial work of the block, sweeping, cleaning, and dispensing supplies to the cells. They also provided the BTs with physical backup. Some tanks had three or four runners, while others had as many as nine. The number of runners included from 175 to 200 inmates.

Cell assignments of these elites reflected their special status. Because of Eastham's telephone-pole design, cells on the first tier (ground level) and immediately off the main hall were the most convenient cells; head BTs always occupied these cells. Other BTs, turnkeys, and bookkeepers typically occupied the middle and last cells on the first tier and the first cell on the second tier. They rarely celled on the third tier because these tiers were too far to climb and were the hottest ones during most of the year. Runners, who occupied the lowest and least-formalized status level in the system, were distributed in no particular pattern throughout the cellblock. **Building Tenders as Snitches.** As always, a major expectation of the BTs was gathering information on the ordinary inmates' behavior and informing the guards. However, they did not report on every rule violation and violator. They screened all information and passed to the staff only intelligence about actual or potential serious rule infractions. Jerry, a head BT, explained: "Look, we don't tell the man [warden or major] about everything that goes on in the tanks. That makes it look bad if I'm running down to the major's office telling somebody, ol' so and so, he's playing his radio too loud, or ol' so and so, he's got an antenna that goes from his cell up to the window. That shows the man up there that I don't have control of that tank and I can't let that happen. It makes me look bad." The BTs handled misdemeanors, or petty rule violations, themselves in the blocks. In the case of serious rule violations, commonly called "major's office business," BTs routinely informed the bosses.

These elites were constantly alert to escape, work strike, or riot plans. For example, one night a cellblock officer found several saw marks on the bars of a cell's air vent, indicating a possible escape attempt. When a shift supervisor arrived to examine the marks, the block's BTs were assembled and asked about the situation. They knew of no hacksaw blades in the block and doubted that the two suspected inmates were the types to be preparing for an escape. They suggested that the cell's previous occupants were the most likely culprits.

These institutionalized snitches also informed the staff about ordinary inmates' homosexual and exploitive behavior. The staff considered this behavior serious because it frequently led to envy, to fights or lovers' quarrels, to retaliation, and to stabbings, as well as to the buying and selling of punks. BTs were very adept at discovering this form of illicit behavior. For example, one night the head BT of a block informed the shift supervisor that one well-known homosexual had entered the wrong cell on the second tier. The shift supervisor and head BT sneaked along the walkway and caught the inmates "in the act." In this same way, officials learned which inmates threatened or actually strong-armed weaker inmates into paying protection, engaging in homosexual acts, or surrendering their prison canteen goods.

Although the introduction of drugs into the population was difficult, small quantities occasionally were smuggled inside. Again, the inmate-agents kept this activity to a minimum and assisted the staff in making "drug busts." In one case a head BT told the guards about an inmate who worked as a tractor driver in the farm operation and was supplying marijuana cigarettes to a certain block. Plans were devised to catch the inmate with his supplies. Although no marijuana was found, it was later reported to the staff that the dealer quit trafficking because he was being watched.

The BTs informed staff members about inmates who manufactured, possessed, or sold weapons, especially knives. Inmates with weapons obviously placed the officers and their inmate-agents in physical jeopardy. On one occasion, a head BT informed a captain about a knife in the eighth cell on the first row of his block. Three officers and two BTs searched the cell, finding the knife wedged between the lower bunk and the cell wall. The owner of the weapon received disciplinary action, spent fifteen days in solitary confinement, and was moved to another cellblock. It was common for the BTs to help the guards search suspected inmates' cells because they knew the tricks and places that the inmates used to conceal weapons.

Runners were important to BTs since they gleaned and reported information in the living area. Although the runners' official role was that of inmate-janitor, their primary job was to be loyal to the BTs and act as informants. Some runners were friends with the BTs in the free world, and some were their consensual homosexual partners. Most important, runners were the eyes and ears of the BTs; they were selected to act as snitches. A head BT explained this situation: "You don't pick these people [runners] and tell them now they've got to go in there and tell me what's going on inside the dayroom. By becoming a runner it is expected that you will tell what's going on, it's an unspoken rule that you will inform on the rest of the people in here. If you hear something you are going to come to me with it." The majority of intelligence on the inmates' moods, problems, daily behaviors, friends, enemies, homosexual encounters, misbehavior, plots, and plans came to the BTs from the runners. These inmates had more contact with the ordinary inmates than did the BTs. This contact facilitated eavesdropping and extracting of inmate information. For example, while mopping the runs (walkways on each tier), runners talked to and observed the inmates in their cells. If things were awry, they informed their BT bosses. At work, these inmates listened to, watched, talked to, and interacted with the others.

BTs, like the guards, could not be everywhere at once and, therefore, relied on stool pigeons. BTs could not, for example, observe homosexuality in the cells, but their snitches could. A head BT summed up this situation: "The tanks are run through an information system. Whether this information comes from runners or even other inmates, this is how trouble is kept down." The BTs' snitching system was officially recognized as part of the prisoner control system.

Runners worked throughout the prison and routinely informed the BTs about activities in such areas outside the blocks as the school, shops, hospital, laundry, dining rooms, and shower rooms. A head BT described this activity:

> We BTs all have our people, but we don't fuck with each other's people. If you walk down the hall and hear somebody say "He's one of mine," that means that that particular inmate owes some type of allegiance to a particular BT. The reason he owes that allegiance or loyalty is perhaps the BT got him a job someplace, got him out of the field and into the garment factory. These people are loyal to me. I put them there not for me but for the man [warden] and they tell me what's going on in that particular place. If you don't help me then I'll bust you. I got Bruce the job in the Issue Room [clothing and supply room]. I own Bruce because I got him that job. He tells me if clothing is being stolen or if inmates are trying to get more than they deserve.

Misbehavior, plots, and plans were not confined solely to the living areas and the BTs had extended "ears" in all areas where inmates interacted. Consequently, they kept abreast of developments everywhere, and relatively little happened without their knowledge.

The actual route of information did not always follow a formal chain of command. Runners told the BTs, who, in turn, relayed information only to those ranking officers (sergeants, lieutenants, captains, majors, wardens) with whom they had developed a personal relationship. Some guards were trusted by few, if any, inmate-snitches and were essentially left out of the informer process. Others, who had displayed sufficient consistency and common sense in handling sensitive information, were trusted, respected, and admired by the inmate-elites. Building tenders actively sought alliances with these officers. Indeed, only a "man" could be trusted with confidential information. Such officers were briefed by BTs each day about events on and off their work shifts. Some of these inmate-agents were so loyal to a particular staff member that they refused to deal with other officers in that particular officer's absence.

While informing occurred throughout the prison, the major's office was the official focal point.[20] Elites routinely came here to relay information and to discuss plans of action. The guards and their inmate-guards socialized here as well as conducted the daily "convict business." Throughout the day, BTs (and turnkeys) came in to visit their inmate-bookkeeper friends and mingle with the ranking guards. Together, in this office area, they drank coffee, smoked, discussed sporting events, joked, chatted, engineered practical jokes, roughhoused, and ate food from the prison canteen. Whenever a captain, major, or warden entered, these inmates (sometimes there were eight or nine) would, if sitting, abruptly stand and say, "Hello, Sir." All day a steady stream of these inmate-agents filed in and out. BTs (and turnkeys) entered this office at will, although the major's office was off limits to ordinary inmates except for official reasons. It was a status symbol for the "rats" to hang around this office and interact with ranking guards.

Within this general familiarity, the process of passing along information usually proceeded according to a rather strict etiquette. Head BTs functioned as the block spokesmen, and they channeled the bulk of information to the guards. As one captain explained: "Generally, the head BT brings in most of the information. That serves several purposes. For one thing, it increases the reliability of the information received from the tank because administrators are always dealing with the same person. And it's more convenient for the BTs themselves in that the same person can carry the information up there [major's office] and there's not a squabble as to who's going to take what."

Some ranking guards had a cadre of BTs working for them. Having access to information from these prisoners put a given officer in a better position to anticipate and control problems in the prison. In this way, elite inmates were in a position to confer status on officers and, indeed, to affect, indirectly, their promotions. Some officers often gave their favorite BT special assignments, generally performed only by staff members, such as staking out, shadowing, or entrapping a suspected inmate or officer to gather evidence about rule violations or plans of wrongdoing.

The symbiotic relationship between key officers and elite inmates in TDC at times led to mutual trust and friendships. Over the years, many ranking guards developed close personal relationships with their favorite BTs. It was not uncommon for guards to call their pet BTs by their first names, a sign of respect and status. Some BTs were so fanatical in their loyalty that they openly stated they would kill another if so ordered by their officer.[21]

Building Tenders as Assistant Guards. BTs supported cellblock and hall officers in several ways. First, these prisoners maintained the inmate head counts, an almost hourly tally of where inmates from a given living area were in the building. At prescribed times officers made body counts, and then compared their tallies with those of the BTs. In many blocks, BTs and officers counted the block together.

Second, the BTs assisted the officers during inmate meals. A hall officer stood near the entrance of each dining hall and signaled the living areas to send a wave of inmates to eat. BTs then yelled, "Chow time, Boss" to the cellblock officer, who then let the prisoners out of the cells to go eat.

Similarly, BTs assisted the first-shift officers in getting the regular inmates ready for work each day. For example, each morning the cellblock officers received various phone calls instructing them to send the laundry workers and kitchen workers, among others, to work. These calls were then relayed to the BTs who, in turn, told the officer the row where these inmates lived, so that the officer could open the correct doors. In addition, the BTs called out the hoe squads each morning. Every weekday an inmate-bookkeeper informed the blocks which hoe squads were working that day. When the work bell rang, a BT in the hall called out the hoe squads. While the BT yelled out the squad numbers, the block officer opened the cell doors to let the inmates out for work.

Finally, BTs protected officers. By breaking up fights in the living areas, the BTs kept the guards from getting involved and risking personal injury. If officers did enter a crowded dayroom to quell a disturbance, BTs knew to look to their safety; it was central to their job.

Indeed, on more than one occasion BTs were observed pulling officers away from fights and then breaking up the action themselves.
But this protection had a price: reciprocal respect. Sometimes officers went overboard by shouting orders at everyone, including BTs.
The BTs controlled these officers' actions by subtly reminding the
officer of his protective role. If the officer continued, then the BTs
threatened the officer by saying, "If you don't get off my ass, Boss,
I might not help you if you get in a fight." Statements such as
these seemed humorous, but the meaning was seldom missed by the
officer.

Building Tenders as Mediators.   Building tenders (head and regular
BTs) routinely acted as adjudicators and arbitrators. Interpersonal
disputes are a fact of prison life. At Eastham, there were two general
types of disputes between inmates. First, there were the private disputes that usually involved cell partners arguing over such matters
as poor personal hygiene, snoring, chronic masturbation, or loud
music. These were petty squabbles, which the BTs called "misde-
meanor shit." When BTs heard or were told of two feuding cell partners, they called the disputants together and tried to settle the problem in house without involving the guards. In most cases, this tactic
was successful.

The second type of dispute was more serious and involved theft,
lovers' quarrels, physical or sexual threats, or failure to repay debts.
BTs viewed these problems as serious breaches of the prison order
(they could lead to violence) and actively intervened to settle them.
If an inmate had some personal property stolen or was physically
threatened, he could tell the BTs to resolve such disputes. An inmate who had a problem with his cell partner described the typical
settlement process: "My celly [cell partner] was reading my mail one
day. I caught him, too. I couldn't believe it. Plus he was a real dirty
guy, he was a real cockroach. I told him to pack his stuff. I ran it
down to the BTs. They got him moved to another tank." Another
inmate described how the BTs in his block handled inmate thievery:
"One time I had some punch [Kool-Aid] come up missing. Well I
asked around the tank to see if anybody had seen somebody go in my
house [cell] and steal my bags of punch. Sure enough, I found out
who it was. I told the BTs and they confronted the dude. He copped
to it and they slapped him around real good."

The BTs kept the peace mainly through cell or dorm moves, fear,
and coercion. If two cell partners were not compatible, the BTs informed the staff of the persistent trouble and advised them where to
move one of the disputants. Most moves occurred within the same

living area. However, the BTs also let some inmates settle their differences in supervised fistfights, in which the inmates actually came to the BTs and asked them if they could "settle it like men." If the inmates were about the same size, the BTs allowed the disputants to fight it out. After a fight settled the matter, the BTs told the guards that "nobody was hurt and it's over with." The staff did not investigate the fight and simply abided by the BTs' description of the incident. These fights were rarely lethal since only fists were used. Inmate disputants seldom used knives or other weapons because of the BTs' vast information network; it was difficult for an ordinary inmate to make and keep a weapon in his cell without the BTs' knowledge.

Inmates who "took matters into their own hands" evoked the wrath of the BTs. Certainly, some inmates engaged in self-help and beat, stabbed, or killed other inmates for such crimes as thievery or failure to repay a debt. However, few inmates went this far in settling personal disputes. Two inmates describe what happened to anyone caught beating up another inmate to settle a score without the BTs' knowledge.

> You couldn't whip another inmate's ass outright even if he stole something from you, because you knew of the repercussions. You had to involve the BTs. You had to get their approval first. If you whipped a dude's ass, they'd a whipped your ass, too. You couldn't take things in your own hands. I mean, you could, but you had a price to pay for it.

> Oh, man, if you beat some guy up to get even you just committed a cardinal sin. If you did that you took a big chance. You got your ass whipped by the BTs for jumping on this other guy.

The fear of coercive retaliation encouraged disputants to approach the BTs or forget about the problem. Furthermore, unsanctioned fighting in a living area brought unwanted staff intervention. The BTs tried to avoid or quell these situations because they brought, in their eyes, unnecessary "heat" on a living area. Such incidents also called into question the BTs' ability to manage effectively.

This dispute settlement process was so institutionalized that rarely did an inmate approach the staff about a problem or dispute. As one inmate stated: "If I put tank business on the street, I mean, if I took some business off the tank, I was a dead man. You never went over the BTs' heads, man, that was taboo. If you did, they got your ass. See, it was an unwritten policy that you took care of your business in the tank. If you went to the guards on your own, it made them [BTs] look bad. Oh, no, man, you never made a BT look bad." The threat of coercion kept the majority of inmates from discussing disputes with the guards. This problem-solving role reduced the number of inmate problems in which the guards actually became involved.

Conflicting loyalties, friendships, moods, and differing personalities produced considerable variance in how BTs handled disputes. All of these elites, however, seemed to weigh several factors in their decisions to intervene in personal problems. One factor was where the disputing prisoners lived. In the dormitories, building tenders settled disputes primarily through negotiation instead of force, since these living areas were regularly used by staff as rewards for good behavior. If the problem persisted, one of the disputants was typically moved to another living area.

Cellblocks were divided into three types: protection tanks, what might be called neutral tanks, and bull, or terror, tanks. Protection tanks housed homosexuals, weak inmates, and inmates who were afraid to be in the general population. BTs in these blocks, like the dorms, typically resorted to negotiation first and coercion last. Neutral tanks housed inmates who did not need safekeeping, were not troublemakers, and were not constant rule violators. BTs in these areas used a combination of negotiation and coercion to settle problems. In the bull, or terror, tanks resided Eastham's chronic troublemakers, malcontents, and "strong" inmates, or bulls. The guards perceived these inmates as potential threats to the institution who needed tight control. BTs in these latter tanks reflected their charges; they were the strongest, most physically aggressive BTs. Dispute settlement in the bull tanks frequently involved coercion first, then negotiation. In short, residence was a major factor in how the BTs handled a problem.

The BTs also weighed the personality characteristics of the disputants. They distinguished between "good people" and "shitheads." The former were solid, could stand up for themselves, were mentally tough, or were street friends or acquaintances of the BTs. The latter were "agitators," troublemakers. These disputant attributes affected the nature and extent to which BTs became involved in the settlement process. If a problem existed between an inmate who was good people and a shithead, the BTs typically stayed out of the incident but sanctioned the beating of the troublesome inmate. In this way,

BTs were able to engineer the punishment of an inmate troublemaker while "keeping their hands clean." If an inmate defined as good people told the BTs about a problem, the BTs typically settled the problem in that inmate's favor.

A third factor influencing BT involvement in prisoners' dispute settlement was race and ethnicity. Hispanic and, especially, black inmates were for the most part discriminated against by the BTs. The majority of the head BTs were white, and they constituted a power structure that made Eastham a "white boy's farm." If a dispute arose between a black and a white inmate, the BTs typically sided with the white inmate. Hispanics rarely asked a BT to settle a dispute between them and other inmates. Hispanic inmates routinely avoided the BTs (and guards) and settled their problems by themselves, at the risk of BT retaliation.

Finally, the age of the disputants seemed to be a consideration. If a dispute involved a thirty-year-old and a fifty-year-old inmate, then the BTs tried to settle the problem through negotiation, regardless of the type of living area. Force was typically not used by BTs as a method of dispute settlement among older inmates.

The foregoing discussion suggests that BTs judiciously settled most disputes. In many cases this was true. In many others, however, a BT acted less on the merits of the situation than on the disputant's attitude, appearance, name, face, or even the BT's mood at the moment. Inmates who were friendly with the BTs typically "had it made" since BTs usually took their side in conflicts. Furthermore, to move a dirty cell partner, for example, an inmate had to pay the BTs in such prison store items as tobacco or bags of instant coffee. Favoritism in solving problems had its rewards. At the same time, if a prisoner was not friendly with the BT and could not afford to buy his favor, then he might lose regardless of whether right was on his side in the dispute.

Building Tenders as Managers. Building tenders at Eastham managed and supervised the other inmates in the living areas. Those cellblocks and dormitories were their turf and responsibility, and ranking guards regularly deferred to the BTs when it came to running the tank. To manage the tank, BTs had to attend to tank maintenance, educate prisoners to the tank rules, and enforce those rules.

The physical and mechanical upkeep of the blocks was the responsibility of the BTs. That is, any time some item malfunctioned in the block, such as a clogged commode, a broken window, or a dead light fixture, the BTs told the guards, who in turn notified the maintenance officer. The BTs saw to it that malfunctions were corrected.

In addition to solving mechanical problems, BTs also kept the tanks clean. Runners were the tank janitors. They daily swept and mopped the dayroom and each week helped the BTs collect and dispense linens and towels to the cells. Runners also emptied the cigarette butt cans and took the tank garbage can every morning to the trash truck for dumping. These inmates also cleaned the dayroom windows and assisted the BTs in putting up the tank's Christmas decorations.[22]

In addition to the institutional rules, BTs also expected inmates to comply with several basic important but unwritten tank rules. These rules functioned explicitly to preserve order and discipline in the blocks. Implicitly, these rules served to mark the boundaries of acceptable and unacceptable behavior. In other words, all inmates living in the tanks knew what to expect should they exceed the limits of what the BTs had defined as acceptable behavior.

Inmates learned the tank rules upon arriving at a new block. A BT, sometimes a head BT, explained the tank rules to all new arrivals. This socialization process was described by two head BTs.

> When a new inmate comes on the tank, we tell each new person that whatever you do, we don't want the police [guards] down here. I don't want any trouble from you. Don't bring any heat here. We don't want to see the man around here or anything. We live down here and this is our neighborhood and we're going to abide by the rules of this place. We don't want any fighting, we don't want any trouble from anybody. You know, you can come in here and you can do your own time. If you start trouble then we'll give you trouble.

> Use the garbage cans, keep your cell clean, don't make excessive noise, and go to work when you're supposed to. If you got problems with anything come to me because that's what I'm here for.

All new inmates at Eastham were thus socialized into the system. They knew what to expect and understood from this encounter that the BTs were in nearly complete control of the blocks.

These rules were straightforward and conveyed one message: mind your own business. Yet, BTs did not constantly scrutinize the inmates or look for rule violations. Instead, they ran the tanks through compromise and often let petty violations go by for the sake of expediency. One BT explained the value of compromise. "You have to let some things go by; when you live with that many people you can't enforce all the rules, you can't enforce everything, you know, you've got to cut people slack. It's living by compromise." For the BTs, minor violations, tank or institutional, were tolerable as long as they did not disrupt the harmony or involve groups of inmates. For example, the BTs disliked gambling because debts often led to fights. Yet some petty gambling was allowed if the pots were small and the players did not incur large debts. Fighting was also tolerated, especially if the fighters were long-time tank residents and were good people. In these cases the staff was not alerted. However, if the inmate-combatants were troublemakers or agitators, the fight was often brought to official attention.

The final and most important aspect of tank management involved maintaining and enforcing order. All else, such as dispute settlement, snitching, or socialization of newcomers, was secondary. Most obviously, the BTs enforced order by telling other inmates what to do, when, where, and how. For example, BTs routinely instructed inmates in the dayrooms to be quiet. They enforced a semi-silent system in the living areas. But orders to be quiet were seldom given politely and in most cases they were intimidating and derogatory. Piqued by a noisy dayroom, one BT at Eastham shouted: "Keep the fucking noise down, you bunch of motherfuckers. If you weren't so fucking loud you might be able to hear me. [He had earlier yelled at them to be quiet.] If I punched one of you fuckers in the mouth, I bet you'd shut up then." After this outburst, the inmates remained quiet and whispered to each other.

Building tenders routinely gave inmates orders in support of the guards. When the officers shouted "count time" the BTs also yelled "Y'all get ready for the count" or "Y'all hurry up out of that dayroom so the boss can make the count." They barked orders to the other inmates to assist the guards in routine security matters. The following case from research notes illustrates this point. "While a cellblock officer was searching inmates returning from breakfast, an inmate walked away from the officer. He [the inmate] did not allow the officer to search him properly. He also laughed as he walked away from the officer. The BT in the tank grabbed the inmate around the shirt collar and threw him into the cell block door and yelled at him 'what the hell's so funny? When that boss wants to shake you down [a pat search], you let him shake you down and you get that grin off your face.'" Orders such as these were also meant to intimidate and threaten the inmates.

Although BTs issued orders primarily to individual inmates, they never shied away from giving orders to groups of inmates or even the entire cellblock. The following incident, related by an officer, illustrates order giving on the block level:

One day the BTs on K-line [a cellblock] were really pissed off because the inmates were too slow during "in and outs." [Every hour the block officer opened the cell doors so the inmates in the dayrooms could return to their cells to use the toilet and get coffee or something else to drink. Inmates were generally allowed five minutes to go "in and out" of their cells.] The head BT told the picket boss [block guard] to "get all three rows in the dayroom." All the inmates in the tank filed into the dayroom for a "meeting." The BTs then stood in front of the group and told them to be faster during in and outs and to quit "jacking around."

Though such group meetings were rare, they demonstrated the power of the BTs and their ability to enforce order as they saw fit.

BTs also enforced order in the tanks by making sure inmates with official minor disciplinary court violations served their punishments. Every evening an inmate-bookkeeper brought an updated list showing all inmates who had been given minor punishments. The BTs knew which inmates in the tank had what punishments and informed the guards about violations. For example, if an inmate had cell restriction but was sitting in the dayroom, the staff was notified immediately.

Finally, the BTs used physical force and terror to maintain order in the tanks and to punish prisoners who failed to follow tank rules. For example, tank rules proscribed homosexual activity. The following incident recorded in field notes illustrates how the BTs typically handled inmates who made homosexual advances on unwilling partners:

The BTs waited for the guy [aggressor] to go to the dayroom. They [the BTs] jumped him as he came down the stairs from 2-row. The BTs beat the hell out of him. He was screaming the whole time. Two BTs held him upside down [they each had a leg] while the other kicked him in the body. They dropped him and then one BT really beat the hell out of him. After about five minutes of this two guards broke it up and took everybody to the major's office. The head BT explained to the lieutenant that the one inmate complained to him about being sexually harassed by the other one. The head BT said he told the dude to quit bothering the guy on two separate occasions. Talking didn't work so he [the head BT] said he decided to kick the dude's ass. Well, the lieutenant agreed with the BT's plan and that everything was alright. The lieutenant wrote a case on the inmate for fighting without a weapon.

This example was typical of most force situations involving building tenders. The BTs told the aggressor twice to quit his advances. The inmate ignored these admonishments and was punished. Significantly, the inmate was beaten in full view of a crowded dayroom. Public beatings made examples of inmates as well as underscored the power and the staff support of the BTs.

On another occasion, an inmate told the BTs that his cell partner kept turning off the cell's light in an attempt to scare him. A head BT described what happened: "When I went to tell the guy to leave the light on, he didn't even look at me or answer me. So I went back up there [3-row] and said, 'Listen motherfucker, when I tell you to turn around and listen to me, you turn around.' I told the boss to open up the guy's cell. I went in and hit him in the head with my pipe. Yeah, when he felt that blood coming down his forehead, he knew I meant business. He said he would leave the guy alone too. If they [ordinary inmates] snap that you're weak, they'll inhale you." It is important to note that the staff was not informed about this incident.

Though the use of force by the BTs, as with the guards, was a last-resort tactic, it was not used sparingly, and it often, as in the above case, involved some type of weapon. With the tacit approval of the guards, BTs possessed such weapons as pipes, clubs, knives, and blackjacks in their cells. Under the BT bench outside the dayroom and inside the first-row washroom, weapons were readily available. The regular inmates knew that the BTs had an arsenal of weapons and feared the BTs because of this.

From the point of view of the BTs, coercion, including the use of weapons, was organizationally sanctioned, effective, and necessary. This self-justification is illustrated in the pragmatic statement of an Eastham BT: "How else are you going to keep order in here? In our tank, we try to run it by compromise, we try to tell people the first time to stop, and if they do something a second time, then something is going to happen to them. Look, on my tank, we called four guys out of the dayroom and slapped them around in the washroom. They were fucking around, making noise, and screwing up. Somebody is getting slapped around in here every day or every other day. But if you mind your own business, stay out of trouble and do what you are told, everything is okay."

In sum, the BTs ruled the tanks through fear, intimidation, and physical coercion. For the officials, the elites, and many regular prisoners, BT order made prison life more predictable and stable. For those defined for whatever reason as shitheads or problems, tank life was at best tense and often unsafe.

The Turnkeys

Turnkeys were inmates assigned to open and close the several riot gates in Eastham's main hall. Whenever a fight or disturbance occurred, their job was to slam these metal doors to isolate the problem and prevent it from spreading. They also carried the keys to those gates ostentatiously on long leather thongs. In the morning, usually around five o'clock, the first-shift turnkeys came to the control picket (main security area that contained all the keys and riot gear) and picked up their keys from a guard. These inmates signed out a key for their gate. Often, a key checked out to an officer was tossed to a turnkey, who then performed the officer's job of locking or unlocking cellblock doors.

Like BTs, turnkeys broke up fights if they occurred in the hall, protected the officers from assault, and generally provided the guards with physical backup. On his first day on the job a new guard was told by a turnkey: "I work for the man. Nothing is going to happen to you. We're here to protect you, you've got more friends than you know."

Turnkeys were also institutional snitches. Because turnkeys worked in the hall, they gathered much information about illegal behavior outside the cellblocks. They acquired information about weapons, drugs, or other contraband being passed in the hall, a vital area in the prison because large numbers of inmates were in constant movement there from one point to another. This information was passed on to building tenders and then up the information ladder. Turnkeys also kept a constant vigil in the hall to keep out unauthorized inmates and to maintain order in a very fluid situation. The hall at Eastham (and at most other units) was divided into north and south ends, and inmates who lived on the north end were forbidden to walk to the south end, and vice versa. No inmates were permitted in the hall who were not en route to an official designation. Turnkeys generally knew in which end of the building inmates lived and vigorously watched for "trespassers." Holding down illegal inmate hall traffic suppressed contraband peddling as well as general disorder.

The Bookkeepers

The power of the inmate-bookkeepers derived from their access to information about prison functions, staff, and other prisoners. These inmates were assigned to the prison departments (e.g., kitchen, laundry, garment factory, field forces, farm manager's office) to perform various clerical duties. Although these departmental bookkeepers enjoyed considerable prestige, they were not as powerful as the major's office bookkeepers. These latter clerks were the most influential inmates in the institution because they could observe and participate in key aspects of prison security. Working six- to ten-hour shifts, the major's bookkeepers processed count slips, move slips, job changes, and all information concerning disciplinary violations and punishments. Throughout the day there were from three to six bookkeepers on duty at a time. An important aspect of the bookkeeper's job was typing rule violation reports. When a rule violation occurred, the witnessing officer submitted a brief written statement to a bookkeeper, who then typed the official report. In many cases, however, the guard simply told the clerk what happened, and the bookkeeper determined which offense should be charged. When the bookkeeper and the officer felt the offender needed more punishment than the current incident warranted, they prepared a report to make the rule violation more serious. The major's office was also the site for most tune-ups, ass whippings, and beatings. Bookkeepers heard about and sometimes participated in these events. This important intelligence was then passed on to the BTs so that they were kept abreast of which prisoners were violating which rules.

The major's head bookkeeper was typically the most influential inmate within the population. At Eastham in the 1970s, for example, the head bookkeeper was Raymond Hafti, an intelligent and prison-wise convict who enjoyed an unusually close relationship with the ranking security officers. Hafti, like his counterparts at other TDC units, was a key figure because he maintained records the staff needed and because he could use his office to facilitate order through moving prisoners from one cell to another.

At Eastham, the staff used two types of cell moves as important mechanisms of social control. First, inmates were often moved within the same block. For example, if two cell partners had a minor feud (e.g., snoring, reading all night, petty thievery), one inmate was moved to another cell in the same block. (Sometimes inmates paid BTs in coffee or cigarettes to engineer a cell move.) In-house moves occurred daily and were meant to keep the peace and aid the BTs in tank management. However, if the problem escalated into a fight, one, or both, of the culprits was moved to another block. Cellblock moves were also used to disperse and prevent cliques from forming and to discipline troublemakers (e.g., moving an inmate from a neutral block to a bull block).

BTs approached the head bookkeeper when they needed a cell move. The head clerk discussed the matter with the guards, who typically agreed with the bookkeeper's move plans. The reason for acquiescence by officials was that the elites were usually much more familiar with the inmates and their trouble. Thus, guards at Eastham relied on Hafti's judgment and his knowledge of the inmates for cell placement. He knew which blocks had open bunks, whether or not the moving inmate could make it in his new living arrangement, and when the move should be made. Once the decision to move an inmate was made, Hafti informed the BTs, who then simply told the moving inmate, "Pack your shit." The other bookkeepers typed an official move list, which was circulated throughout the tanks. Clearly, the power to affect where and how prisoners lived placed the head bookkeeper at the top of the prisoner hierarchy.

Rewarding the Elite

In addition to status and power, BTs, bookkeepers, and turnkeys enjoyed a number of privileges that flowed from and defined their positions. Some of these privileges involved distinctive trappings of elite status, such as specially pressed clothes and unique green quilted jackets (while all others wore white, often ill-fitting cotton coats). Some of these elites even possessed pets such as fish, owls, cats, turtles, and rabbits.

A more substantial reward for the elites, of course, was freedom of movement within the prison. For example, their cell doors were open from 3:30 A.M. until 11:00 P.M., permitting them to move freely about the tanks and to have "special" visits from their punks. Head BTs could also roam the halls and spend considerable time in or around the major's office, tagging along with their officers, or in the craft shop. In addition, these inmates had their own formally designated shower and gym periods, which allowed them to avoid the dangers of being in a large crowd of ordinary inmates. They were also able to eat whenever they wanted and often ate two or three times in one meal period.

Because they were charged with protecting officials, prisoners, and themselves, elites also had tacit official permission to have weapons.

Building tenders, runners, turnkeys, and bookkeepers usually kept their knives, clubs, and hammers more or less concealed. Although they sometimes carried weapons on their person, most weapons were secreted in their cells.

Finally, the elites were generally immune from punishment, a reward that encouraged them not only to use but also to abuse their power over other prisoners. If, for example, a fight occurred between a BT and another inmate, the non-BT typically received some solitary confinement time or cell restriction, while the BT typically received no punishment at all. This differential treatment reflected the tacit understanding that the BT was probably "taking care of business" and the tendency of the staff to accept the self-exonerating explanation given by the BT. Not surprisingly, these inmate-agents regularly exercised their influence on behalf of runners (or other friends) who faced disciplinary cases for "helping the man."

Building tenders, bookkeepers, and turnkeys clearly "worked for the man" because of the benefits commensurate with the job. Privileges were important in the prison because they made life easier. Eastham, like any maximum-security penitentiary, was an unpleasant place, and obtaining some privileges softened the daily grind of institutional life. The following quotes from several of these elite inmates suggest that reward was the major reason they agreed to be co-opted:

Well, what do you mean why work for the man? I work for the man because of the privileges I get. That is, I don't get any harassment, I don't have to do hard time.

Hell, I've got a life sentence and I'm going to do it the easiest way I can. You've got to survive, you know.

Hell, I took the BT job because I knew it was the easiest way to do time.

I don't want to do hard time.

Selection of BTs, Turnkeys, and Bookkeepers

The selection of elites in TDC began primarily with the inmates themselves. Potential BTs, turnkeys, and bookkeepers were usually, but not always, identified among the runners whom the BTs had informally distinguished from the population in the cellblock. If a runner appeared to have snap or good common sense, and a willingness to work for the man, then the head BT would talk to the other BTs or turnkeys to gather additional information about the candidate. In many cases, a BT or bookkeeper would have known the candidate in the free world or perhaps in a juvenile facility. If the feedback about the recruit was favorable, the head BT discussed the matter with the head bookkeeper and both would tell a captain, major, or assistant warden that they thought the inmate would "make you a good hand." The officials, for the most part, relied on the inmate-guards to supply them with candidates. The reason was stated succinctly by a captain: "We have to rely on them. What the hell do you think. We don't know these inmates; they do. Look, they simply know the inmates a whole lot better than we do. They live with them; we don't." Once an inmate was recommended for a BT, turnkey, or bookkeeper position, he was informally interviewed by several ranking staff. The interview was essentially a screening device to determine a candidate's loyalty and judgment. The following quote from an officer captures the purpose and meaning of this interview: "I'll ask him things like why he wants to be a BT. 'Why do you want to work for me? You know people are not going to like you, and what do you expect to get out of the job?' These are the kinds of things I'm going to ask; what his motives are, are you going to be loyal to me? These are the kinds of things I want to know. It's very possible for them to lie, but at least you can find out, do they really want to be a building tender or maybe somebody just threw their name out." Answers to such questions revealed attitudes toward staff and possible deportment under stress. Those inmates who were inclined toward violence in every situation were typically rejected by the staff. Thus, instead of violence and extreme authoritarian conduct, the major desirable characteristics appeared to have been common sense and the ability to handle and manage men, as well as the ability to use aggression with some discretion.

From these informal interviews, the guards compiled a list of potential BTs, turnkeys, and bookkeepers that they forwarded to the classification committee (a panel of four TDC officials, all with prison security backgrounds). This committee then reviewed each inmate's file and made the final decisions. Recommendations to the classification committee from the staff were not always honored, and fewer than half of those recommended were selected for BT/turnkey/bookkeeper positions. However, if a BT, turnkey, or bookkeeper left the prison on parole and later returned, he was almost always reassigned to his former post. This review process demonstrates that some checks existed over which inmates filled these elite positions. That is, unit wardens did not have complete autonomy in the selection process.

The inmates who were ultimately selected for these elite positions had certain distinguishing background characteristics. Bookkeepers were selected on the basis of their education, office skills, intelligence, and communication skills. BTs and turnkeys had to possess a strong physical presence. One supervisor who was an active participant in the recruitment process at Eastham expressed his preference for BTs, which was typical: "I've got a personal bias. I happen to like murderers and armed robbers. They have a great deal of esteem in the inmate social system so it's not likely that they'll have as much problem as some other inmate because of their esteem, and they tend to be a more aggressive and a more dynamic kind of individual. A lot of inmates steer clear of them and avoid problems just because of the reputation they have and their aggressiveness. They tend to be aggressive, you know, not passive."

Most individuals selected for bookkeeper, BT, and turnkey positions were physically and mentally superior inmates who appeared to be natural leaders. Generally, BTs and turnkeys were more violent than their clerk counterparts and criminally more sophisticated than the regular inmates. For example, of the eighteen head BTs at Eastham, eight were in prison for armed robbery, five for murder (one was an enforcer and contract-style killer), one for attempted murder, one for rape, one for drug trafficking, and two for burglary. Their average age was thirty-nine and their prison sentence thirty-two years. Of the seventeen turnkeys, three were in for murder, three for armed robbery, six for burglary, two for drug trafficking, one for rape, one for car theft, and one for aggravated assault. Their average age was thirty-one, and their average sentence twenty-two years. In contrast, the average TDC inmate in 1981 had a twenty-one-year sentence, with a modal age category between twenty-two and twenty-seven. Clearly, BTs and turnkeys were older than most inmates and more likely to be violent recidivists.[23] Race and ethnicity also played a significant role in the selection of inmate-guards. Specifically, all of the major's office bookkeepers were white, and the majority of the regular BTs and turnkeys came from the black and white inmate populations. Although both black and white inmates served as BTs, power was not equally distributed between the races. The predominantly rural, white, ranking guards kept the real power in the hands of the white BTs and bookkeepers. That is, of the eighteen head BTs, there were fourteen whites, three blacks, and one Hispanic. Because the ranking staff members were prejudiced, they trusted the white BTs and bookkeepers more than members of the other two races. In short, with the help of the staff, a "white con" power structure similar to a caste system dominated the inmate society.[24]

At the same time, only a handful of Hispanic inmates were ever recruited, and those tended to come from two large cities: Houston and Dallas. These Hispanics often looked down on other Hispanics from West Texas, San Antonio, El Paso, and the Rio Grande Valley, often referring to them as "wetbacks." The staff capitalized on this cleavage. Generally, prison officials distrusted most Hispanic inmates, perceiving them to be dangerous, clannish, and sneaky. With considerable justification, the prison staff saw Hispanic inmates as tight-lipped and generally unwilling to interact voluntarily with the staff.

Official efforts to select and reward inmate-guards produced a tightly controlled and highly authoritarian environment. This system minimized the likelihood that ordinary inmates (as individuals or groups) might engage in collective dissents, protests, or violence. Those who were docile and went along with the system were generally protected and left alone. The level of order resulting from official reliance on inmate-guards is suggested by the fact that only two inmate murders, two work strikes, and one disturbance occurred from 1972 to 1982.

The use of institutionalized elites as snitches and enforcers to control the mass of prisoners was not without human costs. Many prisoners did not feel safe despite TDC's official record of safety; they lived in fear of BT caprice and omnipotence. Building tenders were known, for example, to beat inmates for such minor things as talking too loudly in the dayroom, smoking in the hall, playing their radio too loudly, gambling, acting crazy, not taking a shower, owing money to a BT, or writing writs. The following quotes clearly illustrate life for the ordinary inmates under the BT regime:

When I got here in '75, you were either a BT, worked for a BT, or you was a convict. A convict then didn't talk or associate with BTs. If they [BTs] ran stores, you didn't buy nothing from them. If you did, that's getting along with them. [But] in a sense you had to get along with them, because they had so much pull or power. One time I was standing in the dayroom on F-line and I was supposed to be sitting down. I was watching a domino table. The head BT came in and looked at me and said, "Sit down, motherfucker." I heard him and stood there, I don't know why. I should have sit down. He came over to me and broke my nose.—White prisoner

Agricultural technology in the Texas prison system prior to 1950. Courtesy of the Texas Prison Museum, Inc.

Unloading of new inmates at the Huntsville Unit, ca. 1955; person opening the door on the truck is an inmate. Courtesy of the Texas Prison Museum, Inc.

Overcrowding and its results—third man in a two-man cell was required to sleep on the floor, 1978. Photograph by James Balzaretti; courtesy of the Texas Prison Museum, Inc.

Field bosses retrieving their weapons from an "outside picket," or guard tower, before taking squads to the field after lunch, 1977. Courtesy of the Texas Prison Museum, Inc.

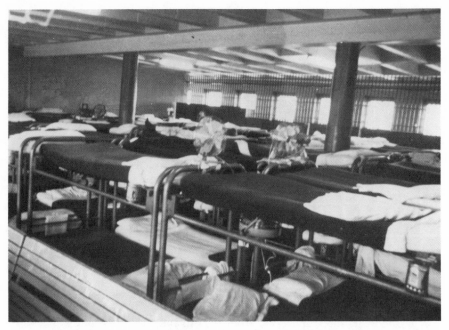

Overcrowded dormitory conditions, 1978. Courtesy of the Texas Prison Museum, Inc.

Example of the "tent cities" erected on many Texas prison units to relieve overcrowding, 1981. Courtesy of the Texas Prison Museum, Inc.

W. J. Estelle, Jr., director of TDC from 1972 to 1983. Courtesy of the Texas Prison Museum, Inc.

George J. Beto, director of TDC from 1962 to 1972. Courtesy of the Texas Prison Museum, Inc.

Oscar B. Ellis, director of TDC from 1948 to 1962. Courtesy of the Texas Prison Museum, Inc.

Warden Carl Luther McAdams, ca. 1950, shortly after the Texas prison system employed tractors and trailers to transport prisoners to the field. Courtesy of the Texas Prison Museum, Inc.

The Honorable William Wayne Justice. Courtesy of William Wayne Justice.

The inmate plaintiffs arriving at the federal courthouse in Houston, October 3, 1978: *left*, Lawrence C. Pope; *center*, O. D. Johnson; *right*, David Ruiz. AP/Wide World Photos, Inc.

Field boss overseeing cottonpickers, ca. 1955. Courtesy of the Texas Prison Museum, Inc.

It was abusive to the niggers. They were the main ones who didn't have a chance back then. I seen 'em get their ass whipped for hollering against a team that was playing against the Dallas Cowboys. That never made sense. Well I was a Cowboy fan from the day I hit this place. I don't like the Cowboys but I went along with it. If you didn't you stayed in the shitter [solitary] all the time, or the field, or on cell restriction.—White prisoner

They [BTs] took it upon themselves to supervise other inmates. A couple of BTs approached me one day [in 1982] and told me they didn't like my attitude. They said that I was on Eastham and you had better go along with it. They said it was a white boy's farm. They said if I didn't, they would bust my head. They hurt you. They threatened me and that was it. You couldn't go to an officer. They expected you to be ignorant. They also told the bosses to keep an eye on me because I was a smartass.—Black prisoner

I got into a fight just over too much noise in the dayroom. My voice was louder than some of the others. I was called out for this [to come out of the dayroom]. The BT didn't say nothing, he just hit me and all of a sudden I hit him back. The next thing you know, I had two or three BTs on me.—White prisoner

If you minded your own business, you weren't antiestablishment or mouthing off, you were left alone. Once you crossed the line, man, you got beat down hard. They ruled through fear. If they didn't like you, you had hell to pay. They'd steal your property, try to make a punk out of you, or else set you up in some way. If you was weak they'd make you pay protection. You know, every time you went to the store [prison commissary] you had to give them some of your stuff. Dudes would pay them off right in the open in front of other people. A lot of dudes paid them off, just to make it. You couldn't win, man. You couldn't fight just one of them, you fought them all, plus them bosses. It wasn't worth fighting the system.—Hispanic prisoner

The ordinary inmates never knew when they might be searched or disciplined on the basis of another inmate's accusation. BTs were not above falsely accusing "insubordinate" inmates for wrongdoing. The staff routinely backed up their allies. Some unruly inmates were framed by the BTs (e.g., having a knife thrown in their cell while at work) and then reported to the staff. Every inmate was suspect, and even lower-ranking guards were dismissed solely on the word of a head BT.

Losing Control of the Inmate Guards

While elite abuse of power clearly occurred, officials did try to limit that abuse. One means of control was by gathering information on the BTs themselves. Although BTs were usually united when confronting ordinary inmates, they regularly engaged in backstabbing each other either for revenge or to help the man. Since the inmates snitched on and policed each other, the staff usually had enough information to divide and control the BT-turnkey-bookkeeper clique. Thus, if an inmate-guard became too abusive, too capricious, or involved in drugs or protection rackets, the guards found out about it and usually fired the offending elite.

This type of control and supervision of elite prisoners appears to be possible only when prison populations are relatively small and growth is limited, as it was in the 1960s and the early 1970s. Over the next decade, however, TDC grew rapidly. Two important consequences of that growth were that the officials became even more dependent on the elites and that the elites became less restrained in the use and the abuse of their power. The two consequences are related, of course; greater official dependence on elites meant less official supervision, and less supervision meant greater freedom among elites to abuse their power.

The situation in the late 1970s parallels that of the 1930s and 1940s. The BT system in both eras was clearly out of control and brutal. Some evidence suggests that the depredations of BTs were worse in the late 1970s than in the 1950s or the 1960s. Interviews with numerous old-time convicts about BT behavior in the 1950s and the 1960s, for example, indicated that, while BTs have always been violent and cruel, they wielded even more discretionary power and were quicker to use violence in the 1970s; physical punishment became a much more routine mechanism of social control.

The primary reason for the greater dependence on elites and the apparent rise in BT depredations was the growing disparity between the number of prisoners and the number of officers. The decade of the 1970s saw an inmate population that nearly doubled, while the guard population remained almost static.[25] These changes at Eastham, which is representative of most other TDC units, are illustrated in Figure 1.

Eastham, like most other Texas prisons in the 1970s, was chronically shorthanded. A single officer was regularly responsible for several cellblocks and hundreds of prisoners. Under these circumstances, it was simply impossible for the guards to oversee by them-

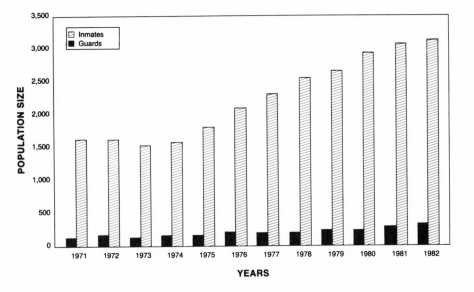

Figure 1. Eastham staff and inmate population between 1971 and 1982.

selves what went on in the blocks. They relied even more on the BTs. Thus, not only were they unable to adequately supervise the regular population, but they also progressively lost control over the building tenders. Yet, even though greater elite violence may have been noted by officials, such behavior was only a change in degree rather than in kind, and the guards tacitly approved.

Conclusion

The control structure created a strong, positive agency image for TDC among the media, citizens, and politicians. The array of frequently informal, and often physical, sanctions used by inmate-guards and staff resulted in relatively few escapes, killings, and stabbings over the decades. This control structure, which was largely unquestioned by outsiders, including the court, reflected the general repressive order that prevailed.

By the mid-1970s, however, there were rumblings of discontent with the prison system, and for the first time in decades questions were raised in the press and the legislature about TDC operations.

These questions were most forcefully pressed by *Ruiz v. Estelle,* the case that found the BT system and most other elements of TDC's control structure to be unconstitutional. The reforms ordered by the federal judge in that case not only dramatically altered the prison's organizational and operational structures but also redefined the nature of prison order. We turn now to a discussion of this historic inmate civil suit.

5

Justice Comes to Texas Prisons

*Old hands in the mule business say that the best way to get a
mule's attention is to hit it hard, right between the eyes, with a
singletree. Similarly, to get the attention of an intransigent government organization, a court must hit it right between the eyes
with an attention-getting order . . .*   —JUDGE WILLIAM W. JUSTICE[1]

THE TDC administrative philosophy initiated by O. B. Ellis,
then supported by George Beto and W. J. Estelle, Jr., produced
a demonstrably efficient and economical organization, relative to
other prison systems. This success, together with the political astuteness of these directors, translated into relatively generous legislative support through two and a half decades. Until the late 1970s,
for example, the department was essentially able to make relatively
unitemized funding requests, and the legislature routinely granted
the bottom line. Legislators, swayed by TDC's reputation, took for
granted that the money would be put to good use.

In the mid-1970s, however, the department's preferred status in
the state and its reputation as an exemplary correctional system began to erode. By the early 1980s, both were gone. This shift in TDC's
fortunes was due to the mounting pressures on TDC during that decade and, most specifically, to the *Ruiz v. Estelle* court case. This
case resulted in a substantial reordering of relations between the
prison system and the legislature, a redistribution of power within
TDC, and a new system of management and control.

Cracks in the Wall

In June 1973, eighteen months after Estelle became director of TDC,
a "work buck" occurred on the Retrieve Unit, south of Houston.
When the warden wanted to send the squads to the field to pick
corn on a Sunday, Father's Day, ten men refused to go. Because wet
weather had hampered the harvest, the warden wanted to take advantage of this first clear day to catch up. The stated plan was for the
inmates to be given a day off later in the week. These few refused to
work on a Sunday and, according to TDC officials, tried to organize a

general work stoppage. Notified of the situation, Estelle told the warden to "put these men to work." Putting them to work reportedly involved a gauntlet of ax handles and rubber hoses through which the prisoners had to run. Although Estelle acknowledged the use of force, TDC's investigation failed to find abuses; it found that a mutinous situation had been met with lawful force.

Neither this incident nor the manner in which it was handled was unique in TDC. Like his predecessors, Estelle believed that all official demands of inmates were appropriate and that noncompliance with those demands simply would not be tolerated. But unlike earlier administrators, Estelle found it increasingly difficult to uphold this prison tradition. His administration would be the first in many years to answer pointed questions from outsiders about the system's style of operation and control.

In the summer of 1974, a joint House and Senate legislative investigative committee began the first official examination in decades of TDC practices. The stated purpose of the investigation was to provide TDC inmates and their relatives a forum in which to speak out on state confinement and to make proposals for changes when the legislature met the following spring. The committee heard testimony from many inmates, including some involved in the so-called Father's Day beatings of a year earlier, who told the investigators of regular beatings. One inmate told the committee that being labeled a troublemaker was likely to trigger an "orgy of revenge" on the part of officers.[2] Testimony further described harassment of "jailhouse lawyers," poor medical care, discrimination against minority inmates, and reliance on building tenders, a practice that violated a 1973 state law against one inmate having power over another.

The lengthy legislative staff report indicted TDC on many counts and recommended many operational changes. Estelle denied any wrongdoing on the part of the staff. In cases of abuse, he pointed out that his officers had a right to defend themselves. He promised, however, that, if any illegal action was proven, he would dismiss the offending official. Responding to claims that inmates could not help each other with their cases and were thus limited in their access to courts, the director pointed out that each unit had a law library and that the system had employed twelve attorneys to handle inmate legal problems. Estelle's reaction to other parts of the committee's report was mixed. He applauded the call for greater medical care and expanded community corrections. In his view, however, allowing conjugal visits and paying inmates for work had no merit.

Despite efforts by several of the joint committee's members, the necessary number of signatures from the full committee could not be gotten. As a result, the staff report could not be brought before the full House of Representatives for consideration. Political sentiment plus the traditional authority of the prison director were just too powerful. Nonetheless, many prison practices, long assumed to be the state of correctional art, had been openly questioned.

These legislative rumblings were actually an early reflection of the shifts taking place in the legislature at the time, shifts that would mean less support for TDC. The old rural, Anglo "good ol' boy" alliances in the statehouse had been weakened by redistricting. Indeed, the vice-chairman of the legislative committee was a black congressman from Houston. Moreover, during this time, legislative staffs were growing and becoming more professional. While these coalitions and a more sophisticated congress failed to change TDC, their work produced a small crack in the solid wall of TDC's reputation.

About this same time, a less official organization began to question the prison system. Calling itself Citizens United for the Rehabilitation of Errants (CURE), this group had less power than a legislative committee, but it would prove to be more tenacious. Made up of friends and relatives of Texas prisoners, ex-prisoners, and others, CURE began as, and remains, a lobby group for prison reform. Its first director was Charles Sullivan, a former Roman Catholic priest. As the only significant prison reform group in the state, the group was rather small and found relatively few sympathetic ears in Austin, the state capital, or elsewhere. It managed to maintain a steady stream of criticism toward the prison, however.

The tenor of that criticism, as well as TDC's attitude toward CURE, was evident in a September 1975 meeting in Huntsville. Estelle was invited to speak. Estelle's invitation had come from State Representative Gonzalo Barrientos, who felt TDC ought to have better communication with CURE. There was understandable hostility at the meeting since the director not only thought that his prison did not need reforming but also had denied CURE's request to set up chapters on each prison unit. Though Estelle had brought a speech, CURE members did not want to hear it; instead they wanted to question Estelle, especially about the tragic Carrasco hostage situation the preceding year, in which two TDC employees and two prisoners had been shot.[3] The first CURE questioner asked Estelle if there had been foul play during that situation. According to witnesses, Estelle began his answer with "There was," at which the audience, having heard the answer they sought, cut him off with applause. At that point Estelle gathered up his speech and left the hall. Barrientos said Estelle's departure was an insult. Sullivan said he was "stunned," although he concluded that Estelle's actions reflected a lack of experience with dealing on an "equal plane" with organized detractors.[4] This observation was, to some extent, true since the prison and its officials were generally in sync with Texas grass-roots sentiments. The only gain by CURE in this encounter was a little media coverage. The organization remained active, however, and by the early 1980s, when the legislature decided to effect some prison reforms, CURE's fortunes would change. Sullivan would be courted, not cursed.

Though a legislative committee and a prison reform lobby sniped at Estelle and the agency he so visibly symbolized, their impact was small compared to the growing pressure of TDC's inmate population.

Rising Prison Population

In 1974 the TDC projected that by the end of August of that year there would be only 125 empty beds. At that time the prison held about 17,000 inmates. By 1976, Estelle reported projections that the population would increase by 50 percent over the next five years and that ten prison units were already overcrowded, with many inmates sleeping on the floors. Crowding problems were certainly not unique to Texas prisons. During the seventies, almost all state prison systems experienced population pressures. Part of the pressure in Texas was due to a booming energy economy that attracted many people to the state. But the prison growth could not be attributed simply to more people being available to be sent to prison. Between 1968 and 1978, the state's population grew 19 percent while the prison population grew 101 percent.[5]

The primary reasons for this growth of Texas prison populations were strong community and legislative attitudes against convicted offenders. Texans have traditionally believed in the use of prisons for punishment. Indeed, until the late 1970s, many counties in the state had no probation capacity at all, leaving prison as the only substantial punishment. In the mid-1970s Texans sent felons to prison at a rate of 143.7 per 100,000, compared to the national incarceration rate of 86.9.[6] These strong attitudes meant longer sentences as well. In 1973, the average maximum sentence was eight years and five months; by 1979, the average sentence was ten years and seven months. Perhaps most important, the actual time served also increased in this period. For 1973, the average time served in TDC was one year and four months; for 1979, it was two years and five months.[7]

Actions by the legislature mirrored the tough sentencing sentiment of Texas communities and, in so doing, compounded the over-crowding problem. In 1967, for example, lawmakers altered the Texas penal code such that an offender who served one-third of his sentence became eligible for parole; previously, that minimum portion was one-fourth. Ten years later, at the urging of Governor Dolph Briscoe, the legislature passed a crime control package that, along with the reinstatement of the death penalty, included elements with direct consequences for TDC's population growth. For example, one action, strongly supported by county sheriffs, redefined, for those convicted felons whose cases were on appeal, who could be automatically sent to TDC. Previously, only those with sentences of fifteen or more years could be moved from the county jails to the state's care. The revision lowered the minimum sentence to ten years and, in the process, added an estimated 5 percent to TDC's population annually.[8] Even more consequential for the prison count was the creation by the legislature of the "aggravated" sentence. This 1977 law called for all persons convicted of committing a felony with a deadly weapon to serve "day for day" one-third of the sentence. That is, the convict would serve one-third of his sentence without benefit of time off for good behavior (good time).

An obvious way to deal with crowding is to parole more inmates, but the Texas Board of Pardons and Paroles has always been conservative, again reflecting public and political sentiment. This attitude dampened the number of paroles awarded to TDC prisoners. In the mid-1970s, for instance, parole accounted for only about half of the annual releases from TDC, compared to a national average of about 75 percent.[9] But state officials became even more stingy with paroles in the late 1970s. That is, from 1977 to 1978, the number of prisoners considered for parole dropped 30 percent, despite a substantial budget increase for the board. More to the point, in 1977, the average number of prisoners actually recommended to the governor for parole each month was 737; in 1978, that figure fell to 469 per month. And, of these, the governor vetoed from 15 to 20 percent.[10]

Given the subsequent growth in the prison population, Director Estelle went to the legislature in 1977 with two proposals. He wanted first to build a new prison and second to keep the officer-inmate ratio near 1 : 10; at the time, that ratio was a "very dangerous" 1 : 12 or worse.[11] Unlike on previous trips to Austin, Estelle found legislators disinclined to fund whatever the agency requested.

It was at this time that the divergent prison philosophies—to build or not to build—began to contend in Texas. Although Estelle had always favored community corrections, he argued that something had to be done quickly about the hundreds of men sleeping on the floor, the third man in the two-man cells. Estelle's call for prison construction had considerable legislative support. The Speaker of the House of Representatives led a group advocating more prisons as well as mandatory sentences. At the same time, however, CURE, the Texas Civil Liberties Union, and the Texas Criminal Defense Lawyers Association argued that the crime package supported by the Speaker (and passed largely intact) was ill advised. These groups instead championed an expansion of community corrections, especially a statewide probation system.

The legislature, in the end, gave something to both sides. It funded a statewide probation program and a new, large prison that would become the Beto Unit. Neither move, however, offered any immediate relief for TDC's population problems. In the seven months prior to May 1978, TDC experienced a 15 percent population increase.

Early Court Involvement

Although rising prison populations made doing time harder for prisoners and managing more challenging for administrators, fundamental practices did not change. The almost total dependence of inmates on their keepers for relief continued since courts had not significantly intervened to that point. Until the early 1970s, judges seldom looked critically at TDC and its operations. Indeed, a Texas district court in 1960 even upheld the use of corporal punishment in prison.[12] The few petitions that inmates did file met with limited success.

This situation began to change in the early 1970s, however, when judges ruled in favor of Texas inmates in several important cases.[13] But these cases were narrowly focused; each addressed only one specific issue. The daily functioning of TDC, the behavior of its officers and its elite inmates, the living conditions, and the general quality of doing time escaped judicial scrutiny. This relationship between the prison and the judiciary began to change, however, when a prisoner named David Ruiz filed a class action suit against the Texas prison system.

The Ruiz Litigation

In June 1972, while serving time on TDC's Eastham Unit, David Ruiz filed a suit in federal court challenging living and working conditions. Ruiz was no stranger to prison or to censorious actions while incarcerated. He compiled a record of at least thirty arrests and four trips to state reformatories. He was first admitted to prison in early 1960 to serve a twelve-year sentence for robbery. Released after eight years, he was readmitted less than a year later to serve a twenty-five-year sentence, again for armed robbery. During this term, Ruiz became a "writ writer," filing petitions and writing letters to draw attention to Texas prison conditions.

Prison officials in Texas viewed all writ writers, including Ruiz, as troublemakers. To better control him and other jailhouse lawyers, Director Beto in 1971 moved them to the Wynne Unit in Huntsville. The idea, apparently, was to house them all in one place so that they could be watched and to minimize their involvement in other inmates' cases. This move did not stop Ruiz. He continued to file writs against officers from the director down, and, in the process, he learned the federal court system and how to use it.

For Ruiz's petition against TDC to be effective, it had to reach a judge willing to take on what one state legislator called the last "sacred cow" agency. William W. Justice, judge of the Federal District Court, Eastern District of Texas, was such a judge. Since his appointment to the federal bench in 1968, Justice had developed a reputation for legal competence and judicial activism. Prior to the Ruiz case, he had ordered dramatic changes in the operation of Texas juvenile reformatories and the creation of a bilingual education program in Texas. These controversial rulings produced among many citizens and state officials quite negative reactions. The judge even became something of a social pariah in his hometown of Tyler, Texas. To many, his pro-underdog posture was too extreme; as one prison official put it, he was a kamikaze liberal. A few irate legislators even introduced bills to have him impeached and to construct a juvenile halfway house next door to his Tyler home.

A more sympathetic observer described Judge Justice and his legal orientation as follows: "He's like the earth he came from. A populist imbued with a sense of righteousness, and most of the time he's right. He's a stickler for the law and adheres to the Constitution and Supreme Court decisions. He is totally honest. I don't think there's enough barbed wire in Texas to whip him with to make him tell a lie. He's a Spartan, an ascetic in a sense, a monk."[14] Committed to civil rights, tenacious, and possessed of a demonstrated sympathy for the powerless, Justice was, from the plaintiff's point of view, the ideal judge for the case.

Early on, the judge decided to combine Ruiz's petition with six similar civil actions also filed by TDC prisoners. This consolidation became a class action suit naming Ruiz as plaintiff and Director Estelle, the board of corrections, and several TDC wardens as defendants. In 1974, Judge Justice directed the United States to appear as amicus curiae.

From 1974 through 1977, both sides engaged in discovery efforts, developing information that would be used at the eventual trial. The issues of the case, clear from the beginning, involved overcrowding, medical care, disciplinary practices, access to courts, security and supervision of inmates, and other conditions of confinement. Regular hearings considered disputed discovery and requests by plaintiffs for protection against harassment by prison officials and other inmates. In December 1975, the court even issued an order enjoining prison officials from interfering with plaintiffs and their access to counsel or courts.[15]

Trial and Opinion

Just prior to the trial scheduled in Justice's district and hometown of Tyler, TDC pushed for a change of venue. State attorneys wanted the trial moved to Houston, contending that the county jail in Tyler was too small to hold and keep secure the nearly two hundred witnesses scheduled to testify. Justice granted the motion, and the trial was moved to Houston. Prison and state officials, however, had an ulterior motive for the venue change; they wanted the trial moved out of Justice's jurisdiction. Although the officials' venue motion succeeded, Justice remained the judge in the case. Another federal judge, who controlled court and case assignments in Houston, reassigned Judge Justice to the case. With the legal maneuvering over, the trial finally began on October 2, 1978.

The trial, with its extensive inmate testimony on brutality and other official misdeeds, was widely covered by the media and closely followed by TDC inmates across the units. Soon after the trial began, inmates at the Ellis Unit initiated a work strike in support of the Ruiz suit. Work stoppages also occurred on six other units. Nearly 1,500 inmates participated in these strikes, and a riot involving an equal number of inmates occurred on the Coffield Unit.[16] In mid-October, Judge Justice, at the request of TDC, made a public statement that "the orderly progress of this trial could be impeded if violence and disruption continue."[17] This statement helped to ease tension and restored some order to the affected institutions.

During the trial, the court received into evidence almost 1,600 exhibits (one was a replica of a cell) and heard testimony from 349 witnesses, including penologists, academicians, current and former employees, and inmates.[18] To interview inmates, the Justice Department enlisted the FBI, which helped screen and question 500 potential witnesses. Thousands of pages of transcripts were obtained from prisoners in TDC and from former Texas prisoners throughout the nation.[19]

Early arguments revealed a confrontation of two quite different perspectives on TDC's operation. State officials, buoyed by the prison's reputation, argued that TDC's practices were quite appropriate and that inmate abuses were isolated events. As to Justice's concern that the prisons were too far from the metropolitan areas where most inmates lived and would return, TDC pointed out that the prison was an efficient, agriculturally based operation and that the farms had to be where they were.

The two different perspectives emerged most sharply, perhaps, in the evidence provided by two former prison officials, Fred T. Wilkinson and Arnold Pontesso, hired by the defense and the plaintiff, respectively. Wilkinson declared the Texas system to be the "best in the world . . . superior to any other state system in physical facilities, quality of personnel and operational programs." He further noted that TDC was handling its problems (e.g., overcrowding) "with realism and integrity."[20]

Looking at the same prison at the same time, Pontesso found it to be "probably the best example of slavery remaining in this country." He was particularly concerned with TDC's solitary confinement practices, crowding, and discipline, which he noted was "unnecessarily harsh, counterproductive and intended to increase the hostility and social isolation of those punished."[21]

Pontesso's perspective was the one taken by Judge Justice. After 159 days of hearings, the longest civil rights trial in the nation's history concluded on September 20, 1979. The weight of the plaintiff's testimony and its support from the bench left little doubt about the trial's outcome. Fourteen months later, the judge issued an opinion that condemned numerous TDC policies and practices and indicated that broad relief was in order for Texas prisoners. The opinion, which ran nearly 250 pages, fairly crackled with rancor at an organization that Judge Justice saw as operating far outside the bounds of the constitution. He concluded:

[I]t is impossible for a written opinion to convey the pernicious conditions and the pain and degradation which ordinary inmates suffer within the TDC units—the gruesome experiences of youthful first offenders forcibly raped; the cruel and justifiable fears of inmates, wondering when they will be called upon to defend the next violent assault; the sheer misery, the discomfort, the wholesale loss of privacy for prisoners housed with one, two or three others in a forty-five foot cell or suffocatingly packed together in a crowded dormitory; the physical suffering and wretched psychological stress which must be endured by those sick or injured who cannot obtain adequate medical care; the sense of abject helplessness felt by inmates arbitrarily sent to solitary confinement or administrative segregation without proper opportunity to defend themselves or to argue their causes; the bitter frustration of inmates prevented from petitioning the courts and other governmental authorities for relief from perceived injustices.[22]

Finding that the totality of conditions in TDC contravened the constitution, Judge Justice ordered changes in nine separate areas of the prison. These areas and the specific alterations within each were as follows:

1. Overcrowding
    a. End triple celling immediately
    b. Eliminate routine double celling in forty-five- and sixty-square-foot cells
    c. Alleviate overcrowding in the dormitories
2. Security and Supervision
    a. Hire more guards to reduce the ratio of 1 : 12
    b. Upgrade preservice training of all personnel
    c. Eliminate staff brutality
    d. Eliminate the building tender system
3. Health Care
    a. Increase staffing of all medical personnel
    b. Restrict the use of inmates in delivering medical and pharmacological services
    c. Improve unit infirmary functions
    d. Upgrade record keeping and improve sick call policy
    e. Provide better living conditions, protection, and medical treatment to all physically handicapped and mentally retarded inmates
4. Discipline
    a. Comply with the provisions for inmate disciplinary hearings outlined in *Wolf v. McDonnell*
    b. Improve solitary confinement
    c. Upgrade administrative segregation procedures
5. Access to Courts
    a. End harassment, intimidation, and coercion by staff on so-called inmate writ writers or others who wish to gain access to courts

6. Fire Safety
   a. Replace deficient extinguishers and improve fire evacuation plans in the housing and work areas
7. Sanitation
   a. Improve water supply, plumbing, solid waste disposal, and food processing procedures
8. Work Safety and Hygiene
   a. Improve workplace safety and develop adequate safety inspection program
9. Unit Size, Structure, and Location
   a. Reduce unit inmate populations
   b. Break units down into smaller organizational entities
   c. Build smaller units near large population centers instead of in inaccessible rural areas

The order included some specific deadlines for ameliorating crowding and supervision in the prison. By August 2, 1981, for example, TDC was to end triple celling and double celling in administrative segregation cells smaller than sixty square feet. By November 1, 1981, the prison was ordered to improve staffing ratios to better than 1 : 10 and to achieve at least forty square feet for each dormitory inmate.

To ensure that TDC complied with these and other aspects of the broad reform mandate, Judge Justice appointed a special master.[23] There were several reasons for this decision. First, the reform order was comprehensive and called for a detailed plan and a protracted effort to remove unconstitutional conditions in TDC. Second, Justice felt that TDC had a "record of intransigence toward previous court orders." And, finally, relations between both sides during the trial had been so fractured that smooth cooperation toward compliance seemed unlikely. A special master would be necessary to facilitate communication among the parties, to report findings, and to recommend solutions to disputed issues.

Both sides in the case were thus invited to submit names from which Justice would select a special master. Although TDC officials were opposed to such an appointment all along, they submitted three names, knowing none was likely to be selected. Plaintiffs submitted only one name, that of Vincent Nathan, whom the judge quickly appointed. Nathan, a University of Toledo law professor, had already had experience as a prison case master in Ohio and Georgia.

Reactions to the order and Nathan's appointment were predictable. Inmates and their attorneys praised the decree for its scope and its demand for reform of the "inhumane and degrading" conditions in TDC. State and corrections officials were outraged and criticized the mandated changes as going beyond the authority of a federal judge. To many, the judge was a meddling "bleeding heart" and "convict lover" whose remedies were frivolous and an invasion of state's rights. They were also vehemently opposed to the special master arrangement since it questioned their ability and willingness to carry out the reforms. Though they had lost at the trial, the defendants remained convinced that they were right. This posture translated into a period of nearly two years of often acrimonious resistance to reform.

Prison and State Resistance

Although the defendants had fought reform before and during the trial, they did not resist all aspects of the ruling. Indeed, prison officials had long been concerned about overcrowding and through the late 1970s had sought legislative relief. Moreover, they recognized that the quality of medical care was often inadequate. Accordingly, TDC had planned for and begun construction of a prison wing onto John Sealy Hospital in Galveston before the trial. Here prisoners would receive much improved major medical care in an acceptably secure facility.

Accordingly, in February 1981, Attorney General Mark White released a partial agreement signed by both parties. This consent decree covered changes in health care, provisions for mentally and physically handicapped prisoners, terms and conditions of solitary confinement, use of chemical agents, work safety and hygiene, and procedures relating to administrative segregation.

Although the issues on which the two sides agreed were certainly important, they were peripheral to the control and discipline mechanisms at the heart of TDC's traditional social order. On noncontrol issues TDC was willing to comply, although officials believed that the scope of reform was often too broad and the deadlines imposed unrealistic. Mandated changes in control practices, however, were considered impossible. Resistance involved formal appeals and informal noncooperation with the special master and his appointed monitors at the units.

Appeal by the State

On June 1, 1981, the state of Texas appealed Judge Justice's reform order to the 5th Circuit Court of Appeals in New Orleans. Later that month, also at the state's request, the court granted a partial stay of the order. Plaintiff attorneys sought to have the stay overturned by Supreme Court Justice Lewis Powell, but he refused. One year later the 5th Circuit's three-judge panel formally concluded that "TDC imposes cruel and unusual punishment on inmates in its custody as a result of the totality of conditions in the prisons."[24] However, the appellate court also substantially modified the scope and overturned some of the provisions of Justice's order. In brief, the 5th Circuit reversed Justice's order:

1. to reduce overcrowding through parole, furlough, and good time (state can decide how it wants to reduce population),
2. to build prisons smaller and closer to large cities,
3. to alter how guards in TDC are trained,
4. to meet National Fire Protection Association fire safety codes (failure here was not cruel and unusual),
5. to give inmates access to law libraries (another lawsuit already required this),
6. to submit all plans for new prisons to the court for approval,
7. to abide by state safety and health laws (out of the trial court's jurisdiction and did not constitute cruel and unusual punishment),
8. to provide each prisoner with a one-man cell by November 1, 1983.

The 5th Circuit panel took a more conservative posture than Justice, arguing that making TDC meet all aspects of the order would be extremely costly and difficult to police. Nonetheless, it dismissed the state's claims that the trial had been unfair, that Justice's findings had been incorrect, and that the U.S. Department of Justice should not have been allowed to intervene in the case, and it did not absolutely rule out the possibility of single celling in TDC.

Despite these last setbacks, reactions among Texas officials to the appellate court decision were generally positive. Texas Governor William P. Clements, Jr., Attorney General White, and the board of corrections hailed the appellate decision as a clear victory for the state. This belief emanated from the appeals court opinion that Judge Justice had actually exceeded his authority on some issues.

The 5th Circuit also ruled on another matter that the state had appealed along with Justice's order, namely, the appointment of a special master. Prison officials had resisted the master appointment in the first place and had hoped the New Orleans panel would remove him and his monitors, lawyers hired to investigate specific aspects of the case. Not only did TDC officials oppose Nathan's appointment, but also, during the year that the appeals court deliberated, animosity between state officials and Nathan increased.

From July through November of 1981, Nathan and his staff made 142 visits to nineteen TDC units. In this time several compliance reports were produced. One of these reports, written by a monitor, concerned the status of building tender compliance. That report revealed that these elite inmates still received such privileges as open cell doors and the possession of stereos, pets, and even weapons in their cells. This report provided ammunition for the move to oust the master. That is, since TDC was experiencing a rash of inmate violence, Attorney General White claimed that Nathan and his staff had been derelict in not reporting the presence of weapons that they had discovered through letters and interviews with inmates on various units. In January 1982, with help from the Fullbright and Jaworski law firm in Houston, White filed a motion to have the master removed. The state claimed that, in addition to not revealing immediately the presence of weapons, the master and his staff were encouraging inmates and employees to file lawsuits against the defendants and were fostering unrest by spreading rumors.

Although Judge Justice set a hearing date for the master-removal motion, the state, at the board's request, withdrew its motion before the hearing. The state decided that the cost, in money and time, of litigating the special master provision separately was too great. Prison officials and attorneys thus agreed to reopen negotiation on the building tender issue, the basis of the report that initially sparked the state's master-removal motion. Of course, prison officials continued to document master and monitor actions for they hoped that the 5th Circuit would remove the special master as the state had requested in the original appeal. In the end, however, the circuit court panel upheld the appointment, although it did stress that the special master's powers should be limited to determining compliance with court orders.

Formal Consent and Informal Resistance

Of the many issues in the court order, none affected TDC's traditional mode of control quite like the judge's proscription of building tenders and of the unguided use of force by security staff. On both there was eventually formal consent to comply but limited actual compliance, especially with regard to the use of force.

Through the last half of 1981, monitors ranged across the units interviewing TDC prisoners and officers to determine if prison administrators had, in fact, eliminated the use of BTs. The monitors regularly found that, while TDC had renamed the BTs "support service inmates" (SSIs), their duties and behavior remained largely the same. Findings to this effect were presented to the court in January 1982 and (without TDC's foreknowledge) also made public. (This report sparked the state's legal efforts to remove Special Master Nathan.) Soon afterward, a series of hearings presented testimony from inmates and ex-TDC officers about BT privileges, duties, power, and brutality. These hearings, like the trial itself, received wide media coverage.

In May 1982, formal resistance on this issue ended. The prison board approved an agreement to dismantle the building tender system, the existence of which prison officials had steadfastly denied during the trial. The consent decree limited the duties of SSIs to clerical and janitorial functions and only under the direct supervision of a staff member. Inmates selected for these positions generally had to have nonviolent records and were allowed none of the privileges or authority of former BTs. Three units—Eastham, Ellis, and Ramsey 1—had to comply with this decree by January 1, 1983, and other units had to comply by January 1985. The units marked for earliest compliance were designated "target units" by the court because of their reputations for having well-entrenched and particularly violent building tender traditions. The settlement also required that TDC hire additional guards to take over the control and supervision roles once held by BTs.

While the removal of BTs eliminated an extension of the guard force, the proscription against the use of force by staff struck at the officers themselves. As we pointed out in Chapter 3, the willingness and ability to use force on inmates was an integral part of TDC's informal control system and, at the same time, facilitated officers' careers. It is not surprising, then, that there was considerable resistance to efforts to limit the use of force.

On June 1, 1981, as directed by the court, TDC filed with the court a set of standards detailing the circumstances under which officers could legally resort to force and the process by which all force episodes must be recorded. During the following year, both parties in the case met often to negotiate and redraft these standards. Finally, in November 1982, a version emerged that the prison officials, the plaintiffs, and the court found acceptable.

But the distribution of these standards across the units had little apparent effect on staff behavior. According to Paul T. Belazis, the court monitor who wrote the "Ninth Monitor's Report," which dealt with the use of force, there was evidence that unit personnel continued to use force and that they actively resisted the monitor's efforts to investigate force episodes.[25]

This resistance came most often through simple lack of cooperation with the monitor. Belazis presented numerous examples of cases in which officers would not talk about an incident, providing only a brief written account of it to court personnel. When the special master asked Estelle to require officers to discuss force incidents with monitors, Estelle declined to do so.

A second type of resistance reported by Monitor Belazis involved the alteration of records by TDC personnel to cover the use of excess force. One example involved an inmate allegedly beaten in his solitary cell. After a medical assistant had completed a report on the prisoner's injuries, the ranking medical officer ordered all copies of the report retrieved and the prognosis changed from "undetermined" to "good." The monitor inferred from the account that a high-ranking security official was behind these sanitizing efforts. Belazis also found evidence that inmate injuries were selectively recorded. In one case, for example, an inmate's official injury report showed only a laceration above the eye. When interviewed by the monitor immediately after the incident, however, the inmate had facial bruises, swollen and bloodshot eyes, and a hematoma behind one ear.

Resistance also came from central headquarters. In early 1983, TDC created the Operational Audits Office to investigate use of force by officers, and Assistant Director D. V. McKaskle was put in charge. In that role, McKaskle agreed to conduct joint investigations of staff misconduct with court monitors. That cooperation never materialized. McKaskle ordered all communication between the monitors and operational audits to go through him exclusively. According to Belazis and other monitors, however, McKaskle not only was generally unfamiliar with the details of the investigations but also somehow never seemed to be available. After a time, the special master's office abandoned efforts to work with TDC's central office.

Besides resisting monitor investigative efforts, prison officials failed to vigorously follow up on reports of force violations as the court had stipulated. The first level of review of an inmate's complaint of unlawful use of force was the unit warden. Monitor Belazis found, however, that wardens often declared that the charge lacked merit and that wardens seldom interviewed the complaining inmates. Yet, despite this tendency to dismiss charges at the unit level, some complaints did get to the central administration. Here, again, according to the monitor, little was done about them. During much of 1983, for example, Gerald Fall, general counsel for TDC, and McKaskle each claimed that disciplining officers for illegal use of force was not their job; they just passed the cases back and forth.

From 1981 through late 1983, TDC and state officials maintained this posture of tactical resistance. Through that period, most state leaders continued to believe that TDC was adequate in most areas and in others quite unassailable, regardless of reports to the contrary. But, after 1981, there were officials in the state who began to ask questions and to urge greater accountability for TDC; in the next two or three years these voices would grow. But, for the most part, support for the prison system and its director remained strong. In Austin, for example, the Speaker of the House of Representatives, Gib Lewis, declared in his speech opening the legislative session that no judge could tell the state how to run its prisons. And, as we have shown, resistance to compliance and to court staff investigations was generally the norm at all levels of the prison system. That resistance was strongest on those matters that directly assaulted TDC's traditional control structures and the autonomy that the agency had so long enjoyed. By mid-1983, however, the decades-old alliance between state politicos and TDC officials was falling apart, and TDC found itself quite alone.

State Pressure toward Compliance

One of the most pervasive colloquialisms used by TDC personnel is the expression "stuck out." This expression describes the condition of an inmate (or an officer) who, for whatever reason, is where he should not be; fails to get with or stay with a group; or is, in some sense, out of step with the flow. By September 1983, TDC and its administrators were stuck out relative to other state officials. After more than two years of postdecree legal resistance, and millions in attorneys' fees, state leaders began to question seriously TDC's traditional policies and, ultimately, to push hard for compliance. These rumblings in Austin and a confluence of legal, economic, organizational, and political problems snowballed to undermine TDC's legitimacy in the eyes of the legislature.

Population Pressure and the Budget Crunch

Overcrowding had, of course, been a central issue in the trial. In 1971, the TDC inmate population was 15,418, and, at the time of the trial (1978), the figure was nearly 25,000, with some 5,000 sleeping on the floor. TDC officials had been concerned about the crowding problem long before the trial, and in court it was readily acknowledged. But in the early 1980s the crowding problem got worse. By 1981, the population was pushing 30,000 with no relief in sight. This growth, as in the 1970s, was due more to political action than to any rise in crime. In 1980, Governor Clements vetoed 30 percent of the recommended paroles, and the 1981 legislature created thirty-seven new district courts, resulting in a predictable rise in prison-bound felons. Such conditions violated the court's mandate on crowding and further frustrated a legislature that had begun to grow weary of the prison problem.

To cope with this large and growing population and to comply with Justice's order, the state approved plans to build metal buildings adjacent to several units. But construction would take time. Governor Clements instructed the prison to borrow tents from the Texas National Guard for temporary housing. "Tent cities" soon emerged within the walls of many units, with each tent holding 10 prisoners. By the fall of 1981 there were 1,200 men housed in tents; the tent population ultimately reached nearly 4,000.[26] Still, by late spring 1982, TDC had a prison population of 33,000 with a net increase of about 20 prisoners per day, nearly 500 per month.

The situation had become critical. On May 4, Justice ordered TDC to show by mid-month how the state was abiding by his order that each prisoner receive forty square feet of living space, a ruling that the 5th Circuit had upheld. In response, the board of corrections, on May 11, ordered Estelle to accept no more prisoners until the system could comply with the court order. Suddenly, TDC, which had traditionally accepted all convicts from the counties, shut its doors. Local officials and sheriffs were irate since their jails were also full and often overcrowded. Some local officials charged that TDC's action was illegal and that they would file suit to force the prison system to accept more prisoners. Others stated that they would handcuff their prisoners to prison fences. Most of all, however, they complained bitterly to the governor.

The crowding problem soon became the focus of political debate in the 1982 gubernatorial race between Republican incumbent Bill Clements and his Democratic challenger (and attorney general) Mark White. The prison system became a political football, with each candidate blaming his opponent and others for the crisis. Clements recommended that the board of pardons and parole release some inmates who were within six months of completing their sentences.

White countered that the public would not appreciate criminals walking their streets because of a fluke in the criminal justice system. White directly blamed Clements for the overcrowding situation because of his 1979 veto of a $30 million prison construction plan, a move that undermined the state's case in the lawsuit. Clements, in turn, blamed TDC for not having a master plan to anticipate growth in the prison population. He also publicly decried Estelle's inability to cope with the inmate population.[27]

On May 14, 1982, Clements ordered TDC to receive more prisoners. In response, TDC established an inmate allowance for sixteen populous counties. Clements held that the closure was a mistake, and he rebuked the board of corrections for not having consulted with his office prior to closing TDC's doors. These criticisms of the prison board and of Director Estelle were the first negative public comments directed at the department from such high places in decades. This was also the first time in many years that the prison system had been mired in political controversy or had become a real campaign issue in a governor's race.

In late May 1982, the governor called a special legislative session to deal with, among other things, the prison crisis. The board of corrections requested an $85 million emergency appropriation to deal with overcrowding. The legislature instead approved $58 million, of which $43 million went to the construction of a new 500-cell maximum-security unit.[28] Clements immediately criticized this decision and advocated minimum-security dormitories, which could be built more quickly and at less cost. Prison officials and the board clung to TDC's traditional emphasis on maximum-security facilities.

This commitment to maximum-security units, together with continuing overcrowding pressure, led TDC's director to present an enormous budget request during the legislative budget hearings in late 1982. To build traditional units and to comply with Justice's mandate for space, Estelle asked for $1.5 billion, with $674 million designated for construction. The members of the legislature were stunned at such figures. Lieutenant Governor and Chairman of the Legislative Budget Board William P. Hobby called the prison a "bottomless pit."[29]

Estelle's budget was rejected completely. During the regular session in early 1983, the legislature allocated to TDC only $620 million, less than half of what Estelle and his staff had requested. Funds for construction were budgeted at $89 million, with most of that money earmarked for repair and upgrading of existing institutions, not for new construction. For the first time in decades, state officials, conservatives and liberals, joined forces to severely reduce prison funding. Such cuts came, in part, because legislators thought that the billion-dollar budget was simply impossible; they also believed that a change in state correctional philosophy was in order.

During the 1983 legislative session, the state began to move away from the traditional, conservative "lock 'em up" philosophy toward expanded community corrections, a move prompted much more by fiscal than by humanitarian considerations. Specific suggestions for this new, and less costly, direction for corrections came from a report developed by a blue-ribbon commission appointed in 1982 by Clements. That commission examined prison overcrowding, probation, and parole practices and suggested alternatives that would improve the crowding situation in TDC. The legislature enacted many of these recommendations into law and funded them with money that once would have gone to TDC. Appropriations to the board of pardons and parole were increased by 70 percent; new, more-generous good-time laws would make more inmates eligible for release on parole. And to expedite the release process, the legislature removed the governor from the parole decision-making loop. To make more room for serious offenders, the legislature provided for intensive supervision on probation for minor offenders who could be diverted from prison. Accordingly, the Texas Adult Probation Commission received a 111 percent increase in funding. As a final population control device, the legislature passed a measure requiring the prison director to notify the governor when the prison nears 95 percent capacity. At that point, inmates eligible, or nearly so, would be released to relieve crowding.

Charges of Fiscal Mismanagement

The staggering budget proposed by Estelle sent shock waves through the statehouse. Wondering how a system that had previously seemed to be so well managed could require that kind of money, legislators became very interested in TDC's fiscal planning and policies. Through the spring and into the summer of 1983, the prison system's accounting procedures were put under the microscope, especially by the Legislative Budget Board (LBB).

This scrutiny led to a series of disclosures that further diminished the reputation of the prison system and Estelle. An example was the administration's plan to let an $8 million construction contract to a private firm owned by a man with whom Estelle and a few other prison officials had had real estate business dealings. Although Estelle denied any interest in the firm then or previously, allegations of conflict of interest surfaced, and some legislators began to wonder about graft and corruption within TDC.[30] Questions also arose over the 400 percent escalation of costs for expansion of the Ferguson Unit; expenses rose from the projected $4.7 million to $21 million in one year. Prison business managers also had difficulty accounting for equipment and food that the agency was supposed to have had on hand. At one point, for example, LBB auditors could not find, and TDC could not account for, over 500,000 pounds of beef.

Other fiscal decisions by TDC also came under fire. One of the most controversial involved hazardous duty pay. This pay bonus for selected employees amounted to $84 per year for each year of employment with the state. Originally designed to reward employees who worked directly with inmates, TDC administrators extended the bonus to nearly all employees, including secretaries, clerks, and accountants who did not work around prisoners. Even the director's secretary was receiving hazardous duty pay.[31]

At the same time, TDC's employee emolument program (including such benefits as low-cost housing, paid utilities, inmate "house boys," family food allotments from prison agriculture, and dry cleaning) was investigated, and more problems emerged. The prison's own analysis of employees who drew emoluments revealed that some officials were obtaining two to three times their share of "perks." Representative Ray Keller, chair of the House Law Enforcement Committee, which oversees prisons, accused TDC officials of operating a scam designed to benefit a select few. He called for an outside investigation.

As these problems surfaced, the attacks on TDC and its administration began in earnest. Newspaper headlines declared TDC finances to be out of control, while some state officials hurled accusations at prison officials. One said, "Fiscally, that place [TDC] stinks over there." Others, trying not to fuel the already intense heat on the prison system, maintained that the agency just grew too fast for its accounting procedures and personnel to keep up. One state senator summed up the situation well: "I think they got so big, so quickly, they just got sloppy."[32]

Continuing Staff Abuse of Inmates

On April 4, 1981, Eroy Brown, an inmate at the Ellis Unit, was involved in a fight outside the prison compound that left Warden

Wallace Pack and farm manager Billy Moore dead. During that fight, Pack drowned in a nearby creek while Moore was shot twice with the warden's gun. These deaths were the first staff slayings since the Carrasco hostage situation in 1974; they were the first deaths of a warden or a farm manager in Texas prison history.

At his trial, Brown pleaded not guilty, claiming self-defense. His story was that the two officials were taking him to "the bottoms" (near the Trinity River), a place, he said, where guards regularly took inmates to beat them. During the hearings, Craig Washington, Brown's attorney, as well as a state representative and an outspoken critic of TDC, called inmates and a former guard to testify that Pack and Moore were violent men who had on numerous occasions beaten inmates, particularly writ writers, or had directed building tenders to do so. One witness testified that he knew Warden Pack carried a pistol in his boot and used it to hit inmates. A year and a half and two sensational trials later, the first resulting in a hung jury, Brown was acquitted of the Pack slaying. The jury found that he had, in fact, acted in self-defense. A subsequent trial of Brown for Moore's death in Brownsville, Texas, also ended with a not-guilty verdict.

Extending into 1982, the Eroy Brown trials were in fact retrials of the prison system itself. The deaths of Pack and Moore left prison officials, and much of the Huntsville community, shocked and angered. Prison personnel and administrators saw the event as a symbol of the loss of control (inmates at Ellis were said to cheer on hearing of the officers' deaths) brought about by what was widely viewed as the unwarranted intrusion of the court. Plaintiffs and others sympathetic to the prisoners saw the evidence in the Brown case as verification not only of traditional abuse but also of continued brutality in direct violation of the court order. For the prison officials and the plaintiffs, the Brown case simply hardened positions long held. For many state officials, however, the evidence presented there raised questions about just what TDC was doing and whether its officials were credible.

Credibility questions multiplied with the publication in September 1983 of the "Ninth Monitor's Report" on the use of force by prison personnel. The report presented evidence that staff brutality against inmates had been rampant in the two years since the court order was issued. The report concluded that "the use of force continues to be routine in TDC" and that the abuse was systemwide. Specific examples were cited to document the involvement of high-ranking officers. This report essentially destroyed statehouse faith that TDC, under Jim Estelle, was going to comply with the court mandate on its own.

W. J. Estelle, Jr., Resigns

Prior to 1980, there were cracks in the TDC monolith of tradition and control, but they were small. Prison officials and state leaders presented a united front, a posture that extended through the trial and beyond. But there was a limit even for TDC's staunchest supporters, and events through 1982 and into 1983 conspired to destroy that support. Faced with a net growth of hundreds of inmates per month and a court order on how to provide for them, Estelle took an impossible funding request to Austin. The legislative response reflected a disaffection with TDC and, inasmuch as he so vividly symbolized the agency, with Estelle himself. Newly elected Governor White urged the board of corrections to get control of the prison system. Not only was there still massive overcrowding, but also guards were continuing to abuse inmates, as the September 1983 monitor's report had made clear. Commenting on the abuse report, but also articulating a growing feeling about TDC autonomy, Representative Keller stated: "This is just one more example of the prison system's desire to be accountable to no one. We are trying to change that with a thorough reform of the Texas prison system to make administrators accountable to the prison Board, to the legislature, and ultimately to the taxpayers."[33]

On September 15, 1983, Estelle announced that he would resign sometime in the next six months, a move he had been privately considering for over a year. Because he personified TDC, he recognized that he had become a "lightning rod," attracting criticism of the agency. He believed that he had failed in his dealings with the legislature and was stung by the charges of continuing inmate abuse and mismanagement of state monies within the prison. This time the issue was Estelle's authorization of a 3.3 percent pay raise for some TDC employees. Legislators noted and were incensed by the fact that recipients of these raises included every person who had lost emolument benefits. In their eyes, Estelle, known for championing his employees, had apparently directly defied the legislature. For Representative Keller the raise decision by the director was the "straw that broke the camel's back. That was insubordination that couldn't be tolerated."[34] Director Estelle did not get six more months. On October 7, 1983, Estelle met in the capitol with the board and other state officials to submit his resignation.

The Court Order's Impact on the Organization

Starting in late 1983, officials began actively to institute new policies aimed primarily at maximizing control of the prison staff. The board of corrections and top state officials rightly saw that this was the key to compliance. Specifically, the security staff had to give up traditional methods of handling inmates. To this end, the board increased its involvement in the system's operations, and the system, in turn, experienced a revolving-door directorship. These organizational changes heightened staff uncertainty and exacerbated inmate control problems.

Board Involvement in Prison Operations

The board of corrections in Texas is a policy-making panel appointed by the governor. Each of the nine members serves a six-year term, with the terms staggered to reduce undue influence from a newly elected governor. Members can be, and often are, reappointed. The board elects one of its own to serve as chairman. Besides its policy-making function, the board serves as the organization's liaison with the governor and legislature.

For two decades, from 1955 to 1976, the board operated under the strong leadership of Chairman H. H. Coffield, who worked closely with directors Ellis, Beto, and Estelle to determine TDC's direction. Once Coffield and the director had made the basic decisions, they took those decisions to a board that consistently, and unanimously, supported them. In this way, the board and the organization worked informally, in tandem, and quite effectively.

This comfortable relationship began to show signs of strain after Coffield's resignation in 1976. After his departure, the chairmanship changed hands several times, leaving the board without the firm leadership of the past. It was during this period of chair succession that Director Estelle began to gain influence over the prison board. One board member commented on Estelle's increased power: "Here was Jim Estelle, very knowledgeable, with these new chairmen coming on the Board, and I think Jim just took up the void. He very autocratically ran the entire system, including the Board." Future board chairman Robert Gunn was even more specific: "Jim Estelle was a tremendously powerful and charismatic person. He just overwhelmed everything and everybody."[35]

Estelle's ascendency over the board began to erode in 1980. That erosion was symbolized by a "no" vote cast in a board meeting, an action that broke decades of uniform support for the director's plans.

The dissenting vote was cast by Harry Whittington, appointed in 1979 to a historically democratic board by the first Republican governor in a century. When Governor Clements lost the gubernatorial race in 1982 to Attorney General White, Whittington rather suddenly became quite vocal in his criticism of TDC and its administration. Some speculated that his public barbs were in large part politically motivated, aimed at embarrassing White. In any case, Whittington's growing criticisms from within the board combined with the more damaging controversies and allegations of 1983 to prompt Estelle's resignation.

With Estelle's departure, the board essentially took over the system. The new Democratic governor, White, told the board to become actively involved in TDC operations and to move the system expeditiously toward compliance with the court order.

The board's first move was to send a memorandum to all parties that it was going to be directly involved in all operations. Indeed, the board directed the department's Office of Internal Audits (in charge of in-house use of force investigations) to report directly to it, bypassing all top TDC officials.

The board's second, and more publicized, move was to put someone in charge of TDC on an interim basis who would actively push the organization toward compliance. Their choice was Red McKaskle, who had for many years served as Estelle's assistant director for special services. McKaskle, in his midforties, had come up through TDC's ranks and served as a unit warden and as director of classification. In his final role under Estelle he had been in charge of security and security staff. McKaskle not only supervised the formal aspects of recruitment, training, and promotions but also maintained an extensive, and quite personalized, information network throughout the prison system and the state. Little went on without his knowledge and approval, making him extremely powerful within the Estelle regime. Indeed, it appeared that, while Estelle handled relations with the legislature, the community, and the media, McKaskle essentially ran the day-to-day functioning of the prisons.

McKaskle's background meant that he had the experience and the connections with the staff to serve effectively. Yet, it also meant that he had long-term loyalties to the old order. But any questions about his orientation in his new role, however, were removed in McKaskle's first appearance before the legislature. He stated: "I am committed to following legislative intent and Board policy . . . I'm going to do whatever the Board tells me to do. There are problems. I'm going to do exactly what the Board wants done and how they want it done."[36] This statement underscored the board's involvement in prison operations.

McKaskle took over at a time when TDC's reputation with state officials, reform groups, citizens, and the media was at a very low point. Along with persistent overcrowding, the brutality issue had seriously damaged TDC's image. This allegation that staff abuse of inmates persisted and was system wide prompted the new director's first actions. In November 1983, McKaskle addressed a memo to all wardens and employees reminding them of the contents of the *Standards for the Use of Force*,[37] a document prepared by TDC and approved by the court almost exactly one year previously. That memo stated that all employees would (1) "cooperate to the fullest extent . . ." with court officials; (2) "respond to all inquiries and requests" from court officials; (3) "refrain from retaliating against or harassing in any manner any inmate, fellow employee, or other person for such cooperation"; and (4) suffer disciplinary action or discharge for failure to follow these directives. This memo followed a TDC agreement with a plaintiff's lawyers to administer polygraph tests to guards and inmates during use-of-force investigations. Although TDC's Office of Internal Audits had been investigating force allegations, they had not employed the polygraph.

This new determination by the board and McKaskle to eliminate brutality on the units led to the dismissal of many officers. In December 1983, a sergeant was fired for refusing to submit to a polygraph examination after a force allegation was filed against him. The active disciplining of staff continued vigorously into 1984.[38] By June 1984, TDC's central administration had disciplined (fired, demoted, suspended, or reprimanded) eighty-five officers, including eight unit wardens (two of whom were fired), for violating official guidelines for the use of force.[39] These actions received extensive press coverage, including the names of the officers involved and the nature of their actions. Board Chairman Gunn declared that the disciplinary actions signaled to the employees (and to the court) that the board and Acting Director McKaskle would strictly enforce the new policy. These personnel actions left little doubt about the board's influence in the prison's daily operations. More important, the firings and the publicity surrounding them effectively ended the staff's use of punitive force as a means of inmate control.

Raymond Procunier and a New Administrative Style

While McKaskle was interim director, the board conducted a national search for a permanent prison administrator. There was no shortage of persons interested, including McKaskle. But the board wanted someone not only with extensive prison experience but also with experience in dealing with a prison system in turmoil and change. A more informal criterion was that the new man be an out-sider to both the prison system and the state.

After being turned down by two other nationally prominent prison administrators, the board, in late May 1984, signed Raymond Procunier, then deputy secretary of the New Mexico prison system. Procunier was an experienced administrator, having already managed prisons in California, Utah, and Virginia. He had a well-established reputation in prison circles as a troubleshooter and as a capable manager of prisons in transition. This reputation, plus an intimacy with prison litigation, made Procunier an acceptable choice. When he accepted the job, Procunier said that he was interested only in getting TDC through the tough period of compliance and re-adjustment and that he would stay in the job no longer than two years. On Procunier's arrival, McKaskle retired from TDC.

The new director brought a new personal and administrative style to TDC. Unlike Estelle, who was courtly, articulate, and tightly in control of his words and actions, Procunier, though certainly a prison expert, was profane in any company and something of a "hipshooter." By design, he had no ties to TDC's past and was committed only to moving the agency beyond its difficulties with the court and the leg-islature. He sought first to dispel the fortress mentality that had characterized the prison and its top officials for so long. "We're going to be wide open. If there's a screw-up, there is a screw-up. I never have a 'no comment.'"[40]

At the same time the board hired Procunier, it also hired another outsider to be his deputy director for operations. This man was Colonel Lane McCotter, commandant of the U.S. Army's disciplinary barracks at Fort Leavenworth.

Regaining Control of Inmates

When Procunier took over, he and his new staff faced two fundamental administrative problems. The first was to regain control of an increasingly violent inmate population, and the second, and from the board's point of view more important, was to rebuild and control the staff. In the long run, of course, these two problems are closely linked. From the outset, however, Procunier had to treat them immediately and independently.

The transition that TDC was undergoing produced or permitted a wave of prisoner violence. By the end of 1984, 404 inmates had been stabbed, 25 fatally. This level of violence contrasted sharply with earlier years in TDC when one or two violent deaths of inmates in a year was remarkable. Indeed, 1984 fatalities were up 40 percent over the previous year. This trend was real and alarming, especially since the violence extended to staff as well; at the Coffield Unit, for example, a sergeant was stabbed in the stomach. Following this particular assault, officers searched the unit and found over five hundred inmate-made weapons. Fights, torchings, stabbings, homicides, and disturbances became common at most units. Prison gangs were growing and were regularly involved in the slayings. This violence, as well as increases in homosexual rape, in the availability of drugs, and in inmates' paying protection money, received regular media attention. At the same time, unit officials declared that they had lost control, and many lamented the passing of the BTs and other control mechanisms of the past.

Procunier instituted a multifaceted plan to deter violence and gain control of the institution. To provide immediate help at the units, a number of six-man Special Operations Reaction Teams (SORT) were created to conduct searches and handle emergency situations at the units. The prison also added walk-through metal detectors and hand-held electronic sniffers to aid security. For troublesome inmates, especially gang members, Procunier established "administrative segregation" cellblocks. Additional officers were hired to staff these blocks.

Inmates who assaulted inmates or guards were aggressively prosecuted and, when possible, given consecutive, or "stacked," prison terms. For example, an inmate who stabbed an officer in October 1984 was found guilty of attempted murder and given an additional fifty years. This sentence was added to his current sentence of ten years for burglary.[41] The new administration also instituted a new good-time policy in which inmates found by the authorities to have been involved in violence would lose accrued good time forever. In the past, good time taken away could be, and often was, eventually returned to the inmate.

More fundamental control strategies were involved in a new inmate classification and management plan. Six TDC units were officially designated as maximum security for inmates classified as high risk and in need of the tightest security. The remaining units became either medium or minimum security. This unit redesignation plan moved the prison away from the traditional notion that all prisons should be maximum security. A new, highly detailed prisoner classification scheme was developed that relied on formal committee decisions rather than on a classification officer's convict sense.

The Procunier staff also established a case management system in which counselors maintained inmate caseloads and provided individual counseling on prison and personal matters. The intent of this classification and case management scheme was to keep hardened violent offenders isolated at certain units and to reward others who were not security problems. Inmates not satisfied with their classification plan could appeal the decision.

Organizational and Staff Control

To comply with the specifics of the court order, staff on all units had to know what behavior was appropriate and that deviation would not be tolerated. Accordingly, Procunier's staff assembled and distributed to top-ranking personnel a new, two-volume manual detailing operating procedures. The manual included job descriptions and outlined what procedures wardens and ranking staff must follow in a variety of circumstances. This manual was part of a communication explosion from the central office, with much of the paper modifying, clarifying, or adding to guidelines already sent out to unit managers.

The purpose was to formalize and to standardize TDC's operations. Of course, TDC had always been a large bureaucratic organization, marked by rules and records, mechanisms of accountability, and formal channels of communication. Yet, the formal rules were regularly disregarded. Informal structure and personalized decision-making processes played a major role in the fate of individual officers and inmates and in determining policies. Procunier's plan was to remove such traditional arrangements through greater specification of rules and accountability.

This strategy also centralized organizational control and reversed a trend that had marked TDC administration over the previous five or six years. Through the Beto years, and in the early years of Estelle's administration, the prison system had been relatively centralized. For example, through his regular visits to the units, Walking George Beto was able to exert tight control over almost all aspects of the penitentiaries. When the system was relatively small and the external environment either supportive or neutral, the top administrator could concentrate on maintaining support from the legislature and, at the same time, rest assured that unit officials and programs operated according to his dictates. Through the late 1970s, however, as TDC's environment became increasingly hostile and its population grew, this tight, centralized control of the organization began to break down. Specifically, policy authority and operational control gradually shifted to the unit wardens as the attention and energies of the director were drained by external pressures. This drift toward decentralization created a problem for wardens and ranking staff. They lacked adequate guidance for managing in a rapidly changing environment. That is, the informal, traditional norms that had worked well in an earlier era were rather suddenly either ineffective or illegal. As individual wardens faced and tried to deal with unfamiliar challenges, policy variations across units increased. These variations were regularly highlighted in monitor reports and negative media coverage.

To reduce these variations, Procunier made a number of personnel changes. In his first month as director, the board authorized Procunier to undertake a general housecleaning, and he did not hesitate. He shook the hierarchy by demoting an assistant director to warden and by replacing nearly half of the twenty-seven unit wardens. He insisted that the staff either obey the decree or get out: "I don't want to hear wardens say they cannot run prisons under a consent decree. Systems are run that way all over the country."[42]

To consolidate central administration control over the units the director created three regional directorships. In charge of the northern, central, and southern regions, the new regional directors had such duties as "overseeing the prison operation in their areas, administering security, conducting on-site inspections, ensuring compliance of court order and rules and meeting training requirements for personnel."[43] One duty of the regional directors was to keep the unit administrators on a short leash. They also added another layer to the organizational hierarchy.

Final Ruiz Settlement

While Procunier and his staff were working to reorient the staff and to stem inmate violence, attorneys for both sides had been working toward final settlement of the Ruiz case. With consent decrees on medical care, the use of building tenders, and the use of force already signed by the state, the only major issue outstanding was overcrowding and the related issues of providing adequate supervision and necessities for a given population of inmates. In late January 1985, lawyers from both sides went to federal court with a proposal that they had worked out to end the thirteen-year-old suit. By May of that year, state officials signed a court-sanctioned settlement. At the time, Board Chairman Gunn stated: "I want to inform them [TDC staff] that the war is over. The side of reform has won."[44]

The settlement, committing the state to an expenditure of $173 million,[45] stipulated the changes to be made by the prison system and the deadlines for those changes.

1. TDC must reduce the inmate population at its 26 units from 37,562 to 32,500 by September 1, 1989. Half of that reduction must be made by September 1, 1987. Furthermore, each TDC unit has a specified capacity that cannot be exceeded.
2. Texas can construct new prisons wherever the state chooses, but maximum capacity of each will be 2,250.
3. TDC must adopt the following minimum level of security staffing by September 1, 1987:

Assistant Warden	40
Major	40
Captain	101
Lieutenant	300
Sergeant	415
Correctional officer	7,283

   TDC may not employ less than one security staff member for each six prisoners.
4. Cells in new TDC units must have 60 square feet while double cells must have 80 square feet.
5. TDC must implement a comprehensive maintenance plan to cure health and safety deficiencies.
6. TDC must make minor additions to existing units, including dividers between beds in dormitories, additional showers, toilets, and lavatories, additional outdoor recreations yards, and gyms.
7. TDC must provide all inmates with, and have on hand during the course of each fiscal year, the following linen items:

   8 pants per year
   8 shirts per year
   8 shorts per year
   10 pairs of socks per year
   4 cell towels per year
   8 shower towels per year
   4 sheets per year
   3 pillowcases per year
   4 pairs of shoes per year

Procunier had been hired to move the prison system toward compliance with the courts' orders and ultimate settlement of the case. Knowing that the job would be difficult and being near retirement, he had stated he would stay only two years. But, after several months on the job, Procunier found he had underestimated the task. The scope of that task and his driving personal style took their toll on him physically. Consequently, after only one year in the post, in June 1985, Procunier resigned, citing health problems and general "burn out."

Much had happened in his short tenure, however. He and his staff, with the constant attention of the board, had wrenched the agency from a generally defensive posture and aggressively pushed it in the direction mandated by the court. His primary task had been to restructure the organization, its procedures, and personnel orientations. Change meant formalization, centralization, and strict accountability. No longer could wardens initiate and enforce idiosyncratic rules. The old ways were gone, TDC was becoming homogenized; the locus of power had shifted unquestionably to the central office. Yet, staff resistance and prisoner violence were still significant aspects of unit life.

The McCotter Administration

When Procunier resigned, the board appointed his assistant director, Lane McCotter, to be director of TDC. When McCotter was hired as Procunier's second-in-command, he was no stranger to Huntsville. McCotter had originally been brought to the board's attention by former TDC Director Beto, then distinguished professor of criminal justice at Sam Houston State University. Colonel McCotter had completed a master's degree a decade earlier at the university, and he and Beto were well acquainted. Beto had visited the stockade at Fort Leavenworth while McCotter was in charge there and had been impressed. Consequently, when the board sought a number two man for Procunier, Beto suggested that McCotter be considered.

At the time the two were hired in the late spring of 1984, it was widely rumored that the board's real plan was to let Procunier make the necessary changes and draw the heat, while McCotter stayed in the wings and learned about running a large state prison system. After Procunier's self-allotted two years, McCotter would be relatively unsullied politically and prepared to run TDC.

But the new TDC Director McCotter faced tasks for which he may not have been fully prepared. The prison population was continuing to grow, and the court case, though settled, would involve continued tests for compliance for years. At the same time, relations with the legislature were little improved from the break in 1983. Finally, although Procunier had plotted a new course, the agency had hardly embarked on it. To meet these problems, McCotter could draw on only one year of acclimation to a huge and complex state prison system and on his experience as commandant of a small military prison housing a few thousand prisoners supervised by a few hundred relatively well qualified officers.

McCotter's most immediate problem was continued inmate violence. The new classification plan had not curbed assaults. Indeed, 1985 was the worst year in TDC history for inmate-inmate violence, with 237 stabbings and 27 deaths. These accounted for nearly a quarter of all inmate deaths in the country. Gang trouble worsened and seemed on the verge of getting completely out of hand. For example, on one September Saturday, three inmates died in gang-related violence, and a gang war was taking place between two rival Mexican American gangs, the Texas Syndicate and the Mexican Mafia.

In response, the director ordered an immediate lock-down of nearly 1,700 inmates at thirteen units in the fall of 1985. The purpose was to isolate and control gang warfare. To handle gang affiliates and others who would be locked down, the administration designated, on several maximum-security units, a number of "super" segregation cellblocks, prisons inside prisons. These would be screened off from the main hall and other cellblocks and would house for indefinite periods violent offenders who were known, or even suspected of being, gang members. Gang affiliation was entered on the inmate's computerized record so that other officials would be aware of that affiliation should the inmate be transferred to another unit. The lock-down strategy for dealing with inmate violence and gang warfare was relatively effective. In 1986, the number of inmate deaths dropped to five.

McCotter faced from the outset of his administration a more amorphous problem, namely, following through on the organizational initiatives of his predecessor while dealing with personnel problems, such as continued noncompliance, generally poor performance, and low morale. To help him with these problems, he rather predictably turned to military people, since they shared his perspectives on organizations and employees. McCotter's recruitment of present and former military personnel into administrative positions, such as the internal audits office, began as soon as he went to work as deputy to Procunier in May 1984. Significantly, most of these individuals had little or no experience with prisons or prison problems.

When McCotter moved to the director's office, many of these former military men were promoted with him. The result was a perception that TDC was being militarized. Insiders referred to the agency as Fort Hood East and to McCotter's staff as the "khaki mafia" or as "jeep drivers." The central office was suddenly full of people who did not wear western boots, who were very comfortable with the new bureaucratization, and who seemed to know much more about administration than prisons. One informant reported hearing McCotter's chief of operations (in charge of security), a former military officer, state flatly that he knew nothing about prisons. Longtime employees found that they could walk down the administration building halls and recognize almost no one.

According to one former employee who served as warden under McCotter and his three predecessors, McCotter's military-oriented administration brought in more than formality, distance, and cronyism. It may have subtly encouraged a very different style of leadership at the units. That is, under TDC's traditional philosophy, the warden was to lead personally. If there was a riot, the warden was expected to be up front. In the military, however, the leader sends subordinates, and the action goes according to a prearranged plan, not the personal preferences of the officers in the action.

Of course, if leadership styles shifted in this way, it was as likely due to the general bureaucratization of the agency as to the militarization per se. The significant point is that the influx of so many military people into top TDC posts was troubling to many employees, especially veteran employees. The military flavor of TDC's top administration was also troubling to politicians. Indeed, it became a campaign issue in the 1986 gubernatorial race when White and Clements squared off again.

Conclusion

In less than three years, the state legislature went from a position of unstinting moral and financial support of TDC to suspicion and outright distrust. This initial posture led the board of corrections and state officials at first to resist the court orders. In time, however, as TDC lost credibility, those officials began to stress compliance.

To move the agency toward compliance, Procunier and then McCotter revised TDC's philosophy and restructured its organization. Since, along with overcrowding, it was TDC's traditional control mechanisms that particularly distressed the court, the new administration ordered massive changes in the control practices on each prison unit. We turn now to a closer look at how those changes affected security personnel at the units.

6

Changing of the Guards

*We can't do it; it ain't no way we can control it now. Mostly
it's the monitors and all them other people that's down on us.
Every time you put your hands on one you got to do a lot of paperwork and stuff . . . You got to cuff 'em, kiss 'em, and read 'em
their rights.*   —TDC SERGEANT, 1984

*The greatest change is when we had to quit giving ass whippings.
That was the biggest change. You didn't have to beat the shit out
of them. You slap him two or three times. The next time you talk
to him, he is liable to do anything you ask him to do. He would
know you mean business. Now it's "Fuck you, you ain't got no
business telling me what to do."*   —TDC OFFICER, 1984[1]

AS STATE officials and new TDC administrators began to comply with the court orders, security officers found themselves
pressured from three directions. First, inmates threatened officers
from below by disobeying orders and by verbally, and even physically, abusing them as never before. Second, lateral pressure came
from a massive influx of new security officers hired to improve the
officer-inmate ratio and, in part, to replace building tenders. Finally,
pressure on the security force came from above as the new administration bureaucratized the organization to maximize accountability. These changes greatly distressed officers, especially veterans,
and affected how they defined and carried out their duties. At the
same time, these pressures undermined the traditional officer subculture such that by the mid-1980s the security staff was fractured
and disorganized.

Inmate Aggression and Perceptions of Control

The dramatic rise of inmate violence demonstrated that traditional
control in TDC was rapidly eroding. When, in August 1984, the system experienced a riot and six stabbings in one twenty-four-hour period, Procunier admitted that officers did not have control of the
situation.[2] Prison halls and cellblocks seemed to be more dangerous.
But prisoners were not the only ones who were at risk; inmate aggression was aimed at officers with increasing frequency.

Table 7 *Changes in Prisoner Rule Violations*

Violations	1983	1984	1985	1986
Striking officer with or without weapon	733	1,895	3,703	4,144
	(20)	(53)	(104)	(109)
Threatening an officer	764	1,399	2,150	2,944
	(21)	(39)	(60)	(77)
Refusing/failing to obey orders	776	11,098	12,515	16,357
	(21)	(311)	(352)	(432)
Refusing to work	3,396	3,393	3,565	7,002
	(96)	(95)	(100)	(185)

Source: Management Services, TDC.
Note: Figures in parentheses denote the number of violations per 1,000 inmates in the system.

Emboldened by the reforms that removed the building tenders and sharply limited the conditions under which officers could use physical coercion, inmates were less inclined to follow rules and obey orders. Table 7 reveals how problems of inmate compliance increased over time.

Officers across the system agreed that inmates became less willing to obey orders. Although most inmates complied with orders most of the time, many prisoners began simply to ignore them. As one officer put it: "We can't control 'em. If you tell an inmate something, they laugh at you and keep on going."

Inmates began to verbally abuse the officers as well. After telling an inmate something, an officer might hear: "Fuck all you whores, you can't tell me what to do anymore," or "Quit harassing me, you old country punk," or "Get your bitchy ass out of my face." The extent of such abuse by inmates and its perception by officers are illustrated by the following statement from a ten-year TDC veteran officer. "And to curse [an officer] is nothing; that's an everyday occurrence, cursing an officer and telling him 'the hell with you, the hell with the man. I don't give a damn about no case.' They use foul language, call you everything in the book. Call your wife and momma everything in the book, and you got to stand there and take it."

In addition to verbal abuse, officers in some work settings, such as solitary or administrative segregation, had feces, urine, vomit, or in a few cases, some combination of these thrown on them. Many officers began wearing rain slickers and headgear for protection.

Most officers in the system were ignored or cursed by inmates and had at least heard about the throwing of body wastes. Such behavior frustrated and angered officers not only because it led to injury but also because it reflected so clearly the erosion of respect and authority that TDC officers had traditionally enjoyed. When the inmate aggressiveness toward officers escalated into relatively frequent physical assaults, fear was added to frustration and anger.

Most physical assaults on officers appeared to have been strikes against the uniform rather than planned attacks on specific officers. Moreover, most officer injuries were relatively minor. For example, disturbed by a search of his dormitory for weapons, an inmate on the Retrieve Unit struck an officer with a fluorescent light bulb as the officer was returning to that dormitory. Later that day, after he was in lockup, that inmate attacked a second employee, a TDC attorney who was walking by the cell. The inmate grabbed the attorney's tie, slammed him into the bars, and began hitting him. An officer rescued the man by cutting the tie.[3] In another case, an inmate threw scalding water into the face of an officer who had just delivered a tray of food to that inmate's lock-down cell. The officer was temporarily blinded.[4] That same day, one officer was struck by an extension cord while another was cut when an inmate slashed at him through cell bars with a broken light bulb.[5]

Other instances of inmate assaults involved more lethal weapons. On the Darrington Unit, an officer was escorting an inmate from the shower when the inmate asked him if he wanted to fight. When the officer declined, the inmate struck him in the face, then stabbed him twice with a sharpened nail.[6] At this same unit, in the fall of 1984, officials uncovered a .25-caliber pistol along with a list of five high-ranking officers at the prison. The assumption was that the officers were on a "hit list" to be killed during a riot or escape attempt.[7]

In the eyes of officers and inmates, such aggression reflected a loss of official leverage over inmates. The officers could no longer use force, nor could they obtain information about inmate activities as they once could. Veteran officers saw a direct connection between the inmates' aggressive behavior and the fact that they no longer feared physical reprisals from staff. "It's changed because you can't put that boot in their ass. . . . [In the past] the only thing they had to do was, whatever happened, keep their mouth shut and try to make it through the system. But now it's freedom of speech, the way they try to put it. You can say what you want to say and express yourself the way you want to express yourself. Ain't no fear no more. Back then they had a lot of fear but now they don't." This connection between fear and acquiescence was even acknowledged by prisoners. An inmate explained: "You can stand out there every day, I mean every day and hear these people calling bosses names that nobody should have to put up with, even though you are a boss. . . . The only reason these people are calling bosses names like they are doing [is] because they know nothing is going to happen to them."

Not only did inmates have less to fear from officers, but they were also much more able to plan actions and execute them without the guards' knowledge. Previously, officers regularly received information from BTs and other inmates. As an assistant warden put it: "I used to come in and be able to tell you everything that went on all night long. I knew at least 65 to 70 percent of what happened the night before, and if I wanted to know it, I could know it in fifteen minutes after I stepped in here. If there was going to be a stabbing, well, I knew about it . . ." In the past, possession of timely information meant that officers could anticipate and control inmate activities effectively. Information was power since it permitted security to penetrate the cellblocks and inmate cliques.

By 1984, the situation was drastically different; officials no longer had advance information about inmate activities. Less information reflected the widening gulf between the staff and the population. This sense of distance from inmate action was widespread among officers. In fact, two out of three officers surveyed agreed that "five years ago officials had much better information on what inmates were doing or planning to do than officials have today."

Several factors account for this loss of information. Perhaps the most important and predictable was fear of retaliation from other inmates for snitching. Inmates were very aware that officers and their minions no longer controlled the prison. Instead, emerging gangs and cliques seemed to dominate. Thus, regular inmates were afraid to talk to officers. A captain described the change in the following way: "[Information] is drying up, partially because of the fear element. The other inmates know they'd get killed if they told, especially if they told on the gang. They're putting their life on the line. Plus, three years ago one would talk to you because he knew who you were, how you took care of your business. That's not true anymore." An assistant warden underscored the lack of information and the fact that gangs and fear have limited its acquisition. "You don't find out nothing here. We got to go all the way around the world just to figure out what happened. These gangs ain't telling you nothing. The only way you find out something from a gang is [from] somebody that we planted in there, and then he is at great risk. So we can't plant them anymore. If somebody wants to come and talk to you, you can listen. But that don't mean that he's telling you the truth. Because look at the risk he's taking to tell you."

A second reason for the reduction of communication from inmates to officers was that the bureaucratization of the control system eliminated discretion to the point that officers no longer had the leeway to "pay" inmates for information, to help them in some way. One guard explained: "Officers aren't as likely to find things out as they used to. There's no reward for snitching today, so they don't find out things."

Finally, the loss of information, and the control that information facilitated, resulted from personnel changes that accompanied the court-ordered reforms. Specifically, TDC engaged in a massive hiring program, adding hundreds of officers to meet new staffing requirements. That influx of new staff and the resultant turnover made almost impossible the delicate business of collecting information from inmates and protecting them in the bargain. One veteran officer commented: "The turnover is so tremendous, the inmates don't know who to trust anymore. The man they talk to today may not be there tomorrow. Most of these young officers do not know how to handle information without making it obvious who gave them the information. They put these inmates in jeopardy."

A New Guard Force

Two central and related elements of the reform order were that TDC eliminate building tenders and greatly increase the number of correctional officers. By early 1983, BTs had essentially been removed from their former positions of authority. Unfortunately, however, TDC found it impossible to increase its security forces as rapidly as necessary. Thus, there was a chronic shortage of staff and supervisors, especially through 1984 and 1985, a problem to which administrators frequently pointed in explaining the rising level of violence.

This staff shortage prompted TDC to step up an already aggressive hiring effort. During the 1985 legislative session, TDC requested $99 million, most of which would go toward hiring additional officers. Administrators sent recruiters not only all over Texas but into other states as well. This effort produced significant increases in the number of uniformed officers at the units. For example, in 1979 the TDC security staff totaled approximately 2,500, and by 1985 that figure had risen to approximately 9,000; the guard force expanded more than three and a half times in that period. The entry of these "new" guards, with backgrounds that were usually urban and frequently non-Texan, changed the composition of the security force and, in the process, created problems for veteran officers and for officer-inmate relations.

Problems with New Officers

The rural, conservative values held by most TDC security officers in years past fit well with and, indeed, helped to shape the organizational culture of TDC. These employees and their values, however, were swamped by the hundreds of new, typically young, urban, and frequently minority officers added so quickly to TDC's guard force. Although many quite competent people were hired, some presented personas strikingly at odds with those of traditional officers. One young uniformed officer, for example, was seen in a convenience store near the Walls Unit in Huntsville just prior to the beginning of his shift wearing black high-top sneakers, hair cut shorter on one side than the other, and a gold, guitar-shaped earring in his left ear. The entry in the early 1980s of such men was certainly unsettling to veteran officers.

A more basic concern among veteran officers (and inmates) was that some of these new officers seemed particularly young and immature. In addition, many new officers often appeared to lack commitment to the job and to work in general; they tended to do the least possible to get by. Although he had been with TDC just slightly over one year, one officer had this to say about other relatively new officers: "A lot of the bosses here don't care nothing about their job. They come in, put in their eight hours, and go on about their business. They don't realize how dangerous it can be. They're just lazy. They don't do their jobs. All it takes is one screw up and you got a dead guard. You can't make them understand that." A lieutenant with six years' experience made a similar point:

When I came here, officers came to work. When he came to the job, like I say, he didn't mind working sixteen hours straight, little griping about it. Supervisors came up and said, "Hey, I need you to work." That's settled. He was right there and didn't mind. The officers we are getting today, they just on the job. It's eight hours, all they want to do is eight hours and go home. They're not interested in their job. They don't know whether they do their job right or not. They don't want no problem; they just want a job. Most of them is fresh out of high school—eighteen, nineteen, twenty years old.

Many new officers seemed to have less respect for rank than did officers of another era. Rank generally, and the presence of ranking officers specifically, seemed less important. Ranking officers did not serve as an important reference for these new men. A sergeant of several years' experience described how his initial orientation toward rank and the job differed from that of the new officers coming into the system.

When I first started back then when I saw a captain or a major, it really did, you know, it concerned me . . . I had a lot of respect for that man just because of his rank that he had. And if I was doing something wrong, I made sure I corrected it before he saw me do it alright. And nowadays a ranking officer to some SOBs, it really don't, it don't, you know, really mean that much to them. . . . It's just the inmates are losing respect for the ranking officers. I think until you can solve that problem you are not going to be able to solve the problem of guards losing respect for ranking officers.

This officer's statement not only characterizes problems with how newer officers respect their superiors but also alludes to a more fundamental problem with newer officers, namely, the extent to which many seem to relate better to inmates than to co-workers. Certainly, many TDC officers over the years have been close to selected inmates, even to the point of being on a first-name basis. In the past, however, such relations were not widespread and, most important, occurred within the prevailing context of paternalism. Despite situation-specific intimacy, there was never any question as to who was in the dominant position. Today, that dominance has become less clear, and many officers, especially newer ones, relate to inmates on an almost equal basis. Such relationships are troubling to veteran officers because they are contrary to tradition and because they can compromise security. A lieutenant and a sergeant, respectively, make the following points:

Back then the boss was king and he could do no wrong. Now you see officers *asking* inmates to do things. Some even call them by their first name. That's the way it is in the federal system.

I think the officers are getting friendlier with the inmates just to make it. If they get along with that inmate, it's easier to get them to follow orders. To make it, they have to get friendly with the inmates. In the future, to make it they'll have to be friendlier with the organizations [gangs]. It's coming. It's sad, too.

Such friendliness is often reflected in the informal, even playful, manner in which some younger officers interact with inmates. This interaction may involve what is known as "horseplaying" or "grab assing." For example, officers may lightly tussle, playfully push, or "rap" with inmates. Whether this interaction reflects a desire to ingratiate themselves with inmates in order to secure compliance or whether it reflects simple immaturity, many more-experienced officers believe that this type of behavior is inappropriate. "There's definitely more [horseplaying]. It's unprofessional, and someone's gonna get hurt. I've seen officers play hand games with these inmates. That wouldn't have happened five years ago. The BTs would have told the officer not to play with the convicts." These "hand games," or playful shoves and pokes, and the relationships with inmates that they signify undermine, or corrupt, the authority not only of a given officer but of the entire security force.[8] A sergeant of thirteen years put the problem this way: "I feel bad about it because they are going to lose respect that way. You see this inmate doing something and you been playing with him and you tell him to stop, he's going to think everything's all right. Going to think he's cool with you or something like that, and he's going to continue to do it. You write him up, you going to have no ground to stand on."

This tendency for many new officers to become overly close to inmates has had a much more pernicious consequence for security than simply difficulty in officers' writing up an inmate friend for a minor rule violation. A growing number of officers have cooperated with inmates to the point of bringing a variety of contraband into TDC units. A warden suggests that the increase is connected with the new officers being hired. "We got more employee problems than probably inmate problems. Two days ago we fired two officers. I fired a woman for bringing in coffee mugs and Christmas cards that play Silent Night and Jingle Bells. If she brought that in, what else will she bring in? I fired another one for getting throwed in jail for marijuana. Before we hired country people. We were a working farm and we hired mostly farm people. Now . . . we're hiring mostly kids from the city."

It is important to note that trafficking by officers did not begin in TDC in the early 1980s. Inmates have always been able to manipulate individual officers, to "weave a web" through sympathy and friendliness toward an officer.[9] The difference by middecade was the extent of the commerce with inmates. That commerce has involved weapons, loans, and drugs and is considered a serious problem by officers across the system. Indeed, 50 percent of the respondents to the officer survey agreed that "a big problem on this unit is officers trading in contraband with the inmates."

Although no officers have been convicted of taking money for bringing in a weapon, free-world weapons have been involved in assaults by inmates and have been found during searches. Such weapons directly implicate officers. For example, though it was not clear that money changed hands, an officer was fired in early 1985 for giving his pocketknife to an inmate who then passed it along to members of the Aryan Brotherhood gang. That knife was used to kill an inmate.[10] The officer involved had been with the department for only four months. More serious was the gun found on the Darrington Unit in late 1984. Of that incident, the unit warden said: "There are only two ways this thing [the gun] could have gotten in [brought in or overlooked by a guard during a search of a returning furloughed inmate]. Either way, a guard had to be involved."[11]

Officers have also taken loans from and done work for inmates. A six-month employee at the Huntsville Unit was arrested for taking a $500 loan from an inmate. The inmate had had the money sent to her Huntsville apartment.[12] Deals between officers and inmates at times went beyond simple loans of money. Several officers, for example, were fired from the Eastham Unit in mid-1985 for taking money from an inmate serving time for aggravated promotion of prostitution. One of the officers was paid for doing some concrete work at one of the inmate's businesses. A second allegedly made a sign for the man's hot tub spa. Two other officers were charged with giving this inmate postage stamps, a copy of his TDC file, a cigarette lighter, and a baseball cap in exchange for free passes to the prisoner's business.[13]

Finally, many officers have been sanctioned for bringing drugs into the prison for money. Typically, a single officer was enticed by inmates, usually gang members, to bring drugs inside. He went to a specified address, picked up the contraband, and delivered it to the unit. Delivery was not difficult since guards were not routinely searched, and security has always been designed to keep inmates in, not officer-carried drugs out. The "mule" then returned to the outside contact for payment. Payment was sometimes even made in advance by inmates at the unit. On one occasion the Texas Syndicate and the Mexican Mafia gangs pooled funds ($450 each) and gave the money to an officer to make a buy. Tipped off, officials found the $900 rolled up in the young officer's sock as he was leaving the unit after his shift.

Changes in the security staff and in the way officers related to inmates must be understood within the context of the changes that TDC was undergoing between 1984 and 1986. Specifically, there were three interrelated factors that combined to produce the patterns of security staff problems discussed above. The most obvious was that TDC was not very selective in who it hired for security during this period. Veteran officers, as well as many of those recently hired, were of this opinion. In fact, nearly nine out of ten agreed with a survey item stating that "TDC should be more selective in who it hires for security."

If TDC was not particularly selective, it was primarily because of the courts' pressure to eliminate BTs and to lower the officer-inmate ratio. That pressure was exacerbated by compliance deadlines. These deadlines and the need simply to find and process hundreds of officers further weakened the personnel department's already limited screening process.

But economic conditions between 1982 and 1985, at least in Texas, where most of the recruitment was done, also worked against TDC. A booming economy made it difficult to attract high-quality people to prison work or even to find "warm bodies" to meet compliance demands. Because of the strong state economy, especially in the oil and gas industry, neither prison work nor state salaries were attractive in comparison with employment in the private sector. Under these circumstances, TDC had to recruit hard and not be too concerned about screening applicants.

Another reason for the pattern of problems with new officers was the socialization process. Although TDC attempted to upgrade its preservice training program, the key to success continued to be the initial experience on the job. Historically, new men were taken in tow by a building tender in the cellblock to which they were assigned. That inmate showed them not only how to complete unit routines but also how to avoid inmate games and injury. And, though most veteran officers usually took a "wait and see" attitude toward the new officer, some might give the new man a few pointers.

Changes in the informal structure of the security relations on the units, however, produced a quite different socialization experience. After going through the classroom training of the academy, the new officer often found that he got help from neither other officers nor inmates. As one officer put it, "Today, unless they have got an officer down there that is willing to teach them, they learn on their own." And finding someone to teach the new officer sometimes depended on luck. "If he's lucky, he'll get to work with a boss who's been here a year. Nowadays you only have a few inmates who'll help you and show you how not to get hurt. If you're lucky, you'll get with a boss who'll show you the ropes. It's changed a lot over the last year and a half."

A final reason for recruit problems involved the quality and extent of direct supervision of a large and expanding security force. Several organizational conditions within TDC compounded the supervision problem. One was simply that there were suddenly hundreds more officers at the entry level who needed supervision. At the same time, Procunier, and then McCotter, created many new positions (e.g., grievance lieutenants and disciplinary captains) which drew on the already small pool of experienced men who could qualify as supervisors. Finally, the rules and regulations not only multiplied but, according to some officers, also seemed to change daily. One result was that supervisors spent much of their time working on procedural details instead of with new officers. One man who holds only the rank of correctional officer but has a hall boss assignment complained about this situation: "See, our rank is so busy doing goddamn paper work, doing bullshit, they don't have time to go down there and tell these people what to do. They tell us [hall bosses] to tell them. Those officers don't give a damn what we say." A lieutenant of four years expressed the same problem more generally: "The inmates are getting to them to buy candy and soda, and that's the problem we have right now. These new guards coming out of high school; they're naïve and getting off on the wrong foot. As much paper work that's been put on the supervisors these days, I really don't know how they show or supervise a new guy."

Female Officers in Men's Prisons.[14]   A sex-discrimination lawsuit originally filed in 1974 against TDC was finally settled in 1982. That suit resulted in a court order that TDC hire enough women to constitute 14.3 percent of its security staff. By mid-1985 TDC had received over 3,700 applications from women seeking employment in security but had hired only 23 percent compared to 45 percent of the male applicants. The number of women hired was well under that necessary to comply with the court's specified percentage.

Beyond general administrative resistance to hiring women, another reason for limitations on their hiring was an order from the same court that women officers in men's prisons be placed in "noncontact" positions. They could have no direct interaction with inmates in their living areas. This stricture often led to shift assignment problems. For example, one warden reported having to assign two women to a post actually requiring only one officer because "there was no place else to put them."[15] And, as violence against inmates and officers increased in 1984, TDC cut back on the number of women being hired, arguing that the need for men in "contact" positions overrode the push to increase the number of female officers.

While some male officers may reject women coworkers because they threaten male status and safety,[16] the most frequently vocalized concern among male officers in TDC involves job assignments. Because of the noncontact requirement, women officers can generally avoid the confrontations and abuse that men endure. Thus, many men see women as getting the choicest assignments, those away from the inmates. Male officers have grumbled about this kind of reverse discrimination and have filed complaints with the Equal Employment Opportunity Commission, alleging that women have unfairly been given easier jobs.[17] For whatever reason, most male officers in TDC do not think female officers meet the performance standards of male officers. Only three in ten agree with this statement: "In my opinion, female officers working security in men's prisons perform as well as male officers." Fifty-six percent disagreed and 14 percent was undecided.

The introduction of women into the guard force has not been easy for them or acceptable to their male counterparts. They represent a departure from the traditional demographics and the masculine orientation of the guard force. And recent changes will probably exacerbate the situation. In February 1988, TDC was forced through the original sex-discrimination suit to "desex" the units, to assign female guards, for the first time, inside male prisoners' living areas.

The Formalization of Control in TDC

When Raymond Procunier became director in mid-1984, his mandate from the board of corrections was to bring the system into compliance with Justice's orders as soon as possible. To achieve this, he had to bring the security staff under control. Only by getting unit officers to carry out new, constitutional practices could TDC reach compliance. The many firings, personnel changes, and internal affairs investigations of 1984 and 1985 reflected this focus on officer behavior. Such administrative actions communicated to line officers that top officials cared about nothing but compliance. Indeed, three out of four guards agreed with the statement that "the concern among top TDC officials seems to be compliance with *Ruiz* regardless of the consequences."

This concern and its divergence from traditional administrative support of staff was illustrated by front-office reactions to the handling of a hostage situation at the Eastham Unit in November 1984. In the early-morning hours, an inmate in solitary confinement was able to disengage a defective locking mechanism on his door. Once out, he released several other inmates, and they took hostage the young officer who was inside the solitary area. By 3 A.M. Warden David Myers, a veteran TDC administrator who knew how to handle such situations, was on the scene. After briefly attempting to talk with the inmates, Myers marshaled several top security officers for an assault. They broke open the door, fogged the area with tear gas, and charged in armed with riot batons. Though the hostage escaped injury in the rescue, the inmates involved did not fare nearly as well. After being subdued very aggressively, some were reported to have been dragged, bleeding, down the hall to the hospital to have their considerable injuries treated.

This rescue followed traditional TDC practices. It was handled by officials on the spot; the central office in Huntsville was notified only after the situation was under control and the hostage freed. Moreover, the assault team physically punished the hostile inmates for taking an officer hostage and for injuring members of the team. In the fray, one officer received a broken arm and others suffered minor injuries. In the past, such immediate and aggressive action by unit officials would have been exemplary. Indeed, at the time, most officers, and even many inmates, felt the actions were appropriate. Afterward, officer morale at the unit was very high because they felt that their warden had done exactly the right thing and because inmates had witnessed what could still happen to them at the hands of officers.

The new administration, however, took a very different view of the matter. For failing to notify headquarters, for failing to call in the SORT specialists, and for allowing officers to abuse prisoners (among other shortcomings during the incident), Warden Myers received a reprimand in the form of a "letter of instruction." Having fallen down at the door, Myers was not involved in the subduing of the inmates and thus not directly accused of abuse. Other officers, however, were found by Internal Affairs to have been too zealous in overpowering the hostile inmates. The guilty officers subsequently received demotions, and several were transferred to other units as punishment. These sanctions confirmed in the eyes of officers at Eastham and all over the system that the old discretionary methods of handling inmates would not be tolerated, even in a hostage situation. Instead, officers would have to follow policy if they wanted to keep their jobs. More generally, the administrative sanctions under-

scored the extent to which unit officers must accede to specialization in security, formalization of procedures, and redistribution
of power.

Specialization and Control Technology

The greater task specialization that accompanied the bureaucratization of TDC starting in 1984 directly impacted the correctional officer role. Under the traditional control system, correctional officers
made a wide range of decisions about inmate jobs, housing, complaints, and punishments. Most of those decisions were informal
and were based on the officers' convict sense. The new operational
procedures, however, called for specialists. For example, disciplinary
captains were designated to preside over the institutional court for
inmate rule violators; these captains had no other duties. Similarly,
grievance lieutenants received, reviewed, and acted on inmate complaints, while housing lieutenants kept track of bed space and cell
changes. Committees ultimately made disciplinary and housing decisions according to written guidelines. In the past, many of these
decisions would have been made by a single officer.

Specialization eliminated the generalist and redistributed power
at the same time. Officers from the wardens down to the line officers
found that they were bound by procedures and often reduced to
doing little more than handling the paper work and channeling an
inmate's problem to the proper individual or committee. As a result,
officials no longer held the power over prisoners or staff that they
once held. This shift in administrative power was widely perceived
in TDC; over 70 percent of the officers in TDC believed that wardens and ranking security staff at the units had much less power
than they did in the early 1980s.

Specialization also affected officers further down the security hierarchy with the introduction of the Special Operations and Response
Teams in September 1984. Established at the larger units, these
teams dealt with problem inmates who assaulted officers, refused
to leave a cell, or were otherwise creating a problem; SORTs also
handled shakedowns and prisoner transfers. Traditionally, these duties had been handled by hall bosses or ranking officers. The SORT
concept was intended to remove the regular staff from such situations as much as possible. SORTs, composed of specially selected,
trained, and dressed (blue uniforms instead of gray) young officers,
were supposed to be called in the event of trouble. Indeed, one of the
allegations made against Warden Myers in the Eastham hostage
situation was that he failed to call in these specialists.

Despite their elite status, SORTs were not unwelcome on the units. Nearly two-thirds of the guard force was of the opinion that the teams were important and necessary. Such support for this special group derived from at least two considerations. First, regular officers were not eager to engage in subduing inmates forcefully; they were increasingly aware that, if they erred, they might be disciplined, sued by the inmates, or both. Moreover, prisoners were more apt to be armed. Thus, line officers were happy to have SORT handle problem cases. A second reason for general support for SORT was that these young men were "gung ho," always prepared to physically control inmates. Their methods, while generally constitutional and often videotaped, were sometimes quite aggressive. If, for example, an inmate refused to move from his cell, a group of four SORT members would enter the cell, grab the man's four limbs, and slam him to the floor, a practice the officers called "flatweeding." Many inmates, especially in administrative segregation, where SORT action most frequently occurred, did not see the teams as much of an improvement over the old days. One noted, "There isn't a time when SORT comes down here that someone doesn't get the hell beat out of him."[18]

An important correlate to the specialization was the increased reliance on technology to control inmates. For example, in late 1983 TDC purchased "stun guns" to replace nightsticks. These devices shot tiny electrically charged barbs into the subject, and the effect was physical incapacitation. Since frisking inmates in the halls for weapons is rather inefficient, officials spent $237,000 in 1985 on walk-through and hand-held metal detectors. A relative bargain at $1,800 was the Tactical Audio Recovery System, an electronic eavesdropping device capable of monitoring conversations through brick walls. Purchased in 1985, this device reflected the administration's concern with the loss of information, especially on gang activities.

By far, the most significant control technology was administrative segregation, or "lock down." Shortly after taking over in 1984, Procunier called for certain cellblocks, first at the Eastham Unit and then at other units, to be designated as administrative segregation blocks. Given the extent to which changes had both emboldened inmates and limited traditional control mechanisms, lock down was thought to be the only means of controlling the rising inmate violence. A new classification system defined those inmates thought to be the greatest security risks, and these were put in "ad. seg."

These cellblocks became worlds unto themselves. The inmates placed there were the most troublesome and assaultive, although some were in administrative segregation because they were under protection. Locked up for indefinite periods in single-man cells, the inmates there not only knew each other but, in many cases, also were sworn enemies. Consequently, through 1984 and 1985, most of the violence that occurred in TDC took place in administrative segregation, a somewhat ironic outcome since lock down was supposed to control violence. Despite strict security, inmates regularly made or obtained weapons to attack people walking in front of their cells. If they could not secure materials for shanks, they spent hours carefully rolling paper into shafts with sharp points. Although not deadly, these "spears" could cause injury. In reaction, prison officials welded wire mesh across the front of these cells. This move kept inmates from reaching through the bars, but spears, paper or metal, could still be effectively thrust through the approximately one-inch-square holes in the mesh. To counter this, officials installed on each tier a rolling, metal shield as wide and as high as the front of a cell. Suspended on a track over the cell doors, the shield was pushed along the row of cells by officers to protect themselves and the inmates they were escorting. Though they were very noisy (the rolling of just one of these shields sounds very much like a subway train passing a station at high speed), they did limit assaults on officers and inmates.

More generally, administrative segregation appears to have been successful in limiting violence in TDC. Instituted in mid-1984, lock down was not extensively used until late 1985. A few months after McCotter took over (and after nearly a year and a half of seemingly unchecked violence in TDC), he ordered several thousand inmates locked in administrative segregation. These were primarily gang members since gang activities were believed to be behind most of the violence. Actually, this lock down action was a kind of dragnet. That is, anyone even thought to have been affiliated in any way with a gang was locked down. This dragnet included persons who were thought to have been with a "biker" gang in the free world or who happened to sport a tattoo suggesting gang connections. Suspicion was a sufficient basis for transferring a prisoner from the general population to lock down. Although some of these inmates were later returned to the population, most were not and remain in lock down.

As a result of this strategy, inmate deaths dropped from twenty-seven in 1985 to five in 1986. It is difficult to determine how much of the decline in homicides and violence can be attributed to the use of administrative segregation. Seven out of ten officers in our survey, however, believed that the extensive use of administrative segregation was the primary reason for the decline in deaths and injuries.

While inmates had to have a bad reputation to get sent to administrative segregation, officers were simply assigned there, in some cases straight out of the training academy. Especially in the first year or two after TDC began to use lock down, ad. seg. was a grim place for officers to work. Being assaulted, grabbed, cursed daily, and splattered with coffee or even urine came with the territory. It was noisy and often wet as inmates regularly flooded their cells in protest over something. In addition to working in these conditions, officers had to take special care in dealing with inmates who were in their cells twenty-two hours per day and who had to have their meals, school books, and medications brought to them. Since failure to meet properly all these needs (hot food had to be 148 degrees by court order, for example) could produce disturbances and more litigation, unit administrators usually tried to keep this area fully staffed, even when they were shorthanded elsewhere. Some officers could not handle the pressure in administrative segregation. Many others, however, found that they liked the challenge and preferred working in administrative segregation, despite the hardships. At several units, the supervisors in charge of lock down obtained caps with the unit name and "administrative segregation" printed on them. These caps symbolized a pocket of solidarity at a time when morale was quite low within the security force generally.

Centralization and Formalization of Security Operations

The new directors effectively shifted power from the units to the central office. Their message was that the units would no longer be outposts; they would become part of a standardized organization, abiding by the same rules.

After replacing most top-ranking unit managers, the Procunier administration began to send to all units new and revised policies on a very wide spectrum of operations. Accordingly, the small rule book of old soon swelled to many volumes. This proliferation of rules was specifically intended to limit discretion by specifying in detail how objectives were to be achieved. Certainly, these rules limited what an officer could do to sanction an inmate. But they also limited the extent to which officers could help inmates. A sergeant expressed this second consequence of the new rules this way: "If [inmates have a] legitimate problem, I'll try to serve them. See, this whole thing is frustrating for the inmates. It's so hard to get anything done now. You have to go through so much b.s. to get one simple thing accomplished. It's so intricate, it's so guidelined where every situation requires this or that action."

The plethora of rules also greatly increased the time officers had to spend filling out forms. Rules meant accountability and accountability meant the documentation of actions, or paper work. Officers overwhelmingly agreed (94%) that the paper work demands on the units had increased tremendously. An assistant warden with fifteen years of TDC experience stated: "It's way too much. All I do is sit here, and I work paper work all day long, 10 hours of it. What they've done is stop the BT system, which stopped the flow of traffic [information]. They added more paper work and stopped you from going to the back [into the cellblocks] to talk to these people. These things have just about shut this son of a bitch down." The warden's opinion about this consequence of paper work is widely shared. Over half of the officers reported that rank spent less time in the halls talking to inmates than they did in the early 1980s.

When compared to the old days, today's paper work demands seem particularly onerous. The most troublesome comparison for officers involved written explanations of their use of force. "It used to be you wrote your offense report or you wrote your little ol' statement. Now you got this goddamn two-page thing you got to fill out. It takes you an hour to write the thing where it used to take twenty minutes. You have to have everybody's name on the thing now, their rank, how many witnesses and what not, and the time. It's unreal. I have been in two where the major use of force was used."

For supervisors, paper work has limited the time they could spend supervising the men. Given the number of new officers, paper work demands indirectly affected order. A sergeant stated: "If you have a use of major force report, that takes four to five hours to complete. If you don't have to do that stuff, [paper work takes] around two hours a day. The paper work keeps me away from the employees. If I didn't have to be tied up with that, I could be down the hall with the bosses showing them what to do. They would feel better if a supervisor was there helping them. The new guys are lost and it's hard for me to get down there and help them. That's our biggest problem. The inmates know it, too."

At the same time, some officers recognize that documentation can benefit officers. A sergeant, a thirteen-year veteran of TDC, noted: "I think [the paper work] is good. It can protect; it can protect guards as much as it can protect inmates." A correctional officer put the same point more prosaically: "We have all this paper work to do. It's a pain in the ass, but it really covers our ass. We do all this paper work to avoid lawsuits and cover our ass."

Formalization of procedures also directly affected the type and the effectiveness of discipline. As officers learned that traditional, informal discipline was risky under the new regime, they turned increasingly to formal sanctions, namely, writing up inmates for rule violations. In fact, most officers (73%) agreed that they now write many more disciplinary reports on inmates than they did before the court-ordered changes.

The most immediate consequence of this increase in formal sanctioning was a flood of cases to be handled by the unit disciplinary courts. In prereform days, the unit court operated with a minimum of ceremony, and little time was spent finding the inmate guilty. Those proceedings barely allowed the inmate to relate his side of the story. Reforms introduced due process into TDC's unit disciplinary hearings. Under the new court system, the tape-recorded sessions permitted inmates to present documentary evidence, make statements, call witnesses, confront the accusing officer, and have a counsel substitute. Beginning in early 1987, TDC began experimenting with inmate advocates from the free world. Restrained by these more elaborate proceedings disciplinary panels on the units simply could not accommodate the growing tide of cases that officers were writing.

The response of some unit court officials to this pressure was to try to exclude or alter the cases coming in. As one officer noted, "It's getting to the point where if you misspell a word, they'll kick the case out." Others reported that the court functionaries were inclined to reduce cases from major to minor in order to process them more quickly. "A lot of times I know for a fact that something will come in [to the court] and they'll say, 'Oh, shit, man, we're backed up. Why don't we just make this a minor case?' And they'll hold court. [A guy may have] 40 minor cases and he'll walk it; [they'll] give him a verbal reprimand. So great! So the guy still had eight wrenches and a screwdriver in his cell and he gets verbal reprimand. . . . Some actions should be taken toward that, but they're so backlogged."

As this statement suggests, many officers came to believe that the formal court processing of errant inmates had little impact on maintaining control. "It's not solving any problems. It's not keeping them under control. Plus, it's too time consuming. As far as disciplining the inmates, the effect is none or nil. We got to have some form of punishment, and it's [the court] the best we can do. They're not afraid if you take their time or class. They get it back. . . . Solitary, cell restriction is a waste of time. They [officers on the blocks] do not even enforce cell restriction half the time."

The seeming ineffectiveness of the institutional court affected officer morale to the point that some officers became less concerned with enforcing the rules through disciplinary reports. "They say, 'Well, fuck it, man. I write this dude up and they ain't going to do shit. Verbal reprimand or something like that.' A lot of officers have tried to do their job and keep writing dudes up about different things and nothing ever happens. They write a dude up because he cursed them out or called them a motherfucker or whatever . . . And they write him up, send the papers in, and the dude is still on the tank. When they [the officers] go back to work they steady got to deal with the same problem."

Impact of Changes on Individual Officers

Changes in the workplace did not affect all TDC officers in the same manner. How long an officer had been in the system was a critical variable in the perception of change. Veteran officers, who had experienced an earlier social order, had a basis for comparison that newer officers did not share. Those who had worked with the BTs often longed wistfully for the old days. But, regardless of tenure, all security staff wore the same uniform and worked in the same frustrating and frequently violent environment. That environment undermined morale and, for many officers, generated considerable stress on the job.

Declining Morale

Officer morale in TDC deteriorated dramatically beginning in the late 1970s.[19] As the reforms took effect, officers became increasingly disaffected. One officer summarized the feelings of many: "It's [morale] low; it's worse now than ever. Three or fours years ago [1980] I liked it. I came in and felt fresh and ready to work. I felt like somebody."

An obvious source of dissatisfaction with the job was the alteration of administrative procedures and structures at TDC headquarters and at the units. Officers, especially veterans, disliked the formalization, the new rules, and the paper work aimed at holding them more accountable. Yet, organizational and procedural changes were probably not the primary source of lowered morale. Even if they did not like the new, more formal policies, officers reported being relatively comfortable with them by 1986. For example, most (61%) disagreed with the statement "The rules that I am supposed to follow here never seem to be very clear." Similarly, 66 percent agreed that the rules were clear enough so that they knew what they could and could not do on the job.

A more likely basis for lowered morale seems to be the widespread sense of having been abandoned, even betrayed, by the central administration.[20] Traditionally, the director and headquarters had supported and encouraged effectiveness in work output and control on the units. Through the 1970s, for example, W. J. Estelle, Jr., sometimes called the "employees' director," defended the staff's actions and regularly sought better pay and benefits for them. In 1984, however, after state officials and the board of corrections decided to push for compliance and had hired Procunier to affect that end, correctional officers sensed a radical change in this traditional posture of support. Indeed, in the eyes of most correctional officers, the central administration not only withdrew support but also aggressively worked against its own security staff.

One symbol of administrative and state support for TDC officers in the past was the emoluments program that provided food, low rent, free utilities, and other perquisites of rank. By 1985, as we have seen, most of these perquisites had been withdrawn by the legislature and new TDC administrations. Officers also lost a number of benefits that all enjoyed, regardless of rank, including free laundry and dry cleaning on the unit and access to a separate menu of specially prepared food served in the officers' dining room. The loss of these benefits was bitterly resented. A correctional officer summarized this bitterness: "I don't really know what they're [the central administration] doing. I read the papers, and that's how I get the news. What pisses me off is that we have to eat what the inmates eat. We have the same menu; plus, they took our laundry away. It's the little stuff."

More detrimental to morale than the loss of perquisites, however, has been the officers' perception that the central administration did not trust them. This perception arose most directly from the aggressive investigations of staff misconduct carried out by the TDC Office of Internal Affairs beginning in 1984. Especially troubling from the office's point of view was the use of the polygraph examination on staff. A captain spoke for many: "It's been devastating. It's been absolutely devastating. It's had probably the single greatest effect on morale of anything they could have possibly done. We think it's illegal. We feel like we're being harassed and subjected to treatment that they wouldn't subject an inmate to." Investigations by Internal Affairs (IA) made officers feel harassed and uncertain about their jobs. When officers believed that they had acted correctly and then found they risked being fired following an investigation of that action, the resentment was particularly keen. Reflecting on the investigation of the handling of the hostage situation in the Eastham solitary wing, an officer concluded: "I think that's one of the things we can do without. Why fire somebody just to make an example out of them. Like in the solitary deal. Well, Internal Affairs investigated that, they just looked for someone to nail. We can do without it. Those officers did their jobs to help that officer."

Some officers even saw a pattern in whom Internal Affairs was trying to "nail." The presumed strategy seemed to be to go after men who had been around a long time since veterans would most likely act contrary to the new policies. A thirteen-year veteran put that belief this way: "I feel it could be a good thing by the Internal Affairs coming out and investigating, but they looking at the TDC officers in the wrong. Seem like they trying to cull out all the ones that's been here for a long time. Whenever you go there and they ask you how long you been with the system, seem like you automatically wrong. You going automatically—might as well say, 'get the polygraph test.'" Besides affecting morale, this general fear of administrative scrutiny through Internal Affairs directly affected how officers went about their jobs. A sergeant stated: "Everybody's on pins. Nobody wants to get involved; they're scared for their jobs. They're afraid of the lie detector because if they fail, they're fired. This makes officers turn their heads when they see something happen."

The Internal Affairs division of central administration did not find every officer it investigated to be "dirty." Indeed, the largest portion of the complaints against officers was resolved in the officers' favor. Yet, IA was aggressive, reflecting the administration's concern for stamping out quickly all remnants of traditional control measures. Investigations emanated from the central office in Huntsville and directly affected job security. Even if an officer was eventually found to be "clean," the fact that he had been investigated was widely believed to hurt his chances for promotion. As a result, most officers held negative feelings toward the Internal Affairs office. Nearly two-thirds believed that the office had done more harm than good. More to the point, the presence and aggressiveness of Internal Affairs testified to unit officers that the central administration did not trust them. That realization was a tremendous blow to morale.

Job-Related Stress

Another consequence of changes in the workplace for individual officers, more subtle and more pernicious than declining morale, is job stress.[21] An important source of stress is ambiguity or uncertainty about how to perform the officer's role in a rapidly changing prison environment. Research suggests that this role ambiguity often results from a "double bind" inherent in prisons undergoing litigated reform.[22] Pressured by intractable inmates and violence, officers in such an environment want to "crack down" to regain control. Their superiors, however, fearing more litigation, call for officers to limit control efforts and hold them strictly accountable for doing so. The bind is that officers believe that they must bend some rules to gain control of prisoners. Yet, if they do, administrators will not only fail to support them but also actively punish them in the bargain.

This double bind existed in TDC and certainly produced stressful situations for officers. We have already discussed the extent to which officers felt that administrators did not trust them and would demote or fire them for inappropriate control tactics. Many officers daily juxtaposed this fear for their jobs with a belief that they should be doing "something" to better control the environment. To the extent that this fear and this belief were strongly felt, officers experienced stress. These stressful conditions were not helped by the chronic shortage of both supervisors and supervisory attention, which might have reduced role ambiguity and stress through more guidance.

Stress also came from an increasingly unsettled environment marked by disordered sights and sounds. As reforms dismantled the old control regime, Texas inmates regularly tested their new freedoms. For example, instead of walking single file along the wall of the prison buildings as they had done in the past, inmates began to move down the hall five or six abreast. This limited vision for security staff and communicated a disturbing defiance. At the same time, noise levels rose dramatically as inmates shouted to each other and played radios at full volume on competing stations. These conditions constituted daily pressures from which officers (as well as inmates) could not escape. The following comment by a young officer illustrates the impact of such conditions:

It sounds like Ringling Brothers–Barnum and Bailey Circus. It gets to me every day. I go to work by 2 P.M., and by 3 P.M. I got a headache. I got to take Tylenol everyday. It's the noise; I get tense, too. When I just got here a boss didn't get hit on or stabbed or anything. Now it's an everyday thing for a boss to have a problem with an inmate. During chow it's crazy, I mean it's wide open. . . . I've always been short tempered, but now it's shorter yet. My relationship with my parents has changed. I can't tolerate this bullshit anymore, at all. If they get on me I just get up and leave and stay with others. I'm not considerate anymore. It's hard not to let these inmates get to you.

Finally, as the possibility and actuality of inmate aggressiveness increased, so too did stress levels. Because all types of inmate assaults on staff were widely reported by the press and the prison grapevine, officers throughout the system were painfully aware of the details. Consequently, they did not have to experience assaults for violence to affect their view of the job as dangerous. An officer's perception that correctional guard work is dangerous was widespread in TDC, regardless of whether he had been personally assaulted. Moreover, evidence indicates that that perception was more widespread in the mid-1980s than in earlier years. A survey of TDC guards completed in 1979 asked respondents to indicate their agreement with the statement that being an officer was quite dangerous; 75 percent agreed.[23] Though a relatively large percentage, it is still markedly less than the 89 percent who viewed the job as dangerous in 1986.[24]

The significance of stress among correctional officers in TDC, as in other prison settings, is often denied by administrators and by officers themselves. Texas prison directors Beto and Estelle have both publicly discounted stress as a problem for officers. Such statements and, especially, the traditionally "macho" demeanor that prison work typically calls forth discourage officers from recognizing or admitting the effects of stress, even to themselves. The lieutenant quoted below, therefore, was exceptional in his articulation of the stress problem and in his call for administrative help.

As far as officers, TDC needs some counselors because of the stress. These guys are drinking and using drugs. I'm lucky my wife can put up with me and this fucking job. It's always, "get the convicts this and that," but these officers are going home and hitting the bottle and coming to work hung over. Some are high on pot, but nobody seems to care about us. We're getting paid to do this job and we're neglected. There's no more emoluments, they take that, they took our laundry, our food. They take and take, but we get nothing in return. . . . I feel for those guys working the tanks. The convicts got W. Wayne [Judge Justice] and Ruiz, but the bosses ain't got shit. We need a stress center. I remember Estelle said we don't suffer from stress; well, what the hell is this? It's stress, he was never in a block here having these fools talk constant trash to you. We need help. Police departments have counselors and we need the same. If you give these bosses something and tell 'em it's theirs, you'd see a real rise in morale. I guarantee it.

Coping with Low Morale and Stress

Officers experienced varying degrees of stress on the job, and they coped differently as well. The most common on-the-job adaptations included apathy, tardiness, absenteeism, and resignation.[25] Collective adaptation was limited to unionization.

The most frequent individual coping strategy appeared to be apathy, or "quitting on the job." All three of the changes discussed earlier in this chapter—the flood of new officers, rapid organizational change, and inmate aggressiveness—prompted a tendency among many experienced officers to "just put in their eight." And, as we noted earlier, among some new officers, this minimalist orientation toward work was apparently present from the first; it was only exacerbated by organizational uncertainty, lack of supervision, and inmate defiance. One officer summed up this adaptation this way: "There is apathy, people don't care anymore. Back then people cared about their jobs, you had the authority to do your job. Now when you get here you gotta check to see if your supervisor is still here. Plus, the rules change all the time. Many of them [officers] just say, 'well, fuck it, I'll just sit on my ass and collect a check.' You see fear in them, too. I was in the hall the other day and I saw this inmate in M-line tell a boss that if he didn't let him out he was going to kick his goddamn ass. Sure enough, the boss let him out. If that's not fear, I don't know what is."

Concerned about their own safety and about minimizing problems on the job, some officers cope simply by giving in to inmate demands. They may also note which inmates not to cross. A veteran sergeant candidly explains his own compromises in this respect: "I've been struck several times, been bitten by inmates. Some of them, I'm afraid of. I'm afraid to say something to them because I know what I'm going to get if I do say something to them. A lot of times, I avoid—if I see an inmate do something wrong, I just completely ignore it. I just walk off it. And I know it's not right, but a lot of people are doing it, a lot of supervisors are doing it because it— like I say, I'm afraid of certain people here, I'm not going to say nothing to them 'cause I know them."

One specific form of withdrawal on the job was to seek a post with limited contact with inmates. Such posts include outside pickets, isolated guard towers on the prison perimeter, and inside pickets,

barred enclosures in each cellblock from which the doors are operated. In recent years officers in increasing numbers have wanted to
be assigned to one of these pickets. Significantly, such assignments
were not always desirable; in the past being assigned there by a supervisor was often a punishment. Most officers sought interaction
with inmates because this was how reputations and rank were made.
By the mid-1980s, however, the reverse was true; many wanted to
get away from inmates. "See, it used to be a punishment to work
tanks or pickets. Now it's nothing; all you got to do is turn doors.
You don't have to fuck with all them SOBs in the hall. You don't have
to worry about getting stabbed or hit. Hell, that's the place to be."

Another way to gain respite from job demands was to simply stay
away from the job as much as possible. Indeed, officers and supervisors report marked increases through the mid-1980s in the number
of officers who were tardy in reporting for their shift and who were
calling in sick.

Finally, the combination of pressures on the job prompted some
officers to leave prison work. For the first half of the 1980s, according to TDC personnel officials, security officer turnover was approximately 30 percent annually. Most of this turnover occurred in
the lower ranks, where it has always been highest. But, unlike the
prelitigation period in TDC, there was also growing attrition in the
mid- to upper-level security staff (wardens through lieutenants).
Certainly, some of this latter group were fired, but most who left
simply decided that they no longer wanted to brook the pressures
and changes of the new TDC.

A major result was new people in new positions everywhere.
Prison officials were bringing in many new officers to improve the
officer-inmate ratio. But they also expanded the number of positions
in the interest specialization. More line officers and more posts, plus
vacancies left by departing midlevel supervisors, translated into a
need for hundreds of promotions in a very short time. The result was
an unprecedented number of inexperienced officers at all levels of
the security hierarchy. As an officer with only one year of experience
put it: "It's worse today. We've had such a big turnover in personnel,
even in rank. We got a new warden, a new assistant warden, new
major, new captain. The only people that were here when I got here
are the three shift lieutenants, and that's it."

But even among those still on the job, a significant number were
thinking about quitting. In our survey, 33 percent of the respondents
indicated that they were seriously thinking about leaving TDC,
while another 19 percent was undecided. Among officers at the lock-

down units, these percentages were higher, 41 and 22 percent, respectively. Clearly, this sergeant spoke for many officers: "I have thought about quitting, just outright quitting. Right now I don't even know from one week, one day to the next about whether I really have my job. . . . I need to be here because I need to work but some days I come and I get so frustrated I just feel like giving it up, but for financial reasons I have to be here. I'm not here because I like it. If I could find something that would pay about the same, I would take it, but right now I have to do this. I don't have any choice."

This officer alluded to a condition that has limited turnover in recent years and heightened frustration among many officers, namely, the shrinking Texas economy. In the early 1980s when the economy was robust, frustrated officers could leave and find employment elsewhere relatively easily. By 1985, however, these opportunities had shrunk as the state's oil-driven economy contracted. In 1985 and 1986, according to TDC officials, security staff turnover dropped to about 15 percent per year from 30 percent in the early 1980s. It is possible that the inability to find other employment accounted for this drop in turnover. The point is that having to remain in undesirable employment would certainly make that employment even more frustrating.

Most officers opted to handle the job pressures, low morale, and stress individually. Many "quit on the job," did not show up for work, or simply resigned. Most probably managed by putting up a front: doing the job as well as they could while swallowing the fear and frustration they felt. Some officers, however, sought a collective rather than an individual solution to job problems; they turned to unionization.[26]

Unionization.   The national unionization movement among correctional officers is relatively new.[27] As officers across the country had to deal with more intractable inmates and with administrations they felt failed to support them, they sought to help themselves through collective, union action. These same general factors provided the impetus for union activity among Texas prison officers as well.

The state of Texas has never been friendly toward unions, either in the private sector or in public agencies. This tradition is underscored by state laws prohibiting strike actions by the union chapters that do exist in the state. Texas public employees have always been expected to be loyal to the agencies that pay their salaries. Indeed, when the Texas Public Employees Association (TPEA) was established in 1946, it contained bylaws (reaffirmed by TPEA in 1979) that strictly prohibit "the affiliation or endorsement of any labor union and prohibit the adoption of a policy or principle of strike action."[28] Reflecting this statewide posture, administrators in TDC over the years have actively discouraged unions for officers. For example, in 1979, Director Estelle argued before the legislature that his requests for salary increases must be met if TDC was going to successfully avoid correctional officer unionization.[29] This aversion to unions meant that, essentially, the only organization available to represent prison officers at the state level was TPEA.

Evidence suggests that TPEA drew its membership mostly from management and that state employees in the lower classified jobs were somewhat underrepresented.[30] Though no data were available, TDC membership in TPEA was probably heavily weighted toward higher-ranking officers and administrators. This sense that TPEA was more management oriented and that regular prison guards needed more representation, together with the frustration of officers, prompted the union activity of 1984.

The Texas State Employees Union (TSEU) has been the most active in organizing prison officers. TSEU represents the AFL-CIO's Communication Workers of America, which put up funds for the recruitment drive among Texas state employees, including prison officers. Asked about their actions among guards, TSEU organizers claimed that they were not antimanagement, just proguard. Their argument states that the managers were represented by the attorney general, the inmates by plaintiff's counsel, and the guards by no one.

Yet, despite concerted efforts, TSEU has not been particularly successful in organizing and representing TDC personnel. This failure is not unusual since guard unions even in states more open to unions have not been overly successful at meeting the needs of officers. Research on prison union activity in New York revealed, for example, that, while unions can help raise wages, improve some working conditions, and limit management arbitrariness, they cannot affect the more fundamental problems that prison officers face, such as inmate violence and officer loss of authority and status.[31] A similar inability to affect these more fundamental conditions of guard work in Texas, combined with administrative resistance and state laws prohibiting collective bargaining and strikes, limited union inroads in TDC.

Nonetheless, starting from scratch in early 1984, TSEU claimed to have enlisted approximately 2,000 security and other employees in TDC by late 1986.[32] These officers probably came from among the most disgruntled since the union offered them some leverage or hope for making the job more bearable. As a correctional officer who had joined put it: "We developed a union here because the administration went out of its way to protect the inmates. They screwed us. I'm serious. The pay hasn't increased. Our living conditions aren't worth shit. The state's going to charge us rent for housing. Look at the medical; I'm paying $165.00 a month for Blue Cross and you can't get your money out of them. We don't have no dental care. There's got to be a better way. They don't care about us."

Most officers, however, had more difficulty seeing the benefit of a union. Despite lawsuits filed by the union to help officers secure grievance procedures, overtime pay, and more flexibility in taking compensatory time off, officers did not flock to the union banner. When asked in our survey if they thought unionization would benefit officers, only 32 percent agreed and 40 percent disagreed; significantly, over a quarter (27%) was undecided. Nonsupport of a union apparently devolved from the fact that a union has limited power in Texas. Commenting on his unwillingness to join the union one officer stated: "Well, they're [the union] fighting a losing battle. It won't do no good; you can't strike. What's a union, if you can't strike."

The Demise of the Officer Subculture

Organizational and other changes did more than affect individual security officers. By the mid-1980s, those changes also had undermined the traditional officer subculture, the values and roles that defined guard work in TDC. Those changes eliminated the autonomy that permitted the emergence of the officer subculture and the informal reward system that sustained it for years.

Traditional Subcultural Supports

The autonomy enjoyed by TDC directors and unit staff derived in part from the geographic isolation of many units and from the distance of TDC headquarters from the state capital. George Beto was fond of pointing out, for example, that Texas is the only state in which the prison system's central office is not in the capital city. The real basis for this autonomy, however, was the ability of successive directors to work closely with a strong board of corrections chairman and then with a few key legislators. Deals were made on land, legislation, or programs by a small group of players, and only the details that the department wanted released were ever made public. Some evidence suggests that at times not even the full board had complete knowledge of what the department was doing. Most legislators, most citizens, and the media were completely in the dark.

Such secrecy and the autonomy it fostered permitted prison officials to focus on those TDC hallmarks, control and work productivity.

Unit managers and staff could employ almost any means to achieve these primary prison goals, as long as they stayed within the subcultural guidelines. Wardens were supposed to handle things on the spot, to do whatever it took to maintain the status quo. Certainly, in the case of a "work buck" the director would be notified, but, as in the "Father's Day" work strike, described in Chapter 3, the director might simply say, as Estelle did in that case, "Put 'em to work." How they were to be put to work was up to the warden. Similarly, Warden David Myers at Eastham was following these traditional guidelines when he "handled" the hostage situation at his unit and only notified central headquarters after the fact. In short, officers at all levels were expected to be able to control and work the prisoners under their supervision; those who could not do this one way or another did not get rewarded or promoted.

Within these subcultural guidelines evolved a set of sanctions designed to produce results. Over the years these sanctions (both positive and negative) were imbued with legitimacy within the department, a legitimacy grounded not only in tradition but also in the staff belief that they were necessary and even appropriate. In addition to discretionary sanctions, there emerged approved modes of relating to inmates and other officers. Together, definitions of how to deal with inmates and fellow officers constituted the traditional subcultural values.

Support for these values among officers certainly did not derive primarily from high salaries and emoluments. Perquisites did save ranking officers money on groceries, but they were probably as much a symbolic as a material benefit in that they were a recognition of service and a sharing of collectively produced bounty. And pay, even for wardens, was relatively low. For example, a salary analysis in a 1984 organizational study of TDC by a consulting firm showed that wardens made considerably less than their federal counterparts. Even more striking was the finding that several TDC wardens on large units were responsible for more inmates, more extensive facilities, and larger budgets than the directors of a number of entire state prison systems, yet they had salaries only in the middle to high $30,000 range.[33]

What kept these wardens and many other midlevel managers on the job in the past was a set of intrinsic rewards. Specifically, for supporting established values and behaving in approved ways, officers received status and inclusion or acceptance into an informal, masculine fraternity. Status, as a reward, derived from two sources.

Most generally, officers took pride in TDC's widely touted state and national reputation as a leading system. A sense of status also came from a positive occupational self-image in the belief that they delivered an important public service. More specific status rewards came from officers' unquestioned dominance of all inmates and the deference inmates paid to them.

Another type of intrinsic reward undergirding subcultural values was inclusion in the guard fraternity. Acceptance was informal, rather selective, and typically the basis for formal promotion. But since acceptance was slow (it took time to develop a reputation), so too was formal promotion. This arrangement made rank more special and respected and, as important, ensured that occupants of mid-management positions reflected the subcultural values.

In short, autonomy and secrecy fostered the emergence of traditional practices and values within the officer force. By being a part of TDC and, much more important, by behaviorally supporting those values and practices, officers were rewarded by status and by being tapped for acceptance and promotion.

The Loss of Secrecy, Selectivity, and Status

Reforms clearly undermined the officer subculture and the reward system that sustained it. First, TDC lost its traditional autonomy and, in turn, the opportunity to operate in a relatively closed, secret manner. As we have seen, legislative investigations of TDC's finances eliminated the discretionary use of state funds by the agency. Formalization, which meant that everything had to be written down, sharply reduced secrecy because actions were recorded. The scrutiny of correctional officer actions by the special master and his monitors, the Internal Affairs division of TDC, and the media had the same effect. Ironically, in the past, having information about questionable actions by officers was a mark of acceptance and trust by others. By the mid-1980s, however, having such information could get an officer in trouble, especially if he kept it to himself.

The reforms further undermined the officer subculture by destroying the traditional and highly personalized manner in which officers were selected for advancement. Rapid growth of the security force and specialization opened up the promotions process and greatly reduced the time it took to make rank. For many officers, of course, this opening up meant greater mobility within TDC. Others, however, were concerned about the fact that promotions were less selective and often premature. Commenting on quick promotions, a lieutenant stated: "I think that's the most dangerous thing there is.

Number one, some of these guys don't have the experience to handle these ranking jobs. They're getting promoted too fast, too soon. They're putting too many inexperienced people in top positions and the inmates aren't stupid; they can see that, too." Because of reduced selectivity, rank no longer projects competence or toughness or generates the kind of respect it once did among inmates and officers. A sergeant notes: "[Officers] don't respect it [rank] like they used to. Used to a lieutenant was running something, once upon a time. Now there's so many of them people think they give out rank, or you're a 'kiss ass.'"

Reduced selectivity in promotions and certainly at the entry level also eroded the sense of loyalty, mutual trust, and teamwork that was evident in years past in the TDC guard force. The feeling of solidarity, of belonging to a group of men who would support and back up each other, was an important reward in the past. One nine-year veteran stated in this regard: "We don't have the commitment anymore. Two years ago [1982], TDC was seen as a family, a big family where we all took care of each other and backed each other up." Officers no longer manifest such loyalty. Indeed, 85 percent agreed that there was much less loyalty to supervisors and to TDC than there was prior to 1981.

Some of this loss of teamwork and mutual support is due simply to inmate aggression and officer fear of it: "I haven't heard the word teamwork around here for so long—used to, it was a team. Officer A would cover Officer B's back. Now you don't see that. There are fights in the hall and some officers lock themselves in the tank. Shit, that never happened before. See, these [new] officers talk shit to these convicts and when something breaks, where are they? They're gone."

That officers became less willing to back up their fellows was also due to the fear that such action could cost a man his job. Two officers made the same point.

It's every man for himself. When I first got here, we were like a family; even if a boss was wrong, we got down for him. Well, Procunier fired some, made us take lie detector tests. Everybody is afraid for their job.

. . . there's a few left [who will back you up]. It wasn't like that three years ago. I guess it's job security today. If you fuck up, then you're on your own.

Finally, officers no longer received the kind of status and respect from inmates and other officers that had been central to the reward system. The evaporation of inmate deference and the accompanying aggressiveness, especially the verbal abuse from them, were keenly felt by staff members. A sergeant lamented: "Like I said, four or five years ago, I could tell an inmate to do something. I felt like I was running it. As far as telling them to do something it made me feel good. I got respected, and it made me feel good. Now, even though I'm a sergeant, I don't get respected." As the pressure for accountability eliminated discretion, officers could no longer develop the kind of personal reputations that in the past generated obedience from inmates and acceptance by officers. Forceful discipline was out as both a punishment and a reputation enhancer. At the same time, officers had no leeway under the more formal and universalistic policies to help inmates as they had been able to do in the past.

If officers perceived a loss of status behind the walls, they also sensed a loss of status outside. A 1979 survey of TDC officers revealed that eight out of ten thought guard work enjoyed a positive image in the community.[34] By 1986, the number of TDC officers who believed this was only about three in ten. Officers in TDC have thus become much less positive about their status beyond the walls.

Conclusion

Although court intervention fundamentally altered the workplace, most TDC security officers who remained on the job have attempted to accommodate the changes. Typically very resistant in the beginning, these officers have weathered the organizational turmoil, administrative succession, and inmate abuse and have found that, by the late 1980s, things were not all that bad. They still have a job, are unhurt, and are actually able to gain inmate compliance most of the time. Many of the "new" (and to veterans often suspect) guards hired during 1984 and 1985 have adapted well and have become "good hands."

Although morale remains relatively low, it is probably not because these officers believe they cannot control prisoners. Certainly, 1984 and 1985 were terrible years for inmate violence, and control was clearly limited. But, by late 1986, most officers reported feeling rather confident of their position vis-à-vis inmates. For example, in our survey, 86 percent of the respondents agreed with the statement "If I want an inmate to do something, I can generally find a way to make him do it." Similarly, only 42 percent agreed with the statement "Short of writing a disciplinary report, there is very little I can do to control the inmates around here." These response patterns indicate that officers feel they have considerable control over inmates.

A more likely reason for low morale is the loss of status. Litigation, through the promulgation of bureaucracy, produced a leveling effect among TDC officers.[35] As decisions about inmates became increasingly the province of committees and specialists, the traditional skills, values, and prerogatives that set the inner core of officers apart from and above others were no longer the basis for status.

The changing status of prisoners vis-à-vis officers also illustrates the leveling effect. As inmates gained rights and began to believe a new day of freedom had dawned, they no longer meekly accepted their status of subordination and abuse. Though officers were still officially dominant, the status gap between the keepers and the kept had been narrowed. This greater equality of rights and power made conflict much more likely.

With lingering uncertainties about support from the central office and little of the old sense of solidarity, correctional work in TDC today is for most just a job, regardless of rank. Formal procedures and the specter of the court have removed the traditional bases for identifying with and feeling good about the work. Gone are the "characters" (guards with special reputations for force or cunning) and the interactions among officers and between officers and prisoners that at one time animated guard work. With those characters and interactions has gone the traditional guard subculture in TDC. It must be remembered, however, that the same subculture that made many officers feel good about the work either produced or permitted the abuse and capricious treatment that many Texas prisoners suffered.

7

Prisoner Crisis and Control

Used to, you could fight, but the bosses would break it up quick.
The worst that could happen back then was getting beat up. It's
not that way anymore. People are getting tired of all the noise and
disrespect. They're tired of seeing their friends hogged and fucked
over. My celly got ripped off, [and he] confronted two Mexicans
about it and stabbed one. But he didn't know they were gang
members. They [TDC] shipped [him] to Ellis and the gang over
there killed him.   —TDC INMATE, 1984[1]

AS STATE and prison officials finally began to comply with
the consent decrees in late 1983, TDC's traditional control
structure underwent a fundamental change. Compliance meant restriction of the guard force and elimination of the building tender
system. As a result, prisoners, who already expected the decrees to
bring about rapid change,[2] began to exploit the erosion of traditional
controls. Though many observers characterized this situation as
a "power vacuum," it was actually an "authority vacuum." With
neither building tenders nor guards proactively maintaining order,
powerful prisoners and prisoner groups began seizing the opportunity to control contraband and other prisoners. Compliance thus
altered the official control system and, in turn, the prisoner social
organization. The result was a restructured inmate society, increased
inmate-inmate violence, and the rise of prisoner gangs.

Dismantling the Building Tender System

Our consideration of the consequences of reform for prisoners begins with the BTs' removal because these elites were so central to
traditional control in TDC. Though our account of the removal of
the BTs and of the consequences of litigated reform draws on observations and interviews from across the system, it relies heavily on
data from the Eastham unit. Eastham, because it was a large prison
housing tough inmates and tough guards, was particularly representative of Texas prison practices and conditions that most distressed
the court, and the changes that prisoners experienced there largely
reflected those experienced by TDC prisoners generally.

Although they initially fought Judge Justice's order to remove BTs, prison officials finally signed a consent decree in May 1982 to eliminate BTs by January 1983 at three target units (Eastham, Ramsey I, and Ellis I). At these units, and certainly at Eastham, security staff generally felt dejected, "sold out" by the administration. To these officers it appeared that the state negotiators had given in too easily. They found it difficult to imagine operating and controlling the unit without the inmate "staff." Yet, the state was committed to removing these inmates from their control roles, and the security staff could only comply, however grudgingly. According to the stipulation, TDC had to remove not less than 10 percent of the current BTs/turnkeys/bookkeepers from their jobs, and Special Master Vincent Nathan could remove no more than 25 percent.[3]

At the Eastham Unit, staff began by removing the bookkeepers. Although the decree permitted the use of inmate clerks by TDC, their duties had to be greatly reduced. In particular, they were restricted from handling sensitive information (e.g., medical, psychiatric, and disciplinary files and inmate travel cards, which contained criminal histories). Moreover, the bookkeepers were forbidden from giving orders to inmates or controlling inmate traffic around the major's office. And, consistent with the new rules, each bookkeeper was assigned to a formal shift, and the job responsibilities were specified and posted near the work areas.

Knowing the special master would certainly push for the reassignment of these inmates, the security staff at Eastham and other units demoted these prisoners voluntarily. While this move demonstrated good faith by the unit officials, it also meant the loss to the unit of critical knowledge, since in many cases inmate bookkeepers had handled and processed vital records for years. The officers who replaced the bookkeepers were quite lost. Instead of developing new procedures, these officers simply adopted the former bookkeepers' methods of recording and filing unit information. Indeed, the former bookkeepers usually taught the guards how to decipher the filing system, handle disciplinary reports and witness statements, and make changes on inmate good-time records. This on-the-job training took several weeks, and the new staff-clerk arrangement was fully implemented in August 1983.

Simultaneously, the Eastham officers began to phase out the turnkeys. In early June 1982, these inmates were no longer permitted to carry keys. During the inmate-guard hearings in the spring of 1982, inmate witnesses testified that turnkeys used the keys on straps and key holders (some were lead filled) as weapons to threaten or strike recalcitrant prisoners. While the consent decree permitted the turnkey to keep his post, his key was to be carried by an officer who had to throw it to him when a door needed to be opened. Being on the job with no key in hand was disconcerting to some turnkeys. One remarked, "Hell, now we're like cowboys without any guns." When the guards finally took over the turnkeys' duties completely, these inmates, like bookkeepers, had to teach their guard replacements how to operate the barricade doors and what to do when fights or other trouble broke out in the hall. Actual removal of the turnkeys occurred on December 31, 1982. Old practices die hard, and at Eastham the staff waited until the last moment to comply.

Elimination of the building tenders followed an unusual chronology that actually began in the early 1970s when the state passed a law prohibiting the use of inmates to control other inmates. To comply with this state law, TDC simply changed the official name for building tenders to "building porters." Technically, the BTs were gone, but officials continued to select and use dominant inmates for control as they always had. Then, in 1981, Judge Justice prohibited the use of inmates performing control functions, regardless of their title.

In response, prison officials redesignated the building porters as support service inmates. Support service inmates were easily identified by the SS added to the number stenciled on the backs of their shirts. These support service inmates, the former BTs, continued to run the blocks, however, and received the same formal and informal rewards that they had enjoyed in the past. Yet, officials were aware of court pressure. At Eastham, for example, the security staff repeatedly told the SSIs to avoid using punitive force as much as possible. Eastham's staff knew they could not "ride any more heat" from the court. Informing, giving orders, and protecting officers were encouraged, but physically disciplining inmates was forbidden.

Despite this temporizing, both the staff and the BTs knew that the inmate-guard system, however labeled, was doomed. The phase out began in August 1982. First, the guards informed the BTs in a meeting that the BT regime was officially over and that they were to turn in their weapons. The BTs brought their weapons to the major's office, but no disciplinary action was taken against them. Indeed, most reminisced with the ranking staff about the "good ol' days," recounting with fondness favorite drug busts, fights, ass whippings, weapons seized, troublesome inmates, stabbings, work strikes, brawls, and stakeouts. From that point, the old BTs were told, they had no official or unofficial authority. They were not to break up inmate fights, give orders to the other inmates, perform head counts, deliver messages for officers, or escort inmates anywhere for any reason. They were also to give up their pets and special clothing.

These changes were highly significant for the former BTs, as well as for the staff, and some BTs were angry. Most of the inmate-elites, however, simply accepted the inevitable. A former BT, whose attitude was typical, stated: "Yeah, I knew they had to change the way things were, and I understand that they don't want to change things. I know that TDC is doing things right now against their will because the feds are making them change. I understand this. I know things can't go on the way they have; things change."

The inmate-elites were reassigned to other, less sensitive jobs, such as those in the laundry, shower, kitchen, or craftshop. A handful of the former inmate-guards were eligible to become orderlies, the new name for inmates working in the living areas. Orderlies swept floors, cleaned dayrooms, and dispensed sheets and socks to the other inmates. To help ensure that they did not go beyond these janitorial duties, their job description was posted, as per the court order, in each living area for all inmates to see. Many inmates read and memorized these job descriptions and systematically informed the special master's office of violations. By the end of October 1982, the inmate orderly system developed by the court was basically in operation at Eastham.

Tension, Fear, and Deteriorating Prisoner Relations

Once the elite prisoners lost their authority and the guards quit using unofficial force, the highly ordered inmate society began to crumble. With little or no enforcement, the traditional norms governing inmate behavior, especially in the living areas, held less sway. For some prisoners this new situation meant fear and tension; for others it meant opportunity.

Inmate Fear and Uncertainty on the Blocks

In the postdecree era, the authority vacuum left by the BTs was filled by aggressive, prison-wise inmates who either individually or collectively exerted their influence in the living areas, especially in the cellblocks. A veteran convict described this transition: "People who have leadership qualities will emerge in any situation. All that has happened is that the game plan has changed. There used to be building tenders inside and lead rows in the hoe squad. You still got leaders, but today they're manifesting their leadership potential in different ways. It's more detrimental, but it's still the same thing."

Aggressive inmates began to intimidate and exploit, or "hog," other inmates. Physically and mentally weak inmates, who in pre-*Ruiz* days often benefited from BT protection, were more easily victimized, fair game for any inmate wishing to establish dominance. Survival for many weak inmates meant paying protection in money, prison commissary goods, or sexual favors. One inmate stated: "There was no way not to pay protection there [Coffield] without getting beaten or stabbed. They would just beat you over and over. You might get sent to the hospital but when you came out, it would happen all over again. . . . My cellmate had no money coming in at all. He had to turn homosexual to make it."[4] One board of corrections member described how rational the protection and extortion rings had become: "We had one prison where we found actual written protection policies. [The charge was] $49 a month for complete security, $29 a month for cuts and bruises, that sort of thing."[5] The "law of the jungle" prevailed, and in many respects convict life resembled that of the pre-Ellis years.

These depredations were not unknown to the guards, but their knowledge of details was often limited. With the loss of the BTs, the staff's information network quickly dissolved and, with it, much official capacity to protect prisoners. As one warden explained, "We know who the tush hogs [tough guys] are, but we can't do nuthin' unless they [inmates] tell us who's rippin' them off." Many victims were afraid to tell the staff about their problems because it betrayed weakness. Those who did talk risked further victimization. One powerful inmate described how "his" block handled known informers:

> People just don't talk to the man much anymore. If you tell the man your shit got stolen and point the guy out, man, you done put yourself in the worst position. You're not a sucker or a thief, you're a snitch. That's bad. On our tank if you're seen going into the major's office, somebody here will ask you why. You better have a good story. If somebody gets written up or locked up, they're gonna say he snitched. They'll hold court on him. We take care of that on the block. We'll tell him he's gotta leave. If he don't, we'll send him off the tank. That's only right . . .

Informing continues, but it is no longer official or rewarded by the staff. A longtime convict describes the present situation: "It's not like it used to be. They don't snitch like in the old days. There's a lot less of it going on today. See, there's no benefits in it. Besides, it's downright unsafe." Today, informers are on their own and cannot be protected by the guards or their minions, a condition that has enhanced exploitation and extortion.

Survival, or "making it," in the blocks in the postdecree inmate society depends more on an individual's own ability and willingness to protect his property, "manhood," and personal space. According to one inmate: "Nowadays, the first son of a bitch that disrespects you, you got to get on his ass, win or lose. Back then you had to fight too, but today it's a different kind of toughness. Today there's no more protection without the BTs. You're on your own. You're either gonna survive or perish. No matter which way, it's up to you. That's the way it should be. You take care of yourself. That's how a convict makes it in here." Those strong enough to protect themselves survive, while the weak pay for protection with money or their bodies.

The rise in extortion was also reflected in increases in the availability of contraband, especially illicit drugs and alcohol. The institutions became "wide open," as several prisoners put it, and the inmate economy greatly expanded, again recalling the pre-Ellis years. Table 8 depicts the rapid increase in disciplinary infractions for selected drug offenses. Although infractions for marijuana and alcohol possession plateaued after 1985, they remain at approximately the 1983 level. These data suggest that contraband was more readily available and that more inmates were seeking to obtain it for profit as well as for personal use. Access to drugs also facilitated status and power within the inmate society.

Increases in the amount of contraband were due in large part to the advent of contact visits (visitors brought balloons filled with narcotics or money, which inmates swallowed and later retrieved),

Table 8 *Statewide Infractions for Marijuana and Alcohol*

Infraction	1983	1984	1985	1986	1987
Possession of marijuana	285 (8.07)	318 (8.93)	479 (12.76)	439 (11.43)	387 (9.77)
Possession of alcohol	323 (9.15)	451 (12.67)	641 (17.08)	521 (13.56)	513 (12.95)

Source: Management Services, TDC.
Note: Figures in parentheses denote the number of infractions per 1,000 inmates in the system.

the flood of new officers, and increased numbers of civilian personnel. Corrupt employees were important suppliers of contraband and "green money" (actual cash), as noted in the previous chapter. On the Ellis I Unit, for example, the drug and alcohol counselor was fired for smuggling alcohol into the institution. Greater availability of contraband meant a more diverse market and, in turn, the resources to further expand that market. The old barter system based on bags of coffee ($2.25 per bag) gave way to dealing in hard cash. A guard described the availability and possible use of money among prisoners this way: "And a lot of these guys [inmates] have money. I was running short a few months ago and one prisoner offered me $50. He had a $50 bill! I turned him down, but I thought about it."[6] Bribery and payoffs of guards aided the introduction of narcotics (even heroin and cocaine) into the once relatively drug free units.

Changing Race Relations

An important factor behind much of the conflict among TDC prisoners in the early 1980s, giving it fuel and direction, was race and ethnicity. In this respect, TDC was becoming much like other state prison systems in which race significantly affects prisoner interaction and association patterns.[7] The court's dismantling of TDC's traditional and white-dominated control structure encouraged many minority (as well as many white) prisoners to press their apparent advantages.

Certainly, racial status has always been a factor in Texas prisoner relations. Informal control norms generally cast minority prisoners as second-class citizens. Indeed, prior to 1979, all inmate housing in Texas prisons was racially segregated. The field force was similarly segregated into white, black, and Hispanic squads.

The system ended its official segregation practices due to a consent decree to integrate the units and all work forces.[8] During the integration period, racial tension was heightened, but the interracial brawls and violence expected by the staff did not occur. The main reason overt conflict did not emerge was simply the rigid control system in TDC and, especially, the presence of the BTs. After the integration, the BTs maintained close surveillance on the population; inmates who tried to "stir things up or get some shit goin'," for example, by forming racial cliques, were summarily punished. The security staff used cellblock moves as the primary means of dispersing inmates thought to be "organizers." Clearly, integration went relatively smoothly because it took place under an intact control system. Inmates were integrated, but the official and unofficial methods of control remained the same.

Although the integration of cellblocks became official policy, inmates continued to segregate themselves whenever possible. In the dining rooms, for example, whites and Hispanics occupied the left-side tables and blacks the right. The same held true when they attended church or assembled to watch movies or television. While racism was always present within the prison population, these feelings rarely led to serious individual or collective violence. A long-time convict explained: "I been here since the early '70s and there's always been tension; you'll always have that because you got people being forced on each other. But the BTs kept 90 percent of that trouble down. You know blacks, whites, and Mexicans couldn't go around opening their mouths and stirring up shit, and if they did, they were liable to get a fist put in it."

When interracial fights did occur before *Ruiz*, they seldom involved weapons. Moreover, interracial conflicts involving groups of inmates were rare. Through negotiation and force, authorities and BTs maintained a tentative triracial harmony. Those who challenged this balance were summarily punished.

Predictably, after integration, white prisoners maintained their power. Most units were dominated by a white convict power structure reminiscent of Stateville penitentiary in the 1940s and 1950s.[9] Eastham, for example, had a systemwide reputation as a "white boy's farm," where white prisoners had a closer relationship with and were treated better by the staff than other prisoners. Although some black and Hispanic prisoners were influential, they occupied an inferior position, relegated to the fringe of the power structure.

Once the BTs were removed, however, this status quo among prisoners changed. Long-repressed racial animosities and hatreds rose to the surface of everyday interactions as minority prisoners began to exert themselves. Blacks, for example, soon dictated television programming and controlled the benches and the domino tables in the dayrooms. Not only did blacks effectively take over in many cellblocks, but they also began to exploit white prisoners.[10] White inmates vociferously complained among themselves but rarely told the staff about groups of blacks pressuring them, assaulting them, and openly stealing their property. Survey data revealed that 72 percent of the white prisoners believed that blacks caused the most problems within the prisons.

Their traditional status with the authorities largely gone, whites grew increasingly fearful of the blacks. This general fear was expressed by one white inmate: "The niggers are more intimidating today. They think every white boy can be fucked. Goddamn they sure as hell try to find out, too. If a white girl is on the TV, they yell, 'I'd like to fuck that white bitch.' Plus they go around yelling 'get out of my way peckerwood.' They do it to start shit. They don't fuck with the Mexicans, 'cause they know they'll get killed quick. Mexicans got a reputation for sticking people and the niggers know it. I respect the Mexicans." This new situation was difficult for most white prisoners to comprehend. Their relatively protected position in the past had eroded, and now they were the victims. They were on their own to protect themselves.

Blacks, however, viewed the new situation quite differently. They complained about past discrimination and the overt preferential treatment given to white prisoners. A black prisoner stated: "Yeah, we got an attitude towards whites. Why not? The reason I say this is because the white inmates have always more or less run this farm [Eastham]. This place has always been a white boy's farm, so our attitude is kind of bitter. We washed the floors around here long enough and seen the white boys make trusty quicker than any of us. Yeah, we got a bad attitude awright. So what about it?" A white prisoner more forcefully summarized the current situation: "Jesus, when I got here Eastham surprised me. I mean, a nigger was a nigger. If they got jumped on by a BT, the man in gray supported it. Now they don't have this fear and they finally realized that they are the majority. Slowly but surely the blacks are taking over this unit." After many years of bitter treatment at the hands of the BTs and staff, blacks have become a force to be reckoned with, especially for the whites.

Racial intolerance and animosities, once controlled and contained, became more overt, creating considerable tension. Because that tension can flare into conflict, most inmates began to try to keep interracial interaction to a minimum. One strategy was extreme self-segregation according to race and ethnicity. By promoting greater informal segregation, such tensions seem to have promoted a greater racial consciousness, a "be true to your own" kind of philosophy. A black inmate described the current state of race relations: "The Mexicans stick together, so do the whites, and the blacks are riding together a whole lot more than they used to. The races are sticking together a whole lot more. The Mexicans don't hardly talk to blacks. The whites are afraid of the blacks, so they stay in their cells. They hardly go to the dayrooms because a bunch of blacks always be there. Everybody's scared." In short, Texas institutions had become by the mid-1980s more racially polarized than ever before.

Heightened Noise and Stress

Though less dramatic than increased exploitation or racial tension, increases in noise levels and deterioration in the living areas affect all prisoners and promote considerable stress. The environment becomes cluttered and dirty. Candy wrappers, plastic spoons, aluminum cans, and cigarette ashes and butts litter the floor, even though trash cans are available. Radio antenna wires drape like spaghetti from cell after cell to the cellblock windows, many of which have been intentionally broken so that the wires reach outside for improved reception. The heat and the cold come through the broken windows (which officials very slowly replace), and the wires make the place look disheveled.

Noise levels are also markedly higher than in years past. The authoritarian regime proscribed inmate banter or boisterous congregation. Today inmates are much freer to shout, laugh, and joke with each other. Inmates also carry on shouted conversations from tier to tier when they are locked in their cells. Freedom to use radios adds to the noise, as they blare on several different stations in the same cellblock. And, as the following prisoner complains, the noise can continue all night. "The noise level here is bad and it's getting worse because the officers aren't doing their job. IOCs [Inter-Office Communications, rules] have been put up about radios playing at night. Shit, fuck that. Come nighttime the radios are blaring until 3 A.M. The boss tells these guys to turn it down, but you hear, 'Get the fuck outta here.' The place is crazy. You just gotta try to block it out."

The noise level is equally oppressive in the dayrooms. Each of these recreation areas contains benches, a water fountain, three or four domino tables, and an elevated television set. The dayrooms, especially at night, are filled with inmates. Some yell at the television set, while others play (and openly gamble with) dominoes, loudly slapping the pieces on the tables; few attempt to carry on conversations. The television sets must operate at almost full volume because of the competing noise in the dayroom and tank. Even so, the program may be hard to follow. "It's, aw man, it's chaos. It used to be quiet; you know the building tenders would enforce that, but you can't even go in the dayroom and watch a movie. You can't hear it. I mean, people are yelling and hollering and playing dominoes so loud that you can watch a program but you can't hear it." Many others stated that they only went to the dayroom to watch sports because "you don't need to hear it to know what's going on." Though some prisoners go to the dayroom daily, most go only two or three times a week. Maximum attendance is on the weekends to view and gamble on sporting events.

Another reason many inmates are not "regulars," besides the noise and frequent lack of space, is that dayrooms can be dangerous and unpredictable places. "That's where trouble happens, because if you step on somebody's shoe you're liable to get into it. People stay mad all the time and if you catch them at the wrong time, look out. It used to not be like that. If you fought, the BTs, and the bosses would break it up and quick. Now there ain't no BTs and if you make somebody mad, you'll get into it. You gotta be prepared. Plus, the tank boss, he ain't gonna break it up till some help comes. So if you get into it you better be sure about yourself 'cause you're on your own."

Dayroom danger is magnified by the fact that block guards are not inclined to break up fights, especially those fights involving weapons, until other guards arrive. A Hispanic inmate revealed his concern about the danger: "You're locked in there. That's what scares me. If you say you're not scared, then you're either stupid or crazy. If a fight or something racial breaks out, even if you're a stranger, the chances of getting hurt are pretty high. It's good they got more officers, even though I get watched more, but they won't come in the room. It's just not safe."

The Crisis of 1984–1985

The confluence of several factors—new freedoms, trafficking and trading in drugs, increased exploitation, racial tension and fear, and loss of initiative by guards to maintain control—led to a "crisis in self-protection" among inmates. So serious was this crisis that inmates began arming themselves as never before. In 1984 and 1985, 2,700 inmates received disciplinary cases for possessing a weapon, an all-time two-year high.[11] The combination of fear and weapons led to an unprecedented level of violence that lasted for two years. In 1984, TDC experienced 25 inmate homicides and 404 nonfatal stabbings. In 1985, 27 prisoners died at the hands of other prisoners, and there were 237 nonfatal stabbings.[12]

Media coverage of the violence was extensive. Television news programs, particularly those in the Houston area, gave nightly "prison violence reports." Newspapers throughout the state regularly carried stories of TDC trouble, with some even sending investigative teams to cover the action. One lengthy article in a Houston paper presented material, complete with pictures, on the weapons (e.g., pork chop bones and crude bombs) that inmates had used to kill and injure each other.[13]

Explanations for the Violence

This level of violence was unprecedented in recent TDC history, and, predictably, there was no shortage of explanations. Several had particular currency. One explanation was the "different kind of inmate" theory, often espoused by TDC officials. This theory surfaced in 1982 when a TDC spokesman told a newspaper reporter that prison life was increasingly dangerous due a new type of inmate.[14] He said: "We are seeing a younger, more assaultive type of inmate coming into the institution. They are inmates who rebel against all forms of authority." The criminals being sent to prison were thought to be of a dangerous new breed.

Though this explanation deflected blame from the agency, there was little basis for it. For example, there appeared to have been no special law enforcement action (e.g., cracking down on street gangs or dopers) that would have rapidly changed the character of the population. Moreover, the proportion of prisoners doing time for violent crimes changed relatively little through the 1970s and 1980s. In 1973, for example, 38 percent of the population in TDC had been convicted of a violent crime (murder, rape, robbery); in 1977, 1984, and 1986, those percentages were 42, 41, and 38, respectively.

A second frequently mentioned explanation for the violence was that media coverage actually promoted it. Feelings about the adverse effects of coverage were strong among guards. Typical was the following statement by a lieutenant:

> Every time an inmate gets stabbed it's on television, or it's in the newspapers. It's really interfering. And inmates get to reading this and the way they print this stuff, oh, man! We all know how the media stretches things 'cause it's their business, it's a way to sell their business. Then the inmates see this and figure, you know, they say, hey, if two inmates get killed up north [northern TDC units] they like to get some action, too. You know, kill somebody, too. Soon as somebody do something to them they got to do it, too. They feel like they got to do it. A lot of them, it makes them feel so damn good to their self to hear their names on TV. They sit there and holler and yell, "See me, I'm on TV." To them it's a popularity contest.

Some officers directly blamed the media for the violence, and they also perceived the press as being pro-inmate. It is interesting to note, however, that more than four in ten inmates (46%) rejected the "media causes violence" argument, and nearly as many were unsure.

Many prison officials also suggested a third possibility, namely, that Texas' "aggravated" statute meant many prisoners do not restrain their aggression. This law stipulates that offenders who commit a crime with a weapon must complete a calendar one-third of their sentence (without benefit of good time) before being eligible for parole consideration. For example, an inmate with a sixty-year aggravated sentence must serve a minimum of twenty years. In practical terms, this sentence is, to many inmates, actually a life sentence. A convict with an aggravated life sentence made the following observation: "This law keeps the pen overcrowded and affects the way a man thinks, it makes them not want to work. Why should they work? They can't see any light. The administration can't tell them what to do. Fuck that shit. A lot of dudes with aggravated time don't give a damn. They see very little hope. That aggravated fucks a man's mind up. Man, when I saw my release date, it was the year 2040, shit, goddamn, man. Shit, when I make parole, man, I won't be catching no bus, I'll be catching a motherfucking spaceship." The personal implications for inmates with these sentences are enormous. An inmate whose institutional behavior cannot alter the "flat time" stretching out ahead of him may decide that he has little to lose by noncompliance and even violence. Indeed, some inmates stated that under such a sentence it would be advisable for an inmate to kill another because "that would make your reputation and stop the others from fucking with you for twenty years." And evidence indicates that, in fact, inmates with aggravated sentences have a higher institutional rule infraction rate. Inmates with aggravated sentences have a prison assaultive infraction rate of 98 per 1,000 inmates while those with nonaggravated sentences have an assaultive infraction rate of 60 per 1,000. Further, "aggravated" inmates had a total disciplinary infraction rate of 2,061 versus 1,442 for nonaggravated inmates.[15] Thus, the aggravated sentence may have contributed to the violence levels to some degree.

A fourth explanation focused on the quality of the new guards, whom top-ranking officers regularly criticized. As we saw in the last chapter, veteran guards often cited the recent upsurge of drugs being brought into the institutions by guards as evidence of the low moral quality of the new employees.[16] More to the point, ranking guards defined most of the new recruits as ineffective at controlling prisoners, thus permitting greater prisoner violence.

A final oft-cited explanation of the violence was prison over-crowding. Most prisoners (69%) surveyed believed that crowding led to the escalation in serious violence, and, in fact, as the TDC prisoner population increased from 1983 to 1985, so did the levels of violence. Yet, despite the attractiveness of this explanation, the links between crowding and prisoner violence are difficult to demonstrate. Sheldon Ekland-Olson directly tested the "crowding tension violence" model with TDC data and found only a weak relationship between violence and crowding.

> These data indicate that the crowding model is of limited utility when explaining patterns of homicide and serious assaultive behavior. . . . Prior to 1978 there was a negative relationship between homicide rates and population levels. Between 1979 and 1984 the relationship was positive. However, during this latter period the amount of space per inmate was increasing. Within institutions homicides concentrated in high-security units and tended to be episodic. Neither inmate-inmate nor inmate-staff assaults were related to cross-sectional measures of population size and density or to changes in population and density levels from 1983 to 1984.[17]

Social Disorganization and Inmate Violence

Some of these popular explanations point out factors that might well encourage prisoner aggression, but none alone can account for the rise in violence experienced in Texas prisons, especially in 1984 and 1985. Indeed, overcrowding and the aggravated sentence statute, for example, were realities in the 1970s when prisoner-prisoner violence was relatively low in TDC.

A more adequate explanation is that violence is the result of social disorganization. That is, aggression and violence surged when the once-institutionalized system of dominance and informal understandings and the traditional rules governing inmate relations broke down. There was a widespread sense that the BTs left a vacuum, and the rush to fill it led to exploitation and violence among prisoners. A veteran officer put it this way: "The inmates know they're not going to get their asses whipped by nobody. They know there's no BTs to whip their ass. So they do what they want to do. You know, 'Fuck TDC.' There's nobody to stop them from killing somebody. They're trying to stake their claim now that the BTs are gone." This vacuum theory was supported by most guards (72%) and nearly half (46%) of the prisoners.[18]

It would be more accurate, however, to attribute the violence not to the loss of the BTs alone but to the many changes in the control system, including the great influx of guards, a new accountability, guard uncertainty, crowding, racial tension, and administrative succession. These changes together promoted social disorganization.

To protect themselves in an increasingly uncertain world, many inmates resorted to violent self-help, and in the process violence became a mechanism of social control.[19] This transition can be illustrated by examining dispute settlement norms before and after *Ruiz*.

Dispute Settlement in Transition.   Under the old regime, the primary mode of dispute settlement was the fistfight; BTs routinely allowed quarreling prisoners to "duke it out like men." These fights, moreover, typically occurred without the staff's knowledge. One inmate recalls having the informal rules for settling disputes explained to him:

> When I drove up on the Darrington, the head building tender told me the rules. He said, "Now if you gotta fight somebody, you come tell me and I will take you up on third row, and we'll go in the mop room and you two can fight your hearts out. No one's going to say anything to you or do anything to you unless you pull out a weapon. Then I'm gonna stop it and you won't like it. In the dayroom, I'm gonna stop it and you aren't going to like it. But we all got to squabble every now and then and all you got to do is say 'I got to squabble,' and then I'll take you up to the mop room. Now if you go into the mop room, there's no quittin'. You're going to fight till one of you hits the floor. Not gonna be coming up here for people that want to hit somebody in the eye real quick and then have the man break it up. So, know in advance when you go up in that mop room, one of you's gonna be on the floor when you come out. If you're seriously hurt, I'll take you to the infirmary."

The norms guiding dispute settlement in the building also held sway in the field. An ex–field major gave the following account of field quarrels:

> They fought out there all day long, and you'd hear 'em say, "You whipped me today but I'll get you tomorrow." They fought the next day, too. If they were picking cotton, they'd get out of that cotton sack [remove from their shoulder the strap holding the sack] and tell you they was gonna get him. Well, I'd tell them, "No, we gotta wait till we get on the other side of these rows

because I don't want you tearing up my cotton." They'd pick up their sack and wait till they got through. Then they'd tell you, "I'm gonna get him here boss," and then they'd fight. As long as one wasn't hurting the other one they could fight. Whenever one got to hurting the other one, like kicking him, the fight would stop.

Once the fight was over, a field officer typically asked the combatants, "Is it over with?" If each stated it was over, then they were allowed to return to work. According to veteran officers and prisoners, such fights usually ended the dispute and seldom led to disciplinary cases.

Perhaps more important, inmates rarely settled their disputes with weapons. To do so invited a serious and probably injurious confrontation with the BTs. Moreover, the BTs' extensive information network made it difficult for inmates to make, keep, or sell weapons without officials finding out about it. Fistfights, therefore, were the primary (and safest) means for settling conflicts. Given the control system, nonlethal settlement became institutionalized, and stabbings and deaths were relatively rare.

The drastic alterations in TDC's control structure, however, brought about a major transition in dispute settlement among prisoners. That is, inmates, especially the weak, found that they were on their own if they became involved in some type of conflict or dispute with another prisoner. This was because guards now operated at a distance, and the BTs no longer offered protection. As a result, inmates who faced a dispute of any consequence had three choices for resolving the problem. First, they could tell the guards about problems (e.g., threats, missing property) with other inmates. Those prisoners who went to the guards for help, however, risked being labeled as a snitch, a punk, or a weakling. Guard interviews revealed that inmates were willing to discuss logistics with them (e.g., job changes, cell changes, programming) but avoided discussing interpersonal problems.

Inmates who were too scared to go to the guards and too weak to fight took the second alternative; they submitted. These inmates were the victims of the extortion and protection rackets discussed above. They regularly lost their personal property and sometimes were sexually violated.

The third choice an inmate had was to fight. But, because of the uncertainty and disorganization that marked prisoner relations, those fights took on a different quality. Specifically, in 1983, fights began to more frequently involve weapons rather than fists, a transition that made dispute settlement a much riskier business. An inmate describes this transition:

> Fistfights is going out. Why get scratched up? It's easier to stick somebody and go about your business. This is one of the changes I've seen. Why fight him? It makes no sense. It's better to stick him. If you fight and whip him, you hurt his ego, every convict in here has an ego he's trying to uphold. Fistfighting is too much trouble. Back then, you could fight, catch the wall for an hour and go back to your tank, it was over with. You don't have that protection anymore. Right now, since they got rid of the BTs, a dude has got a complex about another dude telling him what to do. They don't like it. That shit is dead. Today a dude is more likely to get stabbed for any kind of disorder or disrespect.

This perception of a transition from fists to knives was particularly prevalent on TDC's eight hard-core units, which house violent, multiple recidivists.[20] Through 1984 and 1985, 68 percent of the nonfatal stabbings occurred at these units.

To determine the significance of this perception of a shift toward more lethal modes of dispute settlement, we compared the official rates of three serious offenses: fighting without a weapon, possession of a weapon, and fighting with a weapon. Table 9 presents a comparison over time of the rates of serious inmate-inmate assault on eight TDC units that house the system's "hard-core" prisoners. Although systemwide assault patterns parallel those of these eight prisons, we focus on these units because they were the primary concern of the court and were the sites for most of the prisoner violence.

The data in Table 9 indicate that the rate of fighting without a weapon (fistfights) on the tough units did decline somewhat from

Table 9 *Serious Assaultive Behavior Rates, Eight Key Units, 1983–1987*

	1983	*1984*	*1985*	*1986*	*1987*
Fighting without a weapon	37.78	33.39	60.03	86.92	11.72
Possession of a weapon	35.75	53.66	54.74	31.86	9.26
Fighting with a weapon	39.03	52.21	24.46	17.66	11.33

Source: Management Services, TDC.

Note: Numbers represent rates per 1,000 inmates. Units represented are Coffield, Darrington, Ellis I, Eastham, Ferguson, Ramsey I, Retrieve, and Wynne.

1983 (37.78%) to 1984 (33.39%). At the same time, possession of and fighting with a weapon rose markedly. This pattern is consistent with our interview data and suggests that a crisis of self-protection did exist during this period. As an example of the fists-to-knives trend, at the Ramsey I Unit in 1983, there were ninety-nine cases of fighting without a weapon, and in 1984 that number dropped to forty-five. Yet, fights involving weapons went from twenty-five to sixty-five in the same period. Thus, many inmates at Ramsey and other large units believed that "getting down all the way" (using lethal force) was the best solution for a beef with another prisoner. Many more felt compelled to secure and hide weapons, although they never actually used them. This need to have a weapon is illustrated by the discovery at the Coffield Unit of over one thousand shanks or knives in one 1984 cellblock search. In time, as Table 9 shows, prison officials regained control, and weapons offenses and even fistfights waned.

But, at mid-decade, TDC prisons, especially the hard-core units, were dangerous places. Getting a weapon and using it had become a form of social control among prisoners. As one prisoner stated, "It's either me or him, and if I got to, I'll take him out first."

The following incident occurred in 1984 and serves to underscore the fundamental transition in dispute settlement.

> This dude came to me and wanted to borrow a can of tobacco off me. I had enough for myself, so I gave him one and wanted two in return. Several paydays came and went and he didn't pay me back. I went to him where he worked in the kitchen and asked him for my money. He said, "I ain't going to pay, so stop fucking with me." He used vulgar language against me. He disrespected me. He said, "You better stop fucking with me or I'll kill you or pay someone to kill you." I said to myself, man this guy might just pay someone to kill me. So I beat him to it. I caught him in my tank and stuck him.

The rapid structural and control changes prompted by the reforms undermined traditional dispute settlement mechanisms. In the wake of these changes inmates were on their own to solve their problems. Some could not or would not protect themselves and eventually became the prey of the dominant inmates. Others, however, obtained weapons and protected themselves as best they could by resorting to violence in the face of threats. Still others resorted to a collective type of protection, the prison gang.

The Rise of Prisoner Gangs

Texas prisoners have always associated on the basis of ethnicity, criminal patterns and lifestyles, and city or neighborhood affiliations. Having a "home boy," or staying with one's kind, provided psychic and material support and sometimes protection. Rapid organizational changes in TDC, however, exacerbated traditional social cleavages and made protection a more important reason for joining with others.

A major outcome of these trends was the emergence of major prisoner gangs for the first time in TDC. The Texas experience is in many ways reflective of national trends in prison gangs. Thus, before examining the situation in TDC, we sketch the national picture of prisoner gangs.

Prison Gangs in Other State Prison Systems

Despite the place of the gang in prison power structures, systematic, national data on the origins and nature of prisoner gangs are limited. According to one source, formal prisoner gangs (as opposed to cliques of home boys) date from about 1950, when the Gypsy Jokers, essentially a motorcycle group, formed in the Washington state prison.[21] Since then, inmate gangs have spread, generally from the West Coast eastward. A recent survey of state and federal prison systems found gang activity in twenty-nine systems; 114 gangs were identified with an estimated membership of some 12,000 inmates.[22]

Inmate organizations began to be a significant factor in the late sixties and early seventies when many state prisons were undergoing structural changes due, in part, to court intervention. In some states, such changes offered members of street gangs the opportunity to import the identity and power of their gangs into the prison. This coalescence of prisoners into gangs has been particularly apparent among minority groups. In Illinois, for example, black gangs, such as the Black Stone Rangers and the Devil's Disciples, became important players in the prisoner society.[23] Similarly, in California, during the 1960s especially, the Black Guerrilla Family espoused a revolutionary doctrine, while such Hispanic gangs as the Mexican Mafia formed to control prison rackets.[24] For the last two decades, prison gangs have posed a serious challenge for officials.

The composition of contemporary gangs suggests that the most common basis for gang membership is race and ethnicity. Common cultural and street experiences promote the solidarity and cohesion necessary for gang formation. Consequently, among the major prison organizations in state prison systems around the country are the Mexican Mafia (MM) and the Neustra Familia (NF), both Hispanic groups; the Aryan Brotherhood (AB), a white supremacist group; and the Black Guerrilla Family (BGF).

Although in most prisons gang members are relatively few in number compared to the general population, they can have a major impact on prison order. That is, gang members tend to be disproportionately involved in prison violence, as the California prison experience suggests. In 1971, there were 123 attacks with 19 killings in California prisons; in 1972, there were 186 attacks and 34 homicides.[25] Much of this violence was directly attributed to two rival Hispanic gangs—the Mexican Mafia and the Nuestra Familia—who fought for prestige, members, and control of prison rackets. Moreover, from 1975 through 1979, California prisons recorded 124 gang-related killings. This is in addition to thousands of gang-related stabbings and other nonfatal attacks. And, between 1972 and 1975, gang members killed 11 staff members.[26] The Black Guerrilla Family alone was responsible for 6 of these staff fatalities.

The capacity of gangs to have such a disproportionate effect on prison order stems not only from their willingness to use violence, however. Gangs are effective also because of the organizational structures and the procedures that gang leaders can use to control members. Yet, precisely what that gang organization looks like is a matter of controversy and speculation. Some observers argue that the groups are not well organized and are nothing more than loose collections of individuals interested in criminal activity.[27] Many prison officials, however, maintain that the gangs are cohesive and operate as tightly knit organizations. Indeed, a recent survey on prisoner gangs found that the larger gangs do have leadership roles, constitutions that outline strict regulations for members, and clear divisions of labor.[28] The Nuestra Familia, the Mexican Mafia, the Black Guerrilla Family, as well as the Vice Lords and El Rukns, for example, have ruling councils, lieutenants, and soldiers. In many cases, leaders are charismatics with little compunction about using violence to maintain their positions. Moreover, the entrenched groups have strong street ties and are able to control illicit activities (primarily narcotics trafficking) both inside the prison and outside on the street.

Evidence from around the country suggests the hypothesis that the emergence of gangs and related violence closely follows rapid, fundamental changes in a prison. The Texas experience clearly supports that hypothesis.

The Texas Experience

Through the mid-1970s, TDC was known for its "gang-free" institutions. While prison staffs in other states were fighting prisoner gangs for control of the institutions, TDC was relatively gang free. The only "organized" inmate group in Texas prisons was the Black Muslims, who first appeared in the late 1950s. Texas prison officials feared these inmates (because of their reputation in other prisons as troublemakers) and dispersed them across the system to prevent the Muslim movement from gaining momentum as well as membership. In the mid-1960s, however, Director George Beto implemented a different policy; he ordered all known Muslims to be housed at the Ellis Unit and their beliefs to "be treated like a religion."[29] This strategy was ostensibly designed to centralize religious and dietary services, but its primary function was to control the Muslims. Having them confined to one unit reduced their opportunity to proselytize and made surveillance simpler.

Although Muslims were known for their litigiousness in other states, they were not writ writers in Texas. Contrary to staff expectations, these inmates were not particularly disruptive. According to Beto, "they followed the rules and they never gave us any trouble."[30] Yet, limited evidence indicates that these inmates spent more time in solitary confinement than did other inmates.[31] This higher lockup rate probably resulted from prejudicial disciplinary action on the part of a predominantly white security staff.

In the early 1970s, however, a gang emerged that would become known for its inclination toward violence, namely, the Texas Syndicate (TS). This gang initially developed among a group of Texas Hispanics who were doing time in the California prison system, primarily at Folsom. These Texas inmates banded together to protect themselves from the Mexican Mafia and the Nuestra Familia.[32] Some of these TS members migrated back to Texas (particularly to San Antonio and the Rio Grande Valley) in the mid-1970s, maintained their gang affiliations, and eventually organized a chapter in Texas.

In the late 1970s, a number of TS members were identified by Texas prison officials. Though their numbers were small, they were feared because of their reputed willingness to use extreme violence on other prisoners. Officials were cognizant of the TS' presence and used the BTs to maintain surveillance on known members. Yet, although a file on suspected members was developed, TDC's top officials kept this intelligence secret to downplay the presence of gangs.

In fact, the administration even kept most of this intelligence from unit personnel. Texas prison officials felt that any official recognition of the TS would play into the gang's hands. Thus, while many guards knew of the TS, it was to them a group shrouded in mystery, hearsay, and much speculation. More important, the security staff believed that neither the TS nor any other inmate group represented a challenge to institutional control and order. They were wrong.

As the authority vacuum grew, as racial tension surfaced, and as the dynamics of contraband markets, exploitation, and fear expanded in the population, the gang phenomenon took hold in TDC. For some prisoners the gangs meant protection, material benefits, and a social identity; for others they meant heightened danger and death. The first gang-related homicide in TDC, a TS murder, was in 1979.[33] From that point, gang violence became an increasingly serious control problem.

Though the TS is the oldest, it is certainly not the only gang in the Texas prisons. The Aryan Brotherhood, the Texas Mafia (TM, a white group), and the Mexican Mafia, along with the TS, are the most powerful groups in TDC. Several black groups have also emerged (e.g., Mandingo Warriors, Interaction Organization, and Seeds of Idi Amin), but there have been conflicts within and between these groups; no one leader has come forth to solidify competing factions into one organized group. A racially integrated gang called the Self Defense Family also emerged in 1984. Currently, there are gangs and gang members at almost all Texas prison units.

Gang Structure and Organization in TDC.   Generally, the gangs are organized in paramilitary fashion to control members and activities. Some gangs, like the Texas Syndicate, have a hierarchical structure, such as that depicted in Figure 2.[34] Other gangs, such as the Aryan Brotherhood, have a complex command structure dominated by a central ruling elite called the "steering committee," under which there are three regional divisions (northern, southern, and central). (This arrangement mimics TDC's structure.) Beneath the regional divisions are the individual prison unit organizations, which consist of captains, lieutenants (for general population and for administrative segregation), sergeants at arms, members, and prospects.

Membership, Recruitment, and Growth Trends.   Although being white, black, or Hispanic is typically a necessary condition for prison gang membership, it is not sufficient. Beyond race and ethnicity, gang members screen prospective members as to the prospect's character and sense. For most gangs a member sponsors or recommends another inmate, and then the screening process begins. A Hispanic gang member described recruiting: "We look at how you act, your

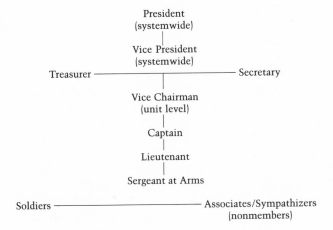

President
(systemwide)

Vice President
(systemwide)

Treasurer ——————————————— Secretary

Vice Chairman
(unit level)

Captain

Lieutenant

Sergeant at Arms

Soldiers ——————————————— Associates/Sympathizers
(nonmembers)

Figure 2. Organizational structure of the Texas Syndicate gang.

character, your heart. Your time is irrelevant. If I thought you were good enough, you don't come to me; I mean, we come to you and ask you to do certain things. Man, it's one way in and one way out. There's no alternative. If you say yeah, then I'll recommend you to the rest of them, throughout the system. If one of them says no, that's it. You'll be able to associate with us, but you won't be accepted, but you'll have your respect for acting like a man." A gang member turned informer described the Aryan Brotherhood's recruitment procedures as follows:

A prospect after being sponsored to the group by an inmate already a member is put on probation for six months. During this time, the prospect is allowed to get to know the other members and more importantly, the other members get to know the prospect, who could be a future brother. The prospect is put through a rigorous investigation around the unit to find out if he has had a good character, or if he is something less than admissible. If the prospect had been on another unit in TDC, the investigation is expanded to the unit and any AB's who knew someone on that unit would write that person and have them ask around about the prospect. The prospect is tested in his basic "convict sense" and is put into situations which would let his brothers know how he could deal with different problems which would be faced as an AB, and if he could do so in such a manner as to keep the

Honor, Integrity and Reputation unsullied and intact. As time passed, and as the prospect came to the end of his probation, he would gradually be allowed to know some of the business and secrets of the AB. He isn't brought into actual meetings, but he is allowed to know certain things which, if he turned out to be less than acceptable, couldn't hurt the group. There is a saying bandied about by outsiders of the AB which goes like so: "Kill to get in, and die to get out." Well, as you can see, a man doesn't have to kill to enter the AB, but he does not leave nor can he terminate his membership except through death. Once in, always in. This holds true even if the member leaves the prison and goes home. He must still contact the organization inside the walls and do so as ordered outside. If, after the complete investigation is through, and nothing has come up to besmirch the integrity of the prospect, and after he has completed his probation/training and has shown he will stand up for his brothers in any situation, he is allowed to put on the patch of the ARYAN BROTHERHOOD.[35]

Evidence indicates that some recruits are attractive to the gang for more than their character and sense. Their frequently violent backgrounds can be an asset. An examination of the criminal backgrounds of the prisoners designated by TDC officials as affiliated with a gang suggests that they are somewhat more violent than most TDC inmates. Table 10 presents TDC data for December 1986,

Table 10 *Gang Membership and Offense of Record (in Percent)*

	Texas Syndicate	*Aryan Brother- hood*	*Texas Mafia*	*Mexican Mafia*	*TDC*
Assault	4	2	5	4	4
Burglary	22	25	18	32	26
Drugs	5	3	2	11	9
Homicide	25	23	16	20	13
Kidnapping	1	2	3	1	1
Larceny	5	2	2	4	6
Robbery	26	29	37	20	20
Sex-related	5	6	4	3	11
Others	6	10	14	4	10
Total population	212	185	92	288	37,777

Source: Management Services, TDC.

showing the offense of record for members of several gangs and for the population as a whole. With the exception of the Mexican Mafia, TDC gang members reflect a greater penchant for robbery and homicide than the general population.

Once in, a new member can identify himself and be identified by a specific tattoo, or patch. For example, the TS tattoo is a "T" superimposed on an "S," while members of the Aryan Brotherhood sport a pair of lightning bolts. Insignia of several major TDC gangs are presented in Figure 3.

Gang membership in TDC has gradually increased since the early 1980s, although the relative number of members is still small. In March of 1983, there were 77 identified members in a prisoner population of 37,227. Members were no more than 0.21 percent of all prisoners. By December 1984, known membership grew to 484, 1.32 percent of the inmate population. Computed for August of 1985, 1986, and 1987, the percentages of TDC prisoners defined as gang members were 2.03, 3.00, and 3.00, respectively.[36] These figures indicate that, while gang growth continues, the percentage of members in the inmate population has plateaued. Consistent with the argument that gang growth is the product of disorganization and fractured control structures, TDC gang expansion has apparently slowed as the organization has moved into a more stable period.

Doing Business Violently. Gangs serve many functions. They provide something to do, protection, a way to "beat the man," and access to illicit goods and services (e.g., narcotics, punks, clothes, and food). Members also ostensibly derive a degree of solidarity or brotherhood. This last point is emphasized by a Hispanic inmate gang member: "Say I get killed and a snitch or somebody is responsible. No matter where they go, we got people on every farm, and the one that's running it there will tell the leaders what went down. They'll pay for what they did. It's a brotherhood, we call each other brother." Gang members believe that if they are threatened, assaulted, or killed they will be avenged. The motto of the AB, for example, is: "An Aryan Brother, Never need fear. For his death shall be avenged, By his Brothers still here."[37] In this sense gangs resemble a surrogate family that offers social and psychological support for its members, both inside and outside the institution.

Although protection, revenge, and brotherhood may be important gang functions, they are secondary to the main business of the gangs, selling protection, acquiring and distributing narcotics and sexual favors, and dealing in other contraband. Through these activities, the gang can expand its influence, and gang members can benefit individually. A former AB member describes these activities:

TEXAS SYNDICATE

ARYAN BROTHERHOOD OF TEXAS

MEXIKANEMI (MEXICAN MAFIA)

TEXAS MAFIA

Figure 3. Tattoo insignia of major gangs in the Texas Department of Corrections.

Most AB members use some form of drug or another and drugs
are a big part of the prison society and also a major way of
making money for the group doing the selling and supplying.
The AB got into this racket much like every other group and that
is to have some officers start to smuggle it in for the group.
These officers get a commission on what they bring in, and can
almost double their weekly pay by this practice. You see, 95% or
more of the convicts used dope on the streets and use them
whenever they can get them in here. And the gang who can supply that dope is the gang who has most of the money on that
unit, and most of the connections throughout the whole society. . . . Not only drugs, but alcohol and intoxicating inhalants
are very precious commodities in demand. Paint thinner or other
things can be sold for quite a good amount of money, fast. . . .
Now, the other main area of money-making enterprise into which
the AB has stepped, much to the disgust of some of the members,
is prostitution. The AB looks at it this way, if a guy is going to be
a punk in the first place, then, if he's white, why let the blacks
make the money off of him when the whites should?

The only thing the homosexual has to do is perform sexual
favors for people the AB tells the punk to perform for, and when
the guy/gal does so, the AB charges the recipient of the sex a
charge for the use of an AB guy/gal. These two goals are primarily for the money involved. The AB feels the need to gain
financial security so its brothers won't have to worry for the
basic necessities of a comfortable prison existence.[38]

A member of the Mexican Mafia, whose major criminal activity in
prison is drug trafficking, describes how they conduct business:

When a young officer is assigned to a cell block, one of us would
start watching him for a few days. Then, I would go up to kind of
talk to him in order to find out where he is coming from. I would
borrow a cigarette or a pen from him. If he goes for it, the next
thing I would do would be to ask him to mail a letter for me. If
he goes for it, I would start showing him pictures of some woman
which I claimed to be my friend. I would tell him to give her a call
because she would show him a real good time. If he calls her and
gets some sexual favors from her, I know I have him.[39]

If the officer "swallows the bait" and brings in drugs, he obtains
some percentage of the profits. However, if the officer takes the bait
but refuses to cooperate, he risks being exposed ("snitched off") to

ranking guards for being involved with an inmate's wife, sister, or other close relative—which usually means termination.

Consolidating lucrative prison rackets is achieved in essentially two ways: by recruiting more members and by eliminating competitors and those who otherwise hamper operations. Gangs have used both strategies, thereby accounting for the very disproportionate contribution of gang members to the violence TDC experienced, especially through 1984 and 1985. For example, between 1980 and 1986, TDC experienced a total of ninety-three homicides, and the TS was involved in thirty-six of them.[40]

Rivalry between two Hispanic gangs in 1985 caused both to step up their recruiting activity; neither wanted to lose influence or be caught with too few troops. The recruiting competition soon led to violence. In fact, in an eight-day period in September 1985, there were eight inmate slayings. On September 9, a triple homicide occurred at the Darrington Unit.[41] The two gangs involved, the Texas Syndicate and the Mexican Mafia, were pressuring recruits to attack rival members as an initiation rite. The murders were also engineered to secure control over such rackets as drug trafficking, extortion, and male prostitution.[42] In October 1985, however, the two gangs proposed a peace treaty to stem the violence. The leaders contacted the Prisoner's Defense Committee, a San Antonio–based prison reform group, to help negotiate a pact ending the hostilities.[43] The leaders of the two gangs issued a statement saying, "It is entirely to each family's benefit to agree to a peace treaty."[44] The violence, according to the gang leaders, only allowed such upstarts as the Aryan Brotherhood to move in on prison rackets.

Despite such truces, violence remained an integral part of gang business and membership. To illustrate, murders were usually fairly well planned, instrumental actions. The gangs maintained hit lists of inmates whom the gang had condemned for betrayal, snitching, failing to complete an assigned hit, attacking a gang member, or welching on a deal. When a hit was decided, contracts were put out on the victims and their names circulated to the other members of the gang via coded messages, such as the following example sent by one TS member to another:

Dear Bro:
How are things on your end? Not much happenin' here. Just wanted to say "hi." By the way, Big Dave got caught by a cop driving the wrong way at 100 miles an hour the other day. What a shitty deal! I always thought that Big Dave was a smart mother-fucker. Sure am disappointed. Hope the judge will take

his license away and never let the son-of-a-bitch drive again. It's people like him that drive up auto insurance costs. Well that's life! Take care.

Your bro till death[45]

Although the content appears harmless, this message is actually a murder contract. Big Dave was on the hit list. While most codes are complex and require intense study to translate, others are so simple that the staff overlook them. For example, a gang member in 1983 received a letter that contained the statement "don't forget to take out the trash." This statement seemed simple enough, but it contained a hidden message. An inmate had the nickname Trashcan, and he was subsequently murdered by a gang member.[46]

As in other states, prison gang influence in Texas is beginning to extend beyond the prison itself. Police and citizens were shaken when, in March 1987, a number of gang leaders committed several high-profile crimes almost immediately after parole. In Houston, for example, police broke up a drug ring run by the TS, and an AB member was arrested for fatally shooting a sheriff's deputy. Gang members have also been implicated in several murders in Dallas and San Antonio. A special state prosecutor commented: "They are operating outside the prisons, but how strong they are, no one knows. When you take an organization as dangerous and vicious as they are, it would be foolish to think they are not operating outside."[47] Texas urban areas, unlike those of Chicago, New York, or Los Angeles, have been, until recently, relatively free of prison-street gang ties. However, these incidents suggest that, as more gang members are released from TDC, the gangs will strengthen their street ties.

Social Fragmentation of the Prisoner Population

Prior to the court's intervention, the co-optation of strong inmates facilitated stability in two important ways. First, it brought those particular inmates under the control of the staff. Second, co-optation helped to repress conflict among ethnic and racial groups. The head bookkeeper on the Darrington Unit for several years prior to the reforms described how BTs helped to limit conflict.

. . . in the count office you had V.S., barrio hardcase Chicano with 650 years, one-half dozen life sentences. There was L.K.G., black, infamous rapist. There was L.L., white, exceptionally brilliant individual. There were the three heads of the population. The Chicanos went to S., the blacks went to G., and the whites went to L. But problems of any magnitude were worked out among the three. [For example,] "If the man does this, the Mexicans are gonna buck. What are the niggers gonna do?" . . . L. would sort it out and take it to the administration . . . When that was done away with, then you had the inception of the gangs which are formed on a racial basis. You have three distinct entities going in three fundamentally different directions, without any communication. That has spilled over into racial tensions.

The reforms disrupted this arrangement for communicating, settling group disputes, and distributing power across prisoner groups. In the process, the prisoner population became increasingly atomized with rifts along racial lines.

While legitimate authority may have been undermined, the coercive power of strong inmates was not. When the BTs vacated their positions, others soon took their places. During the organizational turmoil of the mid-1980s, new inmate leaders stepped in to fill vacated power positions, and their agenda was quite different from that of the BTs they replaced. They worked exclusively for themselves, not for the staff.

That new agenda led to the proliferation of violence and gang activity first by affecting race relations. Black prisoners began to press as reforms redefined the traditional sanctions and stratification system. Without the traditional controls that had favored whites, aggressiveness toward and even assaults on whites by blacks increased. Although fear among whites probably exceeded the actual likelihood of assault, that fear prompted many whites to arm themselves and to look to other whites for protection. Equally fearful blacks reacted in kind. The circular dynamics of racial group aggression and collective response was an important factor in the growth of prison gangs.

Another reason for the emergence of gangs and greater violence in TDC, and also linked to the breakdown of traditional alliances, was the expanded contraband markets within the prison. Expansion occurred, in part, because of the number of new officers that TDC had hired to meet court-mandated staffing patterns. While the proportion of corruptible officers may have been no greater among these recruits than among those in the past, the absolute number of such officers did increase. These officers represented a major source of contraband and were readily exploited by the gangs. But, from whatever source, the amount and variety of contraband, especially drugs and green money to buy them, increased. Prison gangs sought to carve up and control these growing markets.

While the gang phenomenon is perhaps the most visible illustration of fragmentation within the population, it is not the most pervasive. After all, according to TDC institutional records, no more than 3 percent of the population is known to belong to gangs. Even if officials have identified only 20 percent of the members, there is still a full 85 percent of TDC prisoners who are not affiliated with a gang. In what sense then has fragmentation affected the larger segment of the population?

The most immediate impact of the reforms for regular prisoners was the uncertainty of doing time in a changing and dangerous environment. As noted earlier, during the crisis period of 1984 and 1985, many prisoners who had little desire to become involved in trouble or gangs experienced fear and secured weapons for defense. They felt that, since there were no official protectors, they would have to take care of themselves.

Although TDC has become a safer place for prisoners since the mid-1980s, a pervasive consequence of the rapid change and uncertainty remains, namely, a diminished trust of fellow prisoners. Our survey of prisoners clearly indicates that the extent to which inmates trust each other has decreased. Of course, this is a relative observation; prison does not promote much trust in any case. Nonetheless, prisoners indicate that they are less apt to trust other prisoners today than they were before the reforms.

An Emerging Stability

Our account of the impact on prisoners of mandated organizational change in TDC is consistent thus far with a "paradox of reform" argument.[48] This argument holds that, although court-ordered reform may improve conditions for prisoners, it promotes inmate-inmate violence in the process. This is John Conrad's point in a comment on prison conditions in the wake of reforms in American institutions: "Prisoners are no longer so isolated, so poor, so celibate or so restricted in permissible initiatives. Without minimizing the importance of these improvements, they lose most of their significance in prisons where sudden and unpredictable violence has to be expected as a natural part of daily living."[49]

Conrad's conclusions appear to apply to reforms in TDC as well. Indeed, the court's efforts to improve conditions for TDC prisoners did lead to a dissolution of the inmate social order, which, in turn, heightened the risk of injury and death for those same prisoners. The question, however, is whether the violence and danger that so characterized prison life in Texas from the beginning of the court's intervention through the mid-1980s actually became a "natural part of daily living." Our analysis of prisoner perceptions of their environment in the late 1980s suggests that it did not. That is, in time, stability and a sense of safety emerged.

Table 11 presents the results of survey questions designed to assess prisoner perceptions of personal safety over more than a decade in TDC, from the early 1970s through 1987.[50] These data support three important conclusions. The first is that the majority of prisoners in TDC did not view the prison as a safe place prior to the reforms (1970–1978). Though it is true that deaths and stabbings among TDC prisoners in the 1970s and early 1980s were rare, most prisoners perceived TDC to be a dangerous place. They primarily feared the force used by building tenders and staff. The second conclusion is that implementation of the court's decrees prompted prisoners to view TDC as neither dramatically safer nor more dangerous, at least in the short run. Finally, we can conclude that, after 1985, most TDC prisoners came to feel much safer. These patterns generally hold for all groups of prisoner respondents.

The paradox of reform argument predicts an upswing in violence and turmoil after court intervention and a heightened sense of personal risk by prisoners as well. Our data reveal, however, that, while there was a marked increase in prisoner-prisoner violence, especially at middecade, prisoner perceptions of personal safety changed relatively little at first. The explanation is that the reforms, in effect, replaced one threat with another. Once the threat of abuse by guards and BTs was eliminated, a new threat emerged, namely, aggressive

Table 11 *Inmate Perceptions of Personal Safety, 1970–1987 (in Percent)*

	1987	1986	1984–1985	1982–1983	1979–1981	1970–1978
Whites						
safe	67	60	39	28	28	38
unsafe	15	20	37	50	50	42
Blacks						
safe	63	54	24	24	32	27
unsafe	20	23	53	57	55	61
Hispanics						
safe	64	56	45	43	42	45
unsafe	9	16	28	38	41	33
Total respondents	416	411	411	415	410	180

fellow prisoners and gang conflict, as we have shown. Because some element of danger had always been a part of prison life in TDC, the increased prisoner violence of the mid-1980s did not significantly raise the collective perception of risk.

By 1986, however, prisoners saw a more safe and stable environment emerging. Homicides and serious assaults dropped. Specifically, homicides in TDC fell from twenty-seven in 1985 to five and three in 1986 and 1987, respectively. As the apparent threat level dropped, fewer prisoners felt the need even to secure weapons. In 1984 and 1985, for example, between 800 and 1,000 disciplinary cases of weapons possession were processed across the prison system. By contrast, those figures had dropped to approximately 500 in 1986 and to less than 200 in 1987. In short, as Table 11 indicates, two-thirds of each major prisoner group reported feeling safe by 1987.

Changes in safety levels in TDC resulted primarily from measures taken by officials to contain violence, measures that essentially created two prisoner populations. In the summer of 1984, officials began converting existing cellblocks on the larger units (e.g., Darrington, Eastham, Ellis, Coffield, Retrieve, and Ramsey I) into administrative segregation, or lock-down facilities. Entire blocks were designated as ad. seg. wings and retrofitted with metal screening, separate outside recreation areas, and other high-security devices. These control units, in effect, created two distinct populations—those in segregation and those in the general population.

After a triple homicide on September 9, 1985, at Darrington, TDC's director ordered a lock down involving 17,000 inmates on thirteen units.[51] This broad action was designed to save inmate lives and, in the process, deflect growing political concern that the prison was completely beyond official control. The action was also the first step by TDC toward using administrative segregation as a permanent control device. Security staff throughout TDC rounded up known and suspected gang members in the general population and placed them in the new ad. seg. wings. The dragnet continued over the next several months, and hundreds of inmates were sent to administrative segregation. Figure 4 shows the sudden and continued reliance of TDC on administrative segregation to control assaultive and protection prisoners.[52]

Although lock down made the general population inmates feel safer, it isolated in a few cellblocks the most assaultive prisoners and those whose lives, for whatever reasons, were most in jeopardy. This concentration of prisoners in administrative segregation magnified interracial and intergang conflict. Not surprisingly, in 1985,

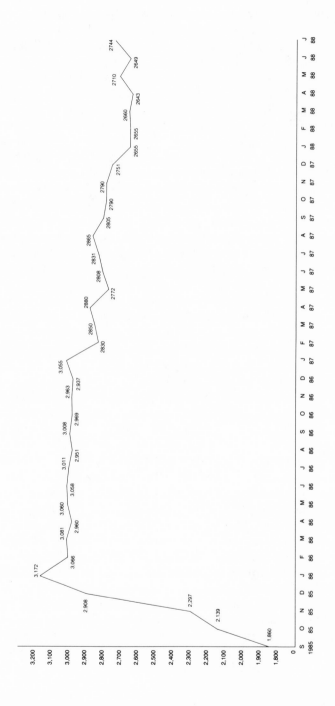

Figure 4. The use of administrative segregation in Texas prisons. (Data from Texas Department of Corrections, *Administrative Segregation Summary*)

ten of the twenty-seven prison homicides in TDC occurred in the administrative segregation blocks.[53]

Prison and state officials are committed to this lock down strategy for problem prisoners. Accordingly, the state has constructed a new prison unit in which five hundred cells are devoted to administrative segregation. This unit, named the Michael Unit and opened in late 1987, is modeled after the high-security federal facility at Marion, Illinois. The lock-down strategy, which guided construction of the Michael Unit, represents the direction TDC has taken in controlling high-risk prisoners.

Many prisoners sense that the general procedural changes in TDC have had an equalizing or leveling effect, in addition to making them feel safer. That is, the mandated standardization of how prisoners are to be treated by staff means that many prisoners have lost the informal perks that they sometimes received in the past. These prisoners are not former BTs or other elites but rather the majority of prisoners, who today, as in the past, dependably work in one of TDC's industries or service areas. These men want to do their time and be left alone. Their inclination to stay out of trouble and do their work was in the past the basis for a kind of entitlement. Their compliant behavior defined them in the eyes of officials as good convicts who deserved special consideration from time to time. Accordingly, many received little favors and rewards, which officers in the past had had great discretion to dispense. Given the current limitations on staff discretion, however, good convicts are less likely to receive special treatment and favoritism.[54] As one longtime prisoner commented: "Fifty inmates out there [are] just waiting to see the administration show me the smallest favoritism so they can file a grievance and keep [the officer] busy all day . . . I think that's one of the bad losses in the *Ruiz* decree . . . Now everybody gets to do the same thing all the time. It's a flat effect . . . It's been stagnated because of equality." This prisoner, like many others, underscores that the present official universalism in TDC has had a cost. The so-called good convicts must today do without the personal and informal advantages that they once gained from "keeping their business straight." This subtle loss is magnified by the fact that, in the new, due process prison environment, problem inmates seem to have been almost elevated in status. Many regular prisoners note and regret that these "shitheads" receive not only the same benefits compliant prisoners receive but more staff attention as well.

Conclusion

The immediate consequences of decree implementation were disorganization and, eventually, considerable violence. In early 1983, the court-ordered reforms dissolved the inmate power structure that had for so long been controlled and defined by the authorities. Dominant convicts soon emerged and filled the authority vacuum left by the building tenders and by a seemingly powerless security force. The transition in control precipitated a crisis in self-protection. While some inmates succumbed to the advances of the stronger aggressive prisoners, others secured weapons. Weapons were increasingly involved in disputes, and few felt safe behind the walls.

These conditions offered fertile ground for the growth of prison gangs. A more wide-open prison and great uncertainty meant that there was opportunity and need for collective action. The gangs that emerged have been responsible for a disproportionate amount of inmate violence. Then, in late 1985, prison officials began a program of locking down for indefinite periods all prisoners defined as gang affiliated or assaultive. According to prisoners and staff, this lock-down strategy was the major reason the prison has become a safer place.

The extensive use of administrative segregation, plus the discovery by the staff that they had not, in fact, lost all power to punish prisoners, produced a marked reduction in deaths and injury among inmates. The prison organization by 1986 was adapting to the reforms and reestablishing order. In the final chapter we will consider the nature of that new prison order.

8

A New Prison Order

Let me state clearly the facts of the Ruiz *case. The lawsuit is
over . . . We must get in compliance as quickly as possible. We
have no choice.*   —TEXAS GOVERNOR BILL CLEMENTS, 1987[1]

WE BEGAN this book on the premise that examining the judicial
transformation of the Texas prison system could shed light on
key questions about the process and consequences of prison reform
litigation: Why did Texas prison officials resist the court's intervention such that implementation was so drawn out and costly in human and financial terms? What was the course of litigated reform in
Texas prisons and how did change affect relations? What does the
post-litigation social order look like in Texas, and is it really different from the pre-litigation order? To address these questions, we
have analyzed the dismantling and the rebuilding of the Texas Department of Corrections in the wake of a reform decree handed down
by Federal Judge William W. Justice.

In this final chapter we offer a conceptual model of TDC's reform
experience, a model that summarizes that experience and provides
answers to each of the above questions. The model, presented in
Table 12, consists of three social orders that Texas prisons, their
staffs, and their prisoners have experienced over the past few decades.[2] Specifically, TDC has moved from a *repressive order* (the prelitigation period) through a *legalistic order* (the period of initial decree and compliance pressure) and into a *bureaucratic order* (the
emergent "new order").

As Table 12 indicates, these orders vary considerably in terms of
prison structures and relations. As court intervention prompted
compliance through legal pressure and a new administration, prison
organization became more formalized and rule driven. These changes
doomed the traditional TDC practices that had supported and defined repressive order. The subsequent legalistic order enhanced
compliance but produced social disorganization. Specifically, a more
formal organizational structure demoralized the staff because it, by
design, limited their actions. At the same time, the new structure
seemed to free prisoners to flaunt efforts to control them. Today, as

Table 12 *Model of Litigated Reform in TDC and Variations in Major Structural Dimensions*

Dimensions	*Repressive Order* (Before 1982)	*Legalistic Order* (1982–1985)	*Bureaucratic Order* (After 1985)
Primary objective of prison administration	Control; discipline	Constitutional legality	Control within judicially approved parameters
Legitimacy of prison actions	Tradition; management personality	Procedural fairness	Procedural fairness
Nature of rules	Many, but weakly binding on officials	Elaborate; strict accountability	Elaborate; tempered accountability
Official discretion and decision making	Pervasive discretion; ad hoc decision making	Very limited discretion; highly centralized decision making; narrow delegation of authority	Some increase in discretion and delegation of authority; much centralization remains
Prisoner control structure Rewards	Informal rewards extensive; important for control	Informal rewards essentially eliminated	Informal rewards very limited

Punishment	Informal, diverse; frequent force and coercion sanctioned officially	Formalized; force strictly limited; staff uncertainty	Formalized controls skillfully used by staff; "legalistic repression"
Prisoner-prisoner relations	Dominance of mass by officially co-opted elites; fear of elites; minorities doubly subordinate	Elite co-operation eliminated; new groups/gangs; rise in racial tensions; fear of inmate aggression	Aggressive prisoners locked down; less fear of aggression; gangs and racial tensions persist
Officer-officer relations	Pervasive guard subculture; personalized interaction, promotion; line-administrative values overlap greatly	Guard subculture dissolved; interaction and promotions highly formalized; line-administrative values do not overlap	Guard work guided by bureaucratic rules and values; line-administrative values overlap somewhat
Institutional relations of court and prison	Little court intervention; little conflict in relations; law subordinate to order in prison	Extensive court intervention; much conflict in relations; order subordinate to law	Reduced court intervention; little conflict in relations due to compliance; order achieved within "letter of the law"

we will show, much of this disorganization has been resolved with the emergence of a bureaucratic order.

Repressive Order and the Primacy of Control

Although Table 12 describes the entire period prior to 1982 as reflective of repressive order, the description applies most appropriately to the period between 1947 and 1981. While Texas prisons before 1947 contained many of the elements of repressive order, they had limited organization, suffered massive neglect, and lacked stability. Beyond a legislative desire that Texas prisons cost as little as possible, there was no strong principle or person to impose a definable order on them. The prisons were essentially anarchies in which state officials and even prison managers largely abdicated responsibility.

Texas prison conditions in the first half of this century were so bad that the regimes of Ellis, Beto, and Estelle, though authoritarian, stood out in sharp, positive relief. Those powerful directors and their staffs, over a thirty-year period, developed and maintained a management style which epitomized a repressive order. That style of management produced in TDC a level of control, stability, and productivity widely known and envied by other state correctional agencies, but it was also a style that carried considerable human costs for prisoners.

In 1947, the prison board hired O. B. Ellis, the man who began the refinement of TDC's repressive order. His success over the next dozen years produced a favorable national, as well as state, reputation for the agency. During his tenure, the officer subculture that controlled key staff behavior began to emerge. That subculture turned the security force, especially the middle and upper ranks, into a "family" operation based on loyalty, trust, and informal networks. Control and order were paramount. To this end, Ellis systematized disciplinary procedures (punishments) on the one hand and increased inmate programs (rewards) on the other. These changes, coupled with agricultural reforms, produced greater economic efficiency and helped limit violence. Throughout this period, Ellis' skills in dealing with the legislature and the media muted criticism and largely precluded outside interference.

George J. Beto continued and extended the Ellis program. Beto, like Ellis, tightly controlled prison policy and unit-level operations. His penchant for showing up at any hour on a unit to check on staff and talk to prisoners earned him general respect and a nickname (Walking George); his authority was augmented by this personal style of management. Beto's political skills also helped ensure that the prison system enjoyed much autonomy from legislative scrutiny. After all, he could point to a system that boasted minimal prisoner violence, one widely known as "the prison system that worked."

When W. J. Estelle, Jr., became TDC director after Beto's retirement in 1972, he largely maintained the traditional prison operations that were so widely approved. Like his predecessors, Estelle projected a powerful, charismatic persona; he was also a master of public and legislative relations. Although during his administration a number of forces (several issue-specific lawsuits, overcrowding, charges of brutality, and incipient pressure from reform groups and legislators) began to undermine TDC's traditional approach, Estelle and his staff were relatively successful at keeping inmates submissive, violence low, and TDC's reputation intact.

In each of these regimes, staff attitudes and behaviors toward each other and prisoners were consistent with a repressive order. Legitimacy was based on tradition and the personal authority of strong directors and key unit personnel; the management objectives of each were essentially the same—order and control. While there were rules to guide official behavior, they were not especially binding on officials as long as those officials could maintain productivity and control. Consequently, individual officers had much discretion in the treatment and control of prisoners. Even after improvements were wrought by Ellis and his successors, official actions were often idiosyncratic. Coercion, both psychological and physical, was routine and central to repressive order. As we previously noted, the use of force by officers did more than foster prisoner obedience; it also indicated a good officer. This valuation of personal toughness on the part of officers was a key feature of the officer subculture that existed on each unit into the early 1980s in TDC.

Also central to TDC's repressive order, especially on the large units for tough prisoners, was the building tender system. This institutionalized use of inmate-elites to control other prisoners had existed throughout most of the twentieth century. While there were always abuses of authority by these elites, there appear to have been variations in the level of that abuse related to officer-inmate ratios. In the 1940s, when the prison system grew rapidly, yet added few officers, reliance on BTs grew; greater official reliance on building tenders led to greater abuse of other prisoners by these elites simply because official supervision was low to nonexistent. Significantly, the same scenario occurred in the 1970s when the inmate population grew tremendously and the security staff increased only slightly. Line officers again became excessively dependent on poorly supervised BTs. The result in both periods was greater abuse by these inmate-guards. Interestingly, between these periods, during the more stable Beto era (1962–1972), BTs were somewhat better controlled, relatively less free to abuse prisoners.

This recurrent problem with the BTs illustrates a more fundamental point about the style of control and the organizational structure in Texas prisons prior to court intervention. Namely, the prison operated on the basis of a highly personalized infrastructure. Individual reputations, convict sense, control skill, and connections were paramount in all relations among officials and between officials and prisoners. Under stable organizational conditions and limited growth (e.g., the Beto period), this personalized infrastructure could effectively guide the controlling of men (officers and prisoners) and the handling of routine fiscal and political accounting required of a state agency. But pressures during the Estelle administration, especially population growth, began to stretch that personalized infrastructure to its limits. Evidence that the system was badly overextended (e.g., overreliance on BTs, loose accounting practices) made the system even more vulnerable to outside criticisms and, especially, to the courts' tests of constitutionality.

Those tests were not forcefully applied until the *Ruiz* case went to trial in 1978. Through three previous decades, characteristic of repressive order, the courts either would not hear prisoner cases or focused on narrowly drawn legal issues. This judicial inaction or reticence gave tacit approval to Texas prison practices and implied that law was, in a sense, subordinate to prison order. This situation changed drastically, however, as Judge Justice moved TDC from a repressive order toward a legalistic order.

Legalistic Order and the Rule of Law

The *Ruiz v. Estelle* trial and the reform mandates laid down by Judge Justice in 1981 did not immediately bring about change in fundamental TDC operations, despite the appointment of a special master to oversee compliance. For unit staff members through 1981 and into 1982, the status quo remained largely intact. Though old control and operating procedures had been ruled unlawful, new procedures remained ill defined or irrelevant on the units while prison, state, and court officials negotiated or contested various issues.

Even when consent decrees on some issues were signed by state officials, unit staff and even central office administrators in TDC continued to operate in the old ways. After all, Estelle was still the director, and the new procedures seemed to many officers to be important only to the court. This official resistance, central to understanding the Texas prison reform experience, derived from a deep commitment by TDC officials to a management and control system that had become, over at least three decades, not only legitimized but also, in some respects, romanticized; it was solidified on the units through the socialization of staff to subcultural values. This commitment was such that traditional TDC modes of operation were, in the minds of officials at all levels, essentially unassailable; those officials could simply not find acceptable any other way of handling prisoners or running a prison, particularly if that other way was being imposed by an outside agent, the court.

It is important to note, however, that not all points of Judge Justice's decree were equally resisted. On such issues as medical care, crowding, or sanitation, for example, there was relatively little resistance to change. Prison and state officials generally agreed that these were problem areas. The resistance came instead on those points in the decree that directly questioned the dominance of officers and their discretion to maintain control in ways they deemed effective. In short, traditional dominance and discretion were considered critical to the maintenance of order.

Although inmates during this time sensed and seized some new freedoms, they were regularly reminded that the old ways were not quite gone. Official resistance to reform meant that traditional methods of control were still being used though somewhat less openly. Consequently, in the period from 1981 to 1982, the prison system drifted between a suddenly unconstitutional past and an uncertain future defined for staffers only by distant, negotiated settlements by lawyers. Incipient policies growing out of those settlements lacked legitimacy for most unit-level officers, who felt little obligation to carry out those new policies.

After this brief transition period, a legalistic order emerged full-blown when prison officials finally embraced and then imposed downwardly structural changes to comply with the court's mandates. The board of corrections took the first step in this regard. In late 1983, the board accepted Estelle's resignation and declared that the staff would strictly abide by court proscriptions, especially those involving the use of force.

The major move in the erection of a legalistic order, however, was the appointment in mid-1984 of Raymond Procunier to the director's post. Procunier's board-imposed agenda was to bring TDC into compliance, to create as rapidly as possible a constitutional operation. With no concern for or commitment to TDC traditions, he declared that the basis for future operations would be constitutional legality as defined by the court. To ensure compliance, Procunier centralized decision making. This move meant a rapid and immediate expansion of TDC's bureaucracy. Rules and accompanying paper work proliferated. The purpose of this formalization by headquarters was to homogenize operations and to maximize compliance by holding staff members strictly accountable for their actions.[3]

Formalizing procedures severely limited official discretion in rewarding and punishing prisoners. New rules specifically prohibited most traditional control devices, particularly use of force except in very specific circumstances and reliance on building tenders. Faced with emerging policies that were contrary to traditional practices and with scrutiny from the central administration via Internal Affairs, many officers experienced great uncertainty. Security staff morale, quite high under earlier regimes, plunged. Many officers expressed their uncertainty and disaffection by limiting their efforts to control prisoners at all. Clearly, the new operational guidelines greatly reduced the power of staff from the wardens to the lowest cellblock officers.

The centralization and accountability did more than redistribute power among prison officials. These changes also altered the informal power relations within the inmate population. Aware of court-defined limits on official control, of officer uncertainty, and of the elimination of the building tenders, many prisoners began to exploit opportunities to extend their dominance over other prisoners. The result was an expansion of protection rackets, drug trafficking, prostitution, and prisoner-prisoner aggression. Racial animosities, formally squelched under a repressive order, now rose to the surface. Growing fear and racial tension among prisoners, in turn, became both causes and effects of the growth in prison gangs in TDC.

This general disorganization in the prisoner social system, plus a lack of confidence in official protection, especially through 1984 and 1985, greatly heightened fear and increased violence among prisoners. The sense of impending danger from riot, gang attack, or individual assault prompted a tremendous rise in the number of prisoners making or securing some type of weapon, primarily for self-protection. The use of many of those weapons created an unprecedented wave of violence in TDC. Over six hundred nonfatal stabbings and fifty-two inmate-inmate homicides occurred during 1984 and 1985.

The rise of a legalistic order, where control seemed to many officers to be much less important than the promulgation of new, more constitutional procedures, dramatically altered relations between and among staff and prisoners. For staff, a new meritocracy greatly undermined the personal network and traditional values that had sustained the officer subculture. An officer's personal ability to judge and deal with prisoners was no longer valuable in a system driven by paper work, computer files, specialists, and a burgeoning clerical staff.

Generally, new standards for work and rewards on the job had a leveling effect among officers by significantly altering the bases for staff promotions and co-worker esteem. For example, exemplars of the traditional officer subculture were fired and disciplined, while new officers who were more comfortable with paper work were promoted. Old loyalties to supervisors, to other officers, and to the agency were deeply eroded, especially among veteran staff. The rapid influx of new officers, many of whom showed little deference to ranking officers, further aided the erosion of traditional subcultural values.

A leveling effect also became apparent among prisoners. As the building tenders slid from their former elite status, others rose to positions of dominance. At the same time, many regular prisoners, who had in the past benefited from official discretion to reward good behavior, found that limited official discretion no longer permitted the special considerations that they had often enjoyed. They found that the new universalism meant they were being treated no differently than the "shitheads," or problem prisoners.

Bureaucratic Order and Legalistic Repression

In his account of the transition of Illinois' Stateville prison, James B. Jacobs notes that, after much turmoil and violence, the prison eventually reached a period of stability.[4] A similar stage was reached in TDC in the years after 1985. The basis for that stability was the gradual emergence of a bureaucratic order.

During the mid-1980s, despite low morale, uncertainty, and apparent inability to restore order, TDC officials at all levels were, nonetheless, adapting, if not always willingly, to the new, court-approved operational policies. This adaptation to and eventual skillful use of the new rules to achieve official objectives is the essence of the bureaucratic prison order. In short, instead of uncertainty and resis-

tance, TDC officials began to adopt the new methods to achieve traditional ends.

While prisoner control seemed to recede in importance under the
legalistic order, it certainly never disappeared as an important objec-
tive. By late 1985, the fear, violence, and deaths in TDC and the predictable pressure from many quarters for officials to "do something"
forced a reassertion of that control agenda, this time within the parameters set by the court. As we noted in the last chapter, TDC in-
augurated a massive lock down of actually and potentially assaultive
prisoners. This move helped to raise staff morale and reduce fear
among prisoners. Both groups welcomed the lock down, since the
prison environment had become extremely stressful for all. The lock
down communicated that the administration was now interested in
something besides mere compliance. More important, it communicated that the administration had at its disposal and would use legal
means of punishing and controlling prisoners. This new approach to
dealing with prisoners gradually filtered down to the unit level, and
a new control structure began to emerge.

Of course, an important element in that new control structure was
a much larger guard force. By 1987, TDC had been able to meet prescribed staffing levels in almost every area. Recruiting diligence by
TDC, aided by a downturn in the Texas economy, produced through
1986 and 1987 enough people to meet unit needs despite continued
turnover. Simply having officers everywhere helped thwart prisoner
aggression and restore official control.

But a larger force alone was not enough to affect the greatly increased stability and safety that characterized Texas prisons in 1986
and 1987. The difference between these years and the crisis period of
1984 and 1985 was that supervisors and officers had learned how
to use new policies to their advantage. With time, the once new,
unfamiliar rules, procedures, and paper work became routine, and
supervisors, like the staff, learned what would work in the new bureaucratic environment. As newly promoted supervisors gained confidence, they became more able (and perhaps willing) to guide their
subordinates. And most remaining veterans adapted to the new
work demands, albeit in many cases grudgingly. At the same time,
new officers, with little sense of the "old days," had less to overcome
and adapted easily. Regardless of background, officers became more
certain about how to do their work.

Specifically, the security staff learned how to use the sanctions legally available to them for inmate control, especially the write up or
report of rule violation. Prisoners in TDC today believe that the

chance of getting written up for a minor violation is much greater than it was in the early 1980s, and most are aware that these "tickets" can affect their good time and eventual release. By varying how strictly they apply the rules, officers can control the behavior of most prisoners through threat, frustration, and harassment. The result can be as effective as the old tune-up or ass whipping.

Because of the extensive use of tickets and the sheer number of guards today, TDC prisoners perceive that the officers are very much in control. That perception is bolstered by the availability and ready use of administrative segregation to control troublesome prisoners. Today, ad. seg. contains thousands of prisoners whom officials have designated violence prone, gang affiliated, or unwilling to follow prison routines. They remain there indefinitely, and at this writing, some have been locked in an ad. seg. cell for years.

Though officers acknowledge that physical coercion is outlawed except under the strictest circumstances, they have discovered that applying the "letter of the rule" to control prisoners can work. Significantly, this is how officials have resolved the dilemma of law versus order, of maintaining control over inmates while not infringing on their rights under the law. By operating formally and universalistically, even when rules are contradictory or when minor injustices are obvious, staff can be punitive on solid, legal grounds. This tactic is a kind of legalistic repression. Of course, many officers do, at times, bend rules either to punish a prisoner or to help him. But the point remains, officers have become more confident and proactive with respect to the rules, even those rules designed to benefit or protect prisoners.

As the bureaucratic order has solidified in TDC, prison officials have regained at least some degree of discretion and autonomy. Under legalistic order, official discretion was highly constrained; only court-defined and supervised operations were acceptable. As TDC has approached compliance, however, especially on control issues, the court has accorded greater autonomy to TDC's central office. While monitoring continued into early 1988, court officials had become much less aggressive in their oversight of TDC operations.

In a like manner, top TDC administrators, who in the early 1980s centralized policy decisions because unit managers were not trusted, have today returned considerable discretion to those (in most cases new) unit managers. Indeed, Director James Lynaugh, appointed to the top TDC post in early 1987 after serving as acting director for several months, has declared that he is returning considerable decision-making authority to the unit wardens. As an accountant with little prison experience, he stated that his concern would be with fiscal matters and that he would let unit officials handle security. This posture reflects Lynaugh's confidence (and by implication the court's) that compliance is now sufficiently institutionalized and that greater unit discretion will probably not put inmate rights in jeopardy.

Clearly, the emergent bureaucratic order, which has so altered prison relations and structures in TDC, is the result of court intervention. But has intervention actually benefited prisoners and improved the conditions of confinement as it was intended to do?

Inmate Life under Bureaucratic Order.   An important question in any reform litigation is whether the process has been in any sense a success. But defining and measuring success is a difficult business for a number of reasons, including, for example, imprecise judicial decrees, conflicting views about reforms among prison interest groups, and, perhaps most important, the problem of weighing positive outcomes (less severe punishment) against negative outcomes (more inmate violence).[5] Because of these and other complexities, there is no established methodology, no "litmus test," for judging the success of intervention.

But there is one approach to assessing the ameliorative impact of court-mandated prison reform that is reasonably straightforward and defensible: simply ask the supposed beneficiaries of litigated reform, the prisoners themselves. We used this approach to discover whether reorganization in TDC has produced real reform and improvement in the prisoners' lot.

How do TDC prisoners perceive the results of years of litigated reform (1981 through 1987)? First, most prisoners believe that TDC has not changed all that much.[6] In one sense, this is not surprising. The place is still a prison, with its routines, physical barriers, official surveillance, and deprivations. Yet, most prisoners also believe that Justice's reform decrees and TDC's ultimate, general compliance with them have made the prison a better place for the average inmate.[7] One example of that improvement is in the treatment of minorities by officials. Prisoners believe that there is somewhat less racial and ethnic discrimination in 1987 than that which occurred before 1983.

A more fundamental example of improvement, however, is the prisoners' perception that under a bureaucratic order TDC is a safer place. Not only do institutional data reveal less violence, but also inmates in 1987 perceived TDC to be a much less dangerous place compared to the late 1970s and early 1980s. Through 1985, approximately 60 percent of TDC prisoners felt that the prison was a dangerous place; for 1986 and 1987, however, that percentage drops to 36 and 28 percent, respectively. Prisoners also report that inmate-inmate aggression has declined, as has stealing by other prisoners. These perceptions underscore the fact that, while intervention may initially promote disorganization and violence, negative consequences do not necessarily become a permanent feature of the prisoners' world. That is, the paradox of reform is only paradoxical for a relatively short period.

Court intervention produced improvements in other areas of prison life as well, including better medical services, the advent of grievance and appeal procedures, full-time free-world inmate advocates on each prison unit, correctional counselors, and explicit standards to guide official discipline. These changes, as we noted above, have generally become integral, accepted parts of the prison bureaucracy. Judicial intervention has, from the prisoners' point of view, made the incarceration experience in Texas better than it had been in the past.

Court and Prison Relations under Bureaucratic Order.   Such improvements in prison conditions have affected relations between the court and the system. Under repressive order, the court was distant and conflict between these institutions over how the prisons operated was consequentially minimal. An opposite relationship was obtained under legalistic order, however. The traditional control agenda in TDC and the court's constitutional agenda directly clashed. Then, with the advent of a bureaucratic order, prison-court relations have again become less adversarial.

The course of prison-court relations in Texas parallels a national trend. That is, having moved from a hands-off philosophy to activism through the 1960s and 1970s, courts again appear less inclined to intervene in prisons. To a number of commentators, this last is a welcomed trend.[8] Samuel J. Brakel, for example, believes that the "litigation revolution" has been excessive and that courts should be limiting their involvement in prison operations. He writes: "That before the court-ordered revolution many of this country's prisons were in deplorable shape does not justify, in my view, wholesale and continuous intervention that disregards the undesirable side effects of the reform mandate, and the alteration in normal lines of government authority and responsibility that accompanies the process. Rather than unequivocally endorse the revolution and its unabated continuation, I would conclude that the courts have gone far enough fast enough."[9]

A reduction in court activism has been noted, and frequently lamented, by many scholars. They sense that the court is returning to a hands off doctrine in which courts either fail to intervene on behalf of prisoners or rule in favor of prison officials.[10] For example, a federal judge recently ruled against prisoners in *Bruscino v. Carlson*,[11] upholding as a prime control device the use of the long-term, total lock down of prisoners at the federal prison at Marion, Illinois.[12]

Several reasons exist for this generally "less-intrusive" posture of the courts today. First, the increasingly conservative political philosophy of the 1980s has dampened judicial interest in questioning prison authorities.[13] Second, reduced court activism may reflect the fact that today there are fewer young lawyers interested in prisoner rights and that there is less money to support their efforts.[14]

The third, and perhaps most important, reason for diminished court activism is that prisons have simply gotten better at operating constitutionally. Prison administrators have seen the legal reform handwriting on the wall and have increasingly accepted judicially defined guidelines on caring for and controlling prisoners. Even administrators of prison systems not subjected to far-reaching decrees have learned vicariously from the experiences of others.[15] In this connection, Allen Breed, who has served in both state and federal correctional posts and as special master in prison reform lawsuits, suggests that the *Ruiz* case has been particularly instructive. "Most [prison administrators] have moved away from the macho position of having to defend themselves in court and want to be a part of the solution. We are consistently seeing more consent decrees than remedial orders. Texas is the last large system for a remedial order. If the courts could win in Texas, as big and powerful and independent as it was, they [administrators] said, 'We'd better think about that in terms of future intervention.'"[16]

After years of intense litigation in *Ruiz*, Judge Justice seems to be following this national trend of withdrawal in Texas, largely because of compliance in TDC on almost all aspects of the decree. Compliance has progressed to the point that the court today is more apt to view prison administrators as cooperative professionals than as obstructionists. In turn, the court is less inclined to scrutinize every official action and policy.[17] In fact, in April 1987, Judge Justice went so far as to commend in writing the legislature, the governor, and TDC's administration on the progress made in compliance. Monitor reports and the judge's own observations on a tour of three TDC units in early 1987 documented that progress. Since Judge Justice does not have a reputation of compromising his principles, this attitude must be due to real improvements instead of to a lowering of judicial expectations.

The only major decree in *Ruiz* that continues to call for court scrutiny concerns overcrowding. And even here the court has taken a somewhat less combative posture toward TDC and the state. For example, in the spring of 1987, Judge Justice threatened to fine the state $24 million per month if progress was not made on the crowding problem. Subsequent efforts by the state to remedy the problem, however, led the judge to suspend the fine, citing the state's "good faith" efforts to solve the crowding problem.[18]

Conclusion

Our analysis of litigated reform in the Texas prison system describes the course and consequences of that process. We have shown how traditional structures and, especially, subcultural values prompted resistance to the reforms and, in turn, extended the process. We have also detailed, in terms of varying social orders, the stages through which TDC has passed and the structural conditions that existed within each stage. Finally, we have characterized the nature of Texas prisons as the court withdraws. Today, what we have termed bureaucratic order prevails in TDC.

The route to that order has been protracted and painful. But, although the court's intervention initially produced tremendous disorder, stability has reemerged. Today, both the keepers and the kept have made an uneasy peace with each other and with the new procedures. For their part, guards are no longer a relatively elite force manifesting subcultural solidarity and capriciously dominating prisoners; they have become bureaucrats.[19] Because inmate rights are more readily recognized today and because current control mechanisms are not as pervasive or penetrating as they were before intervention, prisoners do enjoy somewhat more freedom. But they have learned that the staff can and will levy lawful and generally effective sanctions. In short, organizational expectations have become clearer for all parties, and Texas prisons have become more lawful and predictable.

The transformation has placed the Texas system in the mainstream of institutional corrections in the United States. No longer does TDC reflect the image of the Texas cowboy: independent, sure of traditional values, and against outside intervention. Indeed, western boots and hats are less often the preferred attire, and, in 1987, TDC for the first time since its inception thirty-five years ago canceled the famous Texas Prison Rodeo. Today, the managerial image in TDC is more that of the corporate man or woman, an image consistent with a bureaucratic order. Administrators in TDC are particularly sensitive to judicial, media, and political interests, managing

themselves and their agency accordingly. They are more universalistic and open to professionalism and training.[20]

As a microcosm of changes in other state prison systems, the TDC
experience suggests several broader conclusions about litigated reform and prisons today. One conclusion is simply that, while court
intervention can bring about very significant improvements in prison
conditions, even when actively resisted by prison officials, those improvements fall short of some ideal notion of "justice." In *Ruiz*, prisoner plaintiffs and prison officials appealed to justice, arguing for
their own version of this illusive ideal. Prisoners argued as a class that
they were denied rights and fair treatment, while officials claimed
that TDC's particularistic approach afforded individual prisoners the
justice each deserved. There is no question as to who won the case;
clearly, the prisoners did. The result was a fairer environment in
which prisoners feel safer, enjoy (at least technically) the major
elements of due process,[21] and receive care defined by external or
free-world standards. But, as we have stressed, the letter, rather than
the spirit, of justice tends to prevail. Abuse, indifference, and injury
still occur.[22]

One reason that litigation is limited in its efforts to extend justice
to prisoners is that judicial reforms are self-limiting; they address
only selected prison issues. Even in totality-of-circumstances cases,
such as *Ruiz*, rulings on a given issue (e.g., crowding) have to be
translated into specific operational terms (e.g., 60 square feet per
prisoner). Once a remedy has been put into operation, it only defines
minimally acceptable actions for prison officials. Those officials
need go no further in compliance than these court-defined minima,
and there is often little internal pressure to do so.

There are also realities in the prison enterprise and in society that
blunt reform efforts. One of these is that prisons are unique worlds,
and that uniqueness makes applying social values through litigation
difficult. Prisons contain hundreds, often thousands, of prisoners,
housed involuntarily in dense populations. Often large and always
coercive, prisons aggregate a high proportion of "the mad and the
bad," among whom racial conflict is likely and violence is routine.
These prison constants make achieving justice through due process,
equality, freedom from arbitrary punishment, and abuse even more
difficult than achieving it in the larger society.[23] The level of state
resources may also limit the quality and the extent of reform. In
many states, including Texas in the 1980s, limited funds mean that,
when the state allots finite resources to comply with court decrees
in one part of the prison system, other needs within that system (or

elsewhere in the state) may suffer. Because of these realities, court-induced progress in prisons is usually slow, uneven, frequently disappointing, and sometimes more suggested than real.[24]

In the same way that litigation has moved TDC into the correctional mainstream, it has served to homogenize institutional corrections in general. Evidence on litigated reform in other state prisons suggests that prison officials across the country, like Texas prison managers, recognize the potential applicability of the same case law to their own, often similar, situations. Having experienced or observed the power of the court to intervene, state prison officials tend to employ operational guidelines for the care and custody of prisoners that have been directly or indirectly court approved. Indeed, the bureaucratic order in Texas is probably the national norm for prison management styles, prisoner-staff relations, and relations between prisons and courts.

A final conclusion is that the litigation-induced bureaucratic order signals not only a withdrawal of the court but also a return of prison control to prison officials. This return of control is fostered by diminished media and legislative attention to prison systems that seem to have achieved stability and legality. Prison officials are thus freer to make their own decisions about how prisoners will be handled, as long as official actions meet minimum constitutional standards and legislative guidelines.

Certainly, regaining autonomy does not mean that officials in TDC or other reformed prisons will move back toward the management and control systems that existed in earlier decades. Indeed, there are at least two reasons to expect that such a retreat is unlikely. First, constitutional standards, once formalized into bureaucratic rules, tend to become legitimate in their own right, accepted by staff as appropriate guides for behavior. Self-perpetuating and conservative prison bureaucracies will outlast personnel who come and go. The second reason is that the current large body of case law concerning prison conditions and prisoner treatment both educates and threatens administrators who would employ policies widely recognized as unconstitutional. We may assume that prison officials will operate in terms of current judicial expectations.

But there is a potential danger in this trend toward greater official autonomy for managers of now-reformed prisons. The danger is that, over time, official autonomy may lead to institutions that are legal but lack justice, humaneness, and hope. A bureaucratic order certainly carries the potential for such an outcome if we do not hold prison managers and staff routinely accountable. The danger is well illustrated by the Texas experience. When outside observers (courts, media, legislators, or citizens) did not closely attend to what was going on in TDC over a thirty-year period, they eventually found that administrative concerns for expediency and control had created unacceptable prison conditions. With little or no outside scrutiny, TDC officials operated according to traditional standards of what they thought prisoners deserved, standards that were probably deemed acceptable in society decades ago. Those traditional standards, however, were found by the court to be unacceptable in the 1980s. Clearly, legal and political definitions of how prisoners should be treated had changed; TDC had not.

Through litigation, Texas prisons have been brought into accord with current standards of prisoner treatment. But, should those standards continue to change, there is no guarantee that prison managers on their own will change their practices accordingly. Consequently, outside agencies must ensure that prison structures and practices remain in tune with evolving standards of prisoner treatment.[25]

The need for outsiders to maintain an interest in the quality of prison life in the future is heightened by the ever-greater use of incarceration to punish criminals in this country. Most states, including Texas, face the joint problems of meeting the public's demand to lock up more criminals and the court's requirement that prisons not be overcrowded or limited in services. While diversion and early parole options help to control crowding pressure and costs, citizens want serious offenders put away; legislators are similarly inclined to equate incarceration and punishment.[26] As a result, Texas, along with California and other large states, has opted to build more prisons.[27] Indeed, current plans call for adding over twenty thousand new beds by 1991 at which time the TDC population will exceed sixty thousand prisoners. There is little doubt that these prisons, and very likely more, will be built. The new units will not all be maximum security; many will be "reintegration" units designed to help, through education and training, less-serious offenders avoid returning to prison. What these and other Texas prisons will be like, however, is an open question. The answer lies in time and in society's recognition that extensive use of incarceration, together with ignorance of what that incarceration entails, is a formula for disaster.

Notes

1. Prison Order and Litigated Reform

1. J. K. Weinberg, "The Bureaucratic Judiciary: The Future of Court-Ordered Change," *Law and Human Behavior* 6 (1982): 169–181.

2. See J. K. Lieberman, *The Litigious Society.*

3. W. B. Turner, "Why Prisoners Sue," *Harvard Law Review* 92 (1979): 612–663. See also J. Thomas and A. Aylward, "Trends in Prisoner Civil Rights Litigation: A Preliminary Overview," 1983 paper presented in part at the Law and Society Association annual meetings, Toronto, 1982; J. Thomas, D. Keeler, and K. Harris, "Issues and Misconceptions in Prisoner Litigation: A Critical View," *Criminology* 24 (November): 775–797.

4. By the mid-1980s at least forty-five states have had some part of their prison systems under some type of federal court order (telephone interview with the National Prison Project of the American Civil Liberties Union, Washington, D.C.).

5. J. DiIulio, "Prison Discipline and Prison Reform," *Public Interest* 89 (Fall 1987): 71–90.

6. Accounts of the impact of litigated reform at specific prison sites include M. K. Harris and D. P. Spiller, *After Decision: Implementation of Judicial Decrees in Correctional Settings;* A. Champagne and K. Haas, "The Impact of *Johnson vs. Avery* on Prison Administration," *Tennessee Law Review* 43 (1977): 275–306; Harvard Law Review, "Implementation Problems in Institutional Reform," *Harvard Law Review* 91 (1977): 428–463; P. Baker et al., "Judicial Intervention in Corrections: The California Experience—An Empirical Study," *UCLA Law Review* 20 (1973): 452–580; C. Stastny and G. Tyrnauer, *Who Rules the Joint?* chap. 8; Harvard Center for Criminal Justice, "Judicial Intervention in Prison Discipline," *Journal of Criminal Law, Criminology, and Police Science* 18 (1972): 200–228. For a general discussion of the impact of litigated reform on institutional corrections, see J. Jacobs, "The Prisoner's Rights Movement and Its Impact, 1960–1980," in *Crime and Justice: An Annual Review of Research*, vol. 2,

ed. N. Morris and M. Tonry, and R. Morgan and A. Bronstein, "Prisoners and the Courts: The U.S. Experience," in *Prisons and Accountability*, ed. M. Maguire, J. Vagg, and R. Morgan. For another account of the Texas experience, see S. Martin and S. Eckland-Olson, *Texas Prisons: The Walls Came Tumbling Down.*

7. M. Feely and R. Hanson, "What We Know, Think We Know, and Would Like to Know about the Impact of Court Orders on Prison Conditions and Jail Crowding," paper prepared for the meeting of the Working Group on Jail and Prison Crowding, Committee on Research on Law Enforcement and the Administration of Justice, National Academy of Sciences, Chicago, October 15–16, 1986.

8. *Ruiz v. Estelle,* 503 F. Supp. 1265, 1277–1279 (S.D. Texas 1980).

9. This dilemma is pervasive in the criminal justice system of a democratic society. See H. Packer, "Two Models of the Criminal Process," *University of Pennsylvania Law Review* 113 (1964): 84–100. On this dilemma in police work, see J. Skolnick, *Justice without Trial,* and, in courts, see A. Blumberg, *Criminal Justice.*

10. In the mid-1970s, the order and efficiency of TDC were featured in a series of articles appearing in *Corrections Magazine* 6 (March 1978). After the reforms were underway, a widely read state magazine carried an article critical of those reforms (see D. Reavis, "How They Ruined Our Prisons," *Texas Monthly* [May 1985]: 152–159, 232–246). Besides periodic coverage in other state newspapers, a national newsmagazine devoted several pages to the changes that TDC was undergoing. (See "Inside America's Toughest Prison," *Newsweek,* 6 October 1986, 46–61.)

11. The reference to prisoners as slaves appears in a nineteenth-century Supreme Court ruling, *Ruffin v. Commonwealth,* 62 Va. 790 (1871). For a more extensive overview of the development of the prisoners' rights movement, see Jacobs, "The Prisoners' Rights Movement and Its Impact, 1960–1980," in *Crime and Justice: An Annual Review of Research,* ed. N. Morris and M. Tonry, pp. 429–470. This section benefited from research material provided by Richard Hawkins and Geoffrey Alpert.

12. See K. Haas, "Judicial Politics and Correctional Reform: An Analysis of the Decline of the 'Hands Off' Doctrine," *Detroit College of Law Review* 4 (1977): 795–831. See also I. Robbins, "The Cry of *Wolfish* in the Federal Courts: The Future of Federal Judicial Intervention in Prison Administration," *Journal of Criminal Law and Criminology* 71 (1980): 211–225.

13. As Sherman and Hawkins note, "Concerning correctional conditions, Romilly's advice to Bentham still applies: the public 'does not care tuppence' about prison conditions" (M. Sherman and G. Hawkins, *Imprisonment in America: Choosing the Future,* p. 125).

14. Illustrations of these prison conditions are found in the prison cases litigated through the 1960s and 1970s. Those cases are discussed in A. Bronstein, "Prisoners' Rights: A History," in *Legal Rights of Prisoners,* ed. G. Alpert, pp. 19–46.

15. An excellent review of literature and discussion of staff abuse of in-

mates are found in L. Bowker, "The Victimization of Prisoners by Staff Members," in *The Dilemmas of Punishment*, ed. K. Haas and G. Alpert.

16. See J. Jacobs, *Stateville: The Penitentiary in Mass Society*; R. March, *Alabama Bound: Forty-Five Years inside a Prison System*; T. Murton and J. Hyams, *Accomplices to the Crime: The Arkansas Prison Scandal*.

17. See G. Sykes, *Society of Captives*.

18. See R. Emerson, "Power Dependence Relations," *American Sociological Review* 27 (February 1962): 31–40, for a theoretical discussion of the links between power and dependence in social relationships.

19. See Sykes, *Society of Captives*.

20. This point was initially developed by R. Cloward, "Social Control in Prison," in *Prison within Society*, ed. L. Hazelrigg.

21. According to "deprivation" theory, or "indigenous" theory, the inmate social system emerges in response to deprivations. The initial statement of this theory is by S. Messinger and G. Sykes, "The Inmate Social System," in *Theoretical Studies in Social Organization of the Prison*, ed. R. Cloward et al., pp. 5–19.

22. Stastny and Tyrnauer, in *Who Rules the Joint?* refer to prisons in the prelitigation era as "bicentric" in that there are only two power centers, one among prisoners in the aggregate and the other among officials in the aggregate.

23. J. Jacobs, "Race Relations and the Prisoner Subculture," in *Crime and Justice: An Annual Review of Research*, vol. 1, ed. N. Morris and M. Tonry.

24. See D. Rothman, "The Courts and Social Reform: A Postprogressive Outlook," *Law and Human Behavior* 6 (1982): 113–119.

25. *Cooper v. Pate*, 378 U.S. 546 (1964).

26. A large and diverse literature has risen to consider the consequences of intervention for the court itself as well as the propriety of that intervention. Writers uneasy about that intervention include R. Gaskins, "Second Thoughts on 'Law as an Instrument of Change,'" *Law and Human Behavior* 6 (1982): 153–168; R. Nagel, "Separation of Powers and the Scope of Federal Equitable Remedies," *Stanford Law Review* 30 (April 1978): 661–724; L. Boatwright, "Federal Courts and State Prison Reform: A Formula for Large Scale Federal Intervention into State Affairs," *Suffolk University Law Review* 14 (1980): 545–576; D. Dobray, "The Role of Special Masters in Court Ordered Institutional Reform," *Baylor Law Review* 34 (1982): 587–603; C. Diver, "The Judge as Political Powerbroker: Superintending Structural Change in Public Institutions," *Virginia Law Review* 65 (1978): 43–106; O. Fiss, "The Social and Political Foundations of Adjudication," *Law and Human Behavior* 6 (1982): 121–128. Commentators arguing in support of court intervention include Haas, "Judicial Politics and Correctional Reform"; B. Falkof, "Prisoner Representative Organizations, Prison Reform, and *Jones v. North Carolina Prisoner's Labor Union*: An Argument for Increased Court Intervention in Prison Administration," *Journal of Criminal Law and Criminology* 70 (1979): 42–56; E. Alexander, "The New Prison Administrator and the Court: New Directions in Prison Law," *Texas*

Law Review 56 (1978): 963–1008; T. Eisenberg and S. Yeazell, "The Ordinary and the Extraordinary in Institutional Litigation," *Harvard Law Review* 93 (1980): 464–517.

27. To gain judicial relief, prisoners must tie their complaints to constitutional standards or state statute. Although courts have based their intervention on several constitutional standards (e.g., due process, first amendment rights), the proscription of cruel and unusual punishment in the Eighth Amendment has been particularly important. Because the meaning of "cruel and unusual" has always been hard to define, courts have recently developed a useful definition for prison reform cases. This definition, called the "totality of conditions," permits courts to combine a large number of prison conditions that alone could not be raised to a constitutional level but when weighed together constitute intolerable living conditions. This is the approach taken by federal judges in landmark reform cases in Mississippi, Arkansas, and Alabama prisons and by Judge Justice in the recent Texas case (see I. Robbins and M. Buser, "Punitive Conditions of Prison Confinement: An Analysis of *Pugh v. Locke* and Federal Court Supervision of State Penal Administrations under the Eighth Amendment," *Stanford Law Review* [May 1977]: 893–930).

28. For a recent review of the literature on the impact of prison litigation, see Feely and Hanson, "What We Know."

29. See J. Conrad, "What Do the Undeserving Deserve?" in *Imprisonment*, ed. R. Johnson and H. Toch, pp. 303–313. A similar argument is set forth in K. Engel and S. Rothman, "Prison Violence and the Paradox of Reform," *Public Interest* (1983): 91–105. See also C. Thomas, "The Impotence of Correctional Law," in *Legal Rights of Prisoners*, ed. G. Alpert, pp. 243–260.

30. C. E. Silberman, *Criminal Violence, Criminal Justice*, p. 379.

31. For an account of how this type of disorganization of a prison led to one of the most violent incidents in American correctional history, see B. Useem, "Disorganization and the New Mexico Prison Riot of 1980," *American Sociological Review* 50 (October 1985): 677–688. For another analysis of this riot, see M. Colvin, "The 1980 New Mexico Riot," *Social Problems* 29 (1982): 449–463.

32. On this change, see H. Toch, *Peacekeeping: Police, Prison, and Violence*; H. Mattick, "The Prosaic Sources of Prison Violence," in *Criminal Behavior and Social Systems*, 2nd ed., ed. A. Guenther; Jacobs, *Stateville*.

33. See G. Alpert, B. Crouch, and R. Huff, "Prison Reform by Judicial Decree: The Unintended Consequences of *Ruiz v. Estelle*," *Justice System Journal* 9 (1984): 291–305. See also Jacobs, *Stateville*, chap. 5.

34. See Jacobs, "The Prisoners' Rights Movement and Its Impact," and L. Carroll, *Hack, Blacks, and Cons*.

35. See Jacobs, "The Prisoners' Rights Movement and Its Impact," pp. 457–463.

36. See Jacobs, *Stateville*, p. 206. For a general treatment of accountability issues, see M. Maguire, J. Vagg, and R. Morgan (eds.), *Prisons and Accountability*.

37. Several studies describe these staff consequences of new administrators and policies: see Carroll, *Hacks, Blacks, and Cons*; Jacobs, *Stateville*; Stastny and Tyrnauer, *Who Rules the Joint?*

38. See J. M. Wynne, Jr., "Prison Employee Unionism: The Impact of Correctional Administration and Programs," National Institute of Law Enforcement and Criminal Justice, 1978; J. Jacobs and L. Zimmer, "Collective Bargaining and Labor Unrest," in *New Perspectives in Prisons and Imprisonment*, ed. J. Jacobs, pp. 145–159.

39. In this connection, D. Black argues that, with much information available, control mechanisms can be quite diverse, tailored to individuals and situations; less information means that control becomes more uniform (see his "Social Control as a Dependent Variable," in *Toward a Theory of Social Control: Vol. 1*, ed. D. Black, p. 19).

40. It is unclear, however, just what has been lost. J. Hepburn's study of guard power suggests that it is only coercive power (force and other informal sanctions) that has been eliminated by court intervention and that guards have lost only the "old days," not complete control. Today, he argues, officers still have legitimate power: see his "The Exercise of Power in Coercive Organizations: A Study of Prison Guards," *Criminology* 23 (February 1985): 145–164. See also his "The Prison Control Structure and Its Effects on Work Attitudes: The Perceptions and Attitudes of Prison Guards," *Journal of Criminal Justice* 15 (1987): 49–64, and "The Erosion of Authority and the Perceived Legitimacy of Inmate Social Protest: A Study of Prison Guards," *Journal of Criminal Justice* 12 (1984): 579–590.

41. For example, S. Christianson reported that, between 1973 and 1979, the per 100,000 incarceration rate for whites increased from 46.3 to 65.1; for blacks the increase was from 368.0 to 544.1 (cited in J. Fox, *Organizational and Racial Conflict in Maximum Security Prisons*, p. 2).

42. The most extensive recent work on sexual violence in prison is D. Lockwood, *Prison Sexual Violence*. See also his "Issues in Prison Sexual Violence," in *Prison Violence in America*, ed. M. Braswell et al. According to research reported by S. Sylvester, J. Reed, and D. Nelson, in *Prison Homicide*, homosexual conflict is the major cause of prison homicide, at least through the 1970s.

43. See Jacobs, *Stateville*, p. 206.

2. From Anarchy to Order

1. Texas Department of Corrections, *30 Years of Progress*, p. 20.

2. See W. R. Hogan, *The Texas Republic: A Social and Economic History*, p. 266.

3. Ibid., pp. 245–266.

4. Huntsville was regarded as a boomtown and important economic area vying to become the state capital. Most important, Sam Houston, former president of the republic and future state governor, resided in Huntsville.

5. See D. Walker, "Penology for Profit: A History of the Texas Prison Sys-

tem," doctoral dissertation, Texas Tech University, 1983; C. Copeland, "The Evolution of the Texas Department of Corrections," master's thesis, Sam Houston State University, 1980; H. L. Crow, "A Political History of the Texas Penal System," doctoral dissertation, University of Texas, 1964.

6. See Texas, Texas Prison System, *Biennial Report of the Superintendent of the Texas State Penitentiary*, 1900–1902.

7. Quoted in Walker, "Penology for Profit," p. 367.

8. Adapted from Crow, "A Political History," pp. 248–249.

9. See ibid., pp. 159–170.

10. See J. Brown, "Plantation System Paved Way for Prisons," *Brazosport Facts*, 13 May 1985.

11. See Crow, "A Political History," pp. 159–170.

12. F. Langston, "Behind the Walls," *Daily Times Herald*, 20 December 1947.

13. R. Holbrook, "Overcrowding and the 'Tanks' Are the Source of Many Problems Found in Texas Prison System," *Tyler Morning Telegraph*, 29 December 1947. See also L. Hale, "Poor Housing, Pay for the Guards," *Houston Post*, 13 September 1948.

14. "Stufflebeme Scores Texas Prison Farms," *Fort Worth Star Telegram*, 3 March 1948.

15. See "Prison Oxen Eaten during Scarcity," *Austin American-Statesman*, 8 April 1948.

16. E. Gaston, "Prisons Breed Crime, Says Board Member," *Austin Texan*, 9 April 1948.

17. See W. Hart, "Prison System to Spend $125,000 on Meat, Feed," *Austin American-Statesman*, 8 March 1948.

18. Texas, Legislature, *Report Made to the Fiftieth Texas Legislature by the Legislative Committee on Investigation of the Texas Penitentiary Including Farm Units*, Austin, Tex., spring 1947.

19. "Convicts Live in Stinking Filth," *Wichita Falls Record-News*, 23 April 1948.

20. See C. Evans, "Prison Dope Running Is No. 1 Problem," *Houston Chronicle*, 7 September 1948.

21. See C. Evans, "Ellis Moves to Curb Prison Dope Racket," *Houston Chronicle*, 9 March 1948.

22. B. Jackson, *Wake Up Dead Man: Afro-American Worksongs from Texas Prisons*, p. 9.

23. Texas, Texas Prison System, *Annual Report of the Texas Prison Board of the Texas Prison System*, Huntsville, Tex., 1944.

24. Ibid., 1928–1945.

25. See "Sorry Shape of Prison Farms Told by Sellars," *Cameron Enterprise*, 22 April 1948.

26. See "8-Time Loser Admits Decapitating Convict," *San Antonio Express*, 16 December 1948.

27. H. Heinecke, "Either Him or Me, Convict Declares in Describing Beheading at Prison," *Fort Worth Star Telegram*, 16 December 1948.

28. See "Convicts Live in Stinking Filth."

29. Langston, "Behind Prison Walls."

30. See Texas, Texas Prison System, *Guard Record—Texas State Penitentiary*, book 5.

31. See Texas, Texas Prison System, *Rules, Regulations, and Statutory Laws*, 1921.

32. See Jackson, *Wake Up Dead Man*, p. 213, for a further explanation of "John Henry."

33. See ibid., p. 31.

34. Texas, Annual Reports, 1928–1945.

35. Jackson, *Wake Up Dead Man*, p. 6.

36. See Texas, Annual Reports, 1927–1947.

37. See Jackson, *Wake Up Dead Man*, pp. 1–27.

38. See R. C. Koeninger, "What about Self-Mutilation?" *Prison World*, March–April 1951.

39. See ibid., p. 5.

40. See Texas, Annual Reports, 1940–1942.

41. "Texas Prisons Called Humanity's Junkpile," *San Antonio Express*, 18 November 1948.

42. Texas, *Annual Report*, 1946.

43. Interview with Billy G. McMillan, August 1979.

44. Interview with Eska McGaughey, September 1986.

45. Texas, *Annual Report*, 1945.

46. See Texas, *Rules, Regulations, and Statutory Laws*, 1921.

47. Ibid., p. 29.

48. Ibid., pp. 26–29.

49. Ibid., pp. 43–44.

50. See Crow, "A Political History," pp. 43–44.

51. Texas, Texas Prison System, Minutes of Texas Prison Board meeting, 24 May 1926.

52. Jackson, *Wake Up Dead Man*, pp. 8–9.

53. See Texas, Prison Board meeting, 8 February 1945.

54. See the Shelby County Penal Farm (monograph), 1946, Sam Houston State University archives.

55. See W. Fowler, "Texas Solution Seen in Model Penal Farm," *Dallas Morning News*, 4 December 1947.

56. Letter from W. C. Windsor, chairman of Texas Prison Board, November 1947.

57. See "State Prison Program," *Dallas Morning News*, 7 December 1947.

58. See Langston, "Behind the Walls."

59. W. Hart, "Ellis Plan Seen as Long Range Penal Solution," *Austin American-Statesman*, 25 December 1947.

60. "Prisons Rotten Says One of Board," *Fort Worth Press*, 5 March 1948.

61. "Texan Bawls Like a Baby after Tour of the State's Prison Farms," *Jacksonville Journal*, 4 March 1948.

62. "Texas Prison Farms Worse Than Nazi Camps," *Galveston News*, 4 March 1948.

63. "Get Better Prison System Now," *Tyler Courier-Times*, 3 March 1948.

64. See "Prison System Firings Revealed after Probe," *Fort Worth Star Telegram*, 21 March 1950.

65. See A. Sample, *Racehoss: Big Emma's Boy*.

66. See "Texas Prison Story," *Victoria Mirror*, 12 December 1959.

67. Ibid., p. 10.

68. Interview with George Beto, September 1986.

69. Texas, Texas Prison System, Minutes of the Texas Prison Board meeting, 10 January 1955.

70. Letter from ex-inmate Paul Maness, 2 February 1986.

71. Interview with George Beto, October 1986.

72. See George Beto's presidential speech to the American Correctional Association, 1970.

73. See Copeland, "The Evolution of the Texas Department of Corrections," p. 240.

74. Interview with director of the Texas Legislative Budget Board, 1984.

75. The prisons at this time were racially segregated. Although Beto desegregated the units, the inmate living areas and field force were still segregated. Black inmates lived in all-black wings, just as white and Hispanic inmates lived in all-white and all-Hispanic wings. The outside field force was also divided into three main forces: Black Line, White Line, and Mexican Line. The institutional living areas and line forces were not desegregated until 1979.

76. For an in-depth analysis of efforts by writ writers to bring prison conditions in TDC to light and Beto's efforts to squelch them, see Martin and Ekland-Olson, *Texas Prisons*. Key cases include *Cruz v. Beto*, 603 F.2d 322 (5th Cir. 1979), and *Novak v. Beto*, 320 F. Supp. 1206 (S.D. Tex. 1970, aff'd in part).

77. See S. Singer, "New Prison Head Views: Dr. Beto as 'Master,'" *Houston Chronicle*, 6 August 1972.

78. W. P. Barrett, "Lifer," *Houston City Magazine*, 1982, p. 85.

79. Ibid., p. 54.

80. Singer, "New Prison Head Views."

81. The term "public entrepreneurship" was used by Eugene Lewis to describe the administrative and political success of Hyman Rickover, J. Edgar Hoover, and Robert Morse (see his *Public Entrepreneurship: Toward a Theory of Bureaucratic Political Power*).

3. Stability and Control, Texas Style

1. K. Krajick, "They Keep You In, They Keep You Busy, and They Keep You from Getting Killed," *Corrections Magazine* 1 (March 1978): 4–8, 10–21.

2. See ibid.

3. See Sylvester, Reed, and Nelson, *Prison Homicide*.

4. See B. M. Crouch, "A Profile of TDC Officers," Department of Corrections Technical Report, no. 5, 1974.

5. On "paternalism," see Van den Berghe, *Race and Racism*. See also B. M. Crouch, "The Guard in a Changing Prison World," in *The Keepers*, ed. B. Crouch, pp. 5–45.

6. Albert "Race" Sample records over 200 nicknames applied to prisoners by officers and by other inmates during his time in TDC in the late 1950s and the 1960s. Among the more colorful are "Slopediddy," "Waterboy Brown," "Look 'Em Down Red," "Squat Low," "Dangalang," "Sheepshit," "Liverlips," "Duckbutter," "Chinaman," and "Mamma Betterdrawers" (see *Racehoss*, pp. 319–320).

7. Sample, *Racehoss*, p. 270. Though this "handbook" is quite likely aprocryphal, it does illustrate exactly the type of collected wisdom that officers shared and worked by.

8. See B. M. Crouch, "Maximizing the Effectiveness of Preservice Training," in *Correctional Officers: Power, Pressures, and Responsibility*, ed. J. Tucker.

9. See B. M. Crouch and J. W. Marquart, "On Becoming a Prison Guard," in *The Keepers*, ed. Crouch, pp. 75–77.

10. See B. M. Crouch, "The Book vs. the Boot: Two Styles of Guarding in a Southern Prison," in *The Keepers*, ed. Crouch, pp. 207–224.

11. Sample, *Racehoss*, p. 199.

12. Ibid., p. 226.

13. See Jackson, *Wake Up Dead Man*.

14. See C. J. Friedrich and Z. K. Brzezinski, *Totalitarianism*.

15. Crouch, "The Book vs. the Boot."

16. See *Wolf v. McDonnell*, 418 U.S. 539 (1974) and *Avant v. Clifford*, 67 N.J. 496 (1975).

17. See J. W. Blassingame, *The Slave Community: Plantation Life in the Ante-Bellum South*.

18. Sample, *Racehoss*, p. 138.

19. Ibid., p. 141.

20. See E. Johnson, "Sociology of Confinement, Assimilation, and the Prisons 'Rat,'" *Journal of Criminal Law, Criminology, and Police Science* 51 (January–February 1961): 528–533.

21. See E. Goffman, *Interaction Ritual*.

22. J. W. Marquart, "Cooptation of the Kept: Maintaining Control in a Southern Penitentiary."

23. Ibid.

24. The observations and analysis in this section on force derive almost exclusively from data collected at the Eastham Unit in 1981 and 1982 (see ibid.). Evidence indicates that quite similar uses of force occurred on other TDC units as well, especially those designated for older, more experienced, and violent inmates.

25. Similar practices have been reported for police: see J. Van Maanen, "On Watching the Watchers," in *Policing: A View from the Street*, ed. P. K. Manning and J. Van Maanen.

26. See E. Goffman, "The Nature of Deference and Demeanor," *American Anthropologist* 58 (1956): 473–501. See also P. K. Manning, "Rules

in Organizational Context: Narcotic Law Enforcement in Two Settings," *Sociological Quarterly* 18 (1977): 44–61. That failure by TDC inmates to show respect to officers led to physical punishment parallels findings from investigations of police (see A. Reiss, *The Police and the Public*; I. Piliavin and S. Briar, "Police Encounters with Juveniles," *American Journal of Sociology* 70 [September 1964]: 206–214). On "disrespective citizens," see R. Friedrich, "Police Use of Force: Individuals, Situations, and Organizations," in *Thinking about Police*, ed. C. Klockars.

27. See J. Reider, "The Social Organization of Vengeance," in *Toward a General Theory of Social Control II: Fundamentals*, ed. D. Black.

28. Police inner circles also encourage a code of secrecy (see W. Westly, *Violence and the Police*).

29. See E. Shills and M. Janowitz, "Cohesion and Disintegration of the Wehrmacht in WW II," *Public Opinion Quarterly* 12 (1948): 280–315.

4. Co-optation of the Kept

1. Letter from former TDC inmate, Paul Maness, 1984.

2. Other southern states, for the same reasons, also co-opted elite inmates for control purposes. In the plantation prison systems of Mississippi, Louisiana, and Arkansas, officials armed selected convicts to guard fellow convicts at work. On Louisiana, see J. C. Mouledous, "Sociological Perspectives on a Prison xocial System," master's thesis, Louisiana State University, 1962; on Arkansas, see Murton and Hyams, *Accomplices to the Crime*; on Mississippi, see W. McWhorter, *Inmate Society: Legs, Halfpants, and Gunmen: A Study of Inmate Guards*.

3. See pp. 365–388 in E. D. Genovese, *Roll, Jordan, Roll: The World the Slaves Made*.

4. It is interesting to note that several prisons were established in Brazoria County, the site of many early, slave-operated cotton and sugar plantations (see T. L. Smith, *A History of Brazoria County, Texas: The Old Plantations and Their Owners of Brazoria County, Texas*).

5. See Texas, Texas Prison System, Biennial Reports of the Directors and Superintendents of the Texas State Penitentiary, 1878–1880.

6. Ibid., 1886–1888.

7. Texas, Texas Prison System, *Minute Book of the Board of Prison Commissioners*, 1914–1915, p. 547.

8. By contrast, in Mississippi, Louisiana, and Arkansas, trusties lived and ate in separate quarters for their own protection.

9. See Texas, Texas Prison System, *Report of the 1910 Penitentiary Investigating Committee*, p. 134.

10. Ibid., p. 920.

11. Ibid., pp. 286–289.

12. B. Deason, *Seven Years in Texas Prisons*, pp. 5–6.

13. Ibid., pp. 12–13.

14. See Texas, Minutes of the Prison Board, 1916–1927.

15. Ibid., 1922, 1923, 1926.

16. See J. W. Marquart and B. Thomas, "Overcrowding and Violence in Texas Prisons: 1927–1939," paper presented at the Annual Southwestern Social Science Meeting, Dallas, 1987.

17. Conversation with George J. Beto, 25 May 1987.

18. See J. W. Marquart and B. M. Crouch, "Coopting the Kept: Using Inmates for Social Control in a Southern Prison," *Justice Quarterly*, 1984, pp. 491–509.

19. Although the following discussion focuses on Eastham, interviews with ex-BTs and ranking staff on other units suggest that the BT system operated virtually the same on other "older" units. That is, Eastham is not a unique or atypical case.

20. See J. W. Marquart and J. Roebuck, "Prison Guards and Snitches," *British Journal of Criminology* 25, no. 3 (1985): 217–233.

21. According to Blassingame (*The Slave Community*, p. 200), this same situation prevailed on the slave plantations where "the master and slave lived and worked together on such intimate terms that they developed an affection for each other, and the slave identified completely with his master."

22. For a description of this holiday, see J. W. Marquart and J. Roebuck, "Institutional Control and the Christmas Festival in a Maximum Security Penitentiary," *Urban Life* 15, nos. 3–4 (1987): 449–473.

23. See C. Schrag, "Leadership among Prison Inmates," *American Sociological Review* 19 (1954): 37–42.

24. A similar situation prevailed at Stateville in the 1940s and 1950s during Joseph Ragen's wardenship (see Jacobs, *Stateville*).

25. These data were collected from the Annual Reports of the Texas Prison System, 1971–1982.

5. Justice Comes to Texas Prisons

1. Excerpt from a speech made by Judge William W. Justice at an Interagency Workshop held at Sam Houston State University, 31 May 1986.

2. "TDC Inmates Testify," *Huntsville Item*, 21 July 1974.

3. See A. House, *The Carrasco Tragedy*.

4. "Estelle's Action Termed Insult to Barrientos," *Austin American-Statesman*, 30 September 1975.

5. See House Study Group, "Overcrowding in Texas Prisons," Special (Texas) Legislative Report, no. 43, 8 April 1979, p. 3.

6. See "State Prison Short of Guards—Estelle," *Lufkin News*, 13 August 1976.

7. See House Study Group, "Overcrowding in Texas Prisons," p. 5.

8. Ibid., p. 6.

9. Ibid., p. 3.

10. Ibid., p. 8.

11. See C. Caldwell, "Politics and Prison," *Texas Observer*, 25 February 1977.

12. *Bryant v. Harrelson*, 187 F. Supp. 738 (S.D. 1960).

13. Issues raised in these cases included religion: *Cruz v. Beto*, 603 F.2d

1178 (5th Cir. 1979); mail privileges: *Guajardo v. Estelle* 580 F.2d 748 (5th Cir. 1978); racial segregation: *Lamar v. Coffield* Civil Action No. 72-H-1393 Consent Decree (D.C. Southern District 1977); and medical care: *Estelle v. Gamble,* 429 U.S. 97 (1976).

14. Z. Franks, "The Devil-Saint Federal Judge: He Rules, Texans Pay the Price," *Houston Chronicle,* 18 January 1981.

15. See A. Bleeker, "An Exceptional Remedy: The Special Master as Administrator in the Texas Prison Case," MPA thesis, University of Texas at Austin, August 1983.

16. See T. Moran, "Riot by 1500 Inmates Acknowledged," *Houston Post,* 19 October 1978.

17. R. Vara, "Striking Inmates Given Warning of Harm to Trial," *Houston Post,* 17 October 1978.

18. See W. W. Justice, Memorandum Opinion, 12 December 1980, p. 4.

19. See L. Rocawich, "Texas Prisons," *Texas Observer,* 22 September 1978, pp. 1–6.

20. "Wilkinson Describes Texas Prisons as the 'Best in the World,'" *Houston Chronicle,* 4 September 1978.

21. "Pontesso Sees State Prisons as Failing to Rehabilitate Cons," *Houston Chronicle,* 4 September 1978.

22. Justice, Memorandum Opinion, p. 205.

23. See Bleeker, "An Exceptional Remedy."

24. R. Vara, "Reforms of Prisons Modified," *Houston Post,* 24 June 1982.

25. See P. Belazis, "Ninth Monitor's Report of Factual Observations to the Special Master," Report on Section IIC of the *Amended Decree* (Use of Force), 1983. The following paragraphs draw heavily on this report.

26. See F. Klimko, "TDC Plans to Start Moving Inmates into New Dormitories over Weekend," *Houston Chronicle,* 15 July 1982.

27. See R. Dunkam, "TDC Shuts Doors to New Inmates," *Dallas Morning News,* 11 May 1982.

28. See G. Smith, "State Officials Now Appear to Support Prison Reform," *Houston Chronicle,* 13 June 1982.

29. Quoted in F. Benavita, "TDC Hard-Hit if Budget Cuts Stand, Panel Told," *Houston Post,* 23 November 1982.

30. See R. Reyes and F. Klimko, "Mattox Assigns Lawyers to Audit Probe of TDC," *Houston Chronicle,* 17 December 1983.

31. See G. Smith, "TDC Investigating Payroll Practices," *Houston Chronicle,* 27 January 1984.

32. Both quotes are from T. Nelson and R. Vara, "TDC Finances: Out of Control," *Houston Post,* 22 January 1984.

33. Quoted in F. West and R. Vara, "White Vows Action if Report of Abuse in TDC Confirmed," *Houston Post,* 30 September 1983.

34. Quoted in M. Reeves, "Problems Toppled TDC Chief," *Dallas Morning News,* 4 December 1983.

35. See ibid.

36. R. Reyes, "Estelle Officially Resigns as Director of Texas Prisons," *Huntsville Item,* 8 October 1983.

37. Following are the key elements of the *Standards for the Use of Force* agreement (see Appendix G, in "Overview of *Ruiz v. Estelle:* A Summary of Relevant Orders, Stipulations, Reports, and Issues," by M. Walter, U.S. District Court, Eastern District of Texas, July 1984):

1. In cases of self-defense against an inmate where the physical safety of a TDC officer or employee is immediately threatened; threatened;
2. Where an inmate must be physically restrained because his conduct presents an imminent and immediate threat to the physical safety of another person or persons;
3. In the prevention of serious damage to property by an inmate, where the danger to property presents an imminent and immediate threat;
4. In the prevention of an escape;
5. In maintaining or regaining control of a TDC institution or facility therein (including any open fields or areas where inmates are employed), in the event of a mutiny, rebellion, riot or disturbance. Authorization for the use of force to quell (one of these) shall be made only by the assistant warden or higher authority, except in case of actual emergency where the officer in charge must take necessary action without delay; and
6. In enforcement of TDC rules and regulations in order to temporarily isolate or otherwise confine an inmate, where lesser means have proven ineffective.

38. See D. Nunnelee, "TDC Firings: Six Ranking Employees Fired, Others Demoted," *Huntsville Item*, 7 February 1984.

39. See P. Belazis, "Nineteenth Monitor's Report of Factual Observations to the Special Master," Report on Section IIC of the *Amended Decree* (Use of Force), 1984, p. 59.

40. Staff Bureau Report, "TDC Names New Director," *Huntsville Item*, 22 May 1984.

41. See M. Fowler, "Prison Inmate Given 50 Years for Assaulting Guard," *Brazosport Facts*, 14 September 1985.

42. "Procunier Sends Shock Waves through System," *Dallas Morning News*, 23 June 1984.

43. J. Brown, "TDC Appoints Two Regional Directors to Aid Management," *Brazosport Facts*, 7 January 1985.

44. Quoted in "Hobby: Tough Choices Ahead as TDC Lawsuit Settled," *Huntsville Item*, 17 May 1985.

45. For a more detailed description, see "Final Ruiz Settlement," *Echo* (TDC), May–June 1985, pp. 1–24.

6. *Changing of the Guards*

1. These quotes were taken from field notes made at the Eastham prison unit of TDC in the fall of 1984.

2. F. King, "TDC: Guards Lack Full Control," *Houston Post*, 28 August 1984.

3. See F. Klimko and J. Toth, "TDC Inmate Attacks Guard, Lawyer," *Houston Chronicle*, 8 August 1984.

4. See "Grand Jury Will Probe Scalding of TDC Guard," *Houston Post*, 15 August 1984.

5. See "2 Guards Assaulted," *Houston Chronicle*, 12 October 1984.

6. See J. Toth, "Guard Is Beaten, Stabbed in TDC," *Houston Chronicle*, 8 August 1984.

7. See J. Toth and F. Klimko, "Possible Hit List, Gun Found in Prison," *Houston Chronicle*, 22 November 1984. Since the 1981 killings of a warden and a farm manager by inmate Eroy Brown, only one officer has died at the hands of an inmate. This was a female officer who was stabbed by an inmate in June 1985. At first believed to be part of an escape attempt, the killing, according to the offender, was actually prompted by her rejection of his love.

8. The classic treatment of this problem of informal relationships corrupting official authority is by Sykes, *Society of Captives*.

9. See ibid.; M. Schneckloth, "Why Do Honest Employees React Dishonestly?" *American Journal of Corrections* 21 (March–April 1959): 6, 24, 27.

10. See F. Klimko and M. Miller, "TDC Suspends Guard after Stabbing," *Houston Chronicle*, 1 February 1985.

11. J. Toth, "Warden Says Guard Helped Smuggle Gun," *Houston Chronicle*, 24 November 1984.

12. See F. Klimko, "8 TDC Employees Arrested in Inmate-Loan Racket, Drug Hunt," *Houston Chronicle*, 8 August 1984.

13. See W. Pack, "Guards Admit Accepting Money from TDC Inmate," *Houston Chronicle*, 4 May 1985.

14. For a general discussion of women officers working in men's prisons, see B. M. Crouch, "Pandora's Box: Women Guards in Men's Prisons," *Journal of Criminal Justice* 13 (1985): 535–548; L. Zimmer, *Women Guarding Men*.

15. F. King, "TDC Cuts Back on Women Guards," *Houston Post*, 9 August 1984.

16. See Crouch, "Pandora's Box."

17. See C. Horswell, "Women Guards Still a Sensitive Issue in Prisons," *Houston Chronicle*, 21 November 1984.

18. J. Toth, "Team of Last Resort," *Houston Chronicle*, 21 October 1985.

19. To assess levels of officer morale over time, we asked survey respondents to indicate their general morale level on a scale from 1 (very low) to 7 (very high) for each of four time periods: 1979–1981, 1982–1983, 1984–1985, and 1986. Following are the time periods and the percentage of officers who reported morale levels at or below 4 (low morale) on the scale for that time period: 1979–1981, 10 percent; 1982–1983, 27 percent; 1984–1985, 55 percent; and 1986, 57 percent.

20. This reaction by officers following organizational and administrative change in other prisons has been noted elsewhere: see, for example, Carroll, *Hacks, Blacks, and Cons*, and Jacobs, *Stateville*.

21. Over the past decade a significant literature has developed on the nature, extent, and basis for correctional officer stress: see F. Cullen et al.,

"The Social Correlates of Correctional Officer Stress," *Justice Quarterly* 4 (December 1985): 505–534; C. M. Brodsky, "Long-term Work Stress in Teachers and Prison Guards," *Journal of Occupational Medicine* 19 (February 1977): 133–138; H. A. Rosefield, Jr., "What's Killing Our Officers?" in *Correctional Officers: Power, Pressure, and Responsibility*, pp. 5–9; J. J. Dahl, "Occupational Stress in Corrections," in *Proceedings of the 110th Annual Congress on Corrections*, pp. 207–222.

22. See F. Cheek and M. Miller, "A New Look at Role Ambiguity," in *Correctional Officers: Power, Pressure, and Responsibility*, pp. 11–16; see also F. Cullen et al., "The Social Correlates of Correctional Officer Stress."

23. See B. M. Crouch, "Prison Officer Training, Supervision, and Turnover," report prepared under Grant Number BG-2 from the National Institute of Corrections, U.S. Department of Justice, October 1980.

24. Data from the officer survey permitted us to determine a number of correlates of stress. First, stress was measured by a six-item scale developed by Francis Cullen (see Cullen et al., "The Social Correlates of Correctional Officer Stress"). Other scales in the survey, adapted from John Hepburn's work, measured perceived loss of authority and control (seven items), perceived danger (five items), role strain, and satisfaction (see his "The Exercise of Power in Coercive Organizations"). An original scale tapped the extent to which officers felt a decline in trust and loyalty among officers. Stress was correlated with these attributes of the work setting in the following way: sense of control over inmates ($r = -.44$); danger ($r = .43$); role strain ($r = .38$); satisfaction ($r = -.47$); and extent of co-worker loyalty ($r = -.35$).

25. Anecdotal evidence indicated that some officers may have relieved stress through alcohol and soft drugs.

26. On unionization of guards, see B. M. Crouch, "Prison Guards on the Line," in *The Dilemmas of Punishment*, ed. K. Haas and G. Alpert, pp. 177–210; Jacobs and Zimmer, "Collective Bargaining and Labor Unrest," pp. 145–159; Wynne, "Prison Employee Unionism."

27. An examination of the dates that guard unions in state prisons were established reveals that, even in strong union states in the northeast and north-central parts of the country, guard unions generally emerged in the 1970s (see T. Flanagan, D. van Alstyne, and M. Gottfredson [eds.], *Sourcebook of Criminal Justice Statistics—1981*, pp. 138–139).

28. G. Keith, "State Employees, Part Three: Public Employee Organizations and Collective Bargaining," House Study Group—Special Legislative Report, no. 62, November 1980.

29. T. Bertling, "TDC Works to Prevent Union," *Huntsville Item*, 4 February 1979.

30. See Keith, "State Employees, Part Three," pp. 31–32.

31. See Jacobs and Zimmer, "Collective Bargaining and Labor Unrest."

32. Telephone interview with Danny Fetonte, executive director of TSEU, Austin, Texas, October 27, 1986.

33. See McKinsey and Company, "Strengthening TDC's Management Effectiveness," Final Report, 14 May 1984.

34. See Crouch, "Prison Officer Training, Supervision, and Turnover."

35. On the "leveling" of bureaucratization in general, see M. Weber, *The Theory of Social and Economic Organization*, p. 47.

7. Prisoner Crisis and Control

1. Statement by a Texas prisoner on the Eastham Unit, November 1984.

2. Between 1 March 1987 and 5 June 1987, we administered questionnaires to a random sample of 460 inmates housed in the Coffield, Eastham, Ferguson, Ellis I, Wynne, Retrieve, Darrington, Ramsey I, and Ramsey II units. We stratified the sample by time served, selecting inmates who began their sentences between 1977 and 1981 and had lived in or experienced both the pre- and the post-Ruiz systems. On this specific point, questionnaire data revealed that 73 percent of inmate respondents agreed with the statement "Right after the court ordered TDC to reform, most inmates thought improvements would come quickly."

3. See W. J. Estelle, Jr., *For Compliance with Ruiz Stipulation Concerning Use of Support Service Inmates*, TDC Unit Operations Manual, 1982, p. 6.

4. S. Blow, "Inmates Do What It Takes to Survive," *Dallas Morning News*, 30 September 1984.

5. P. Taylor, "When Inmates Stopped Running Texas Prisons, Hell Broke Loose," *Washington Post*, 1 October 1984.

6. E. Moore, "Inmates Can Buy Almost Any Item," *Houston Chronicle*, 19 November 1984.

7. See Carroll, *Hacks, Blacks, and Cons*.

8. *Lamar v. Coffield*.

9. See Jacobs' description in *Stateville* of the convict society during Ragen's administration.

10. For an extensive discussion of the forms of prisoner exploitation, see L. Bowker, *Prison Victimization*.

11. Data on disciplinary offenses were compiled by TDC's Management Services.

12. See F. Klimko, "TDC Director Gives Tentative OK to Early-Release Plan," *Houston Chronicle*, 16 January 1986.

13. See E. Moore and F. Klimko, "From Bones to Bombs: Make-Shift Murder Weaponry Limited by Inmates' Imaginations," *Houston Chronicle*, 19 November 1984.

14. See F. Klimko, "TDC Violence on the Rise: Increase Blamed on Younger, More Hard-core Criminals," *Houston Chronicle*, 5 November 1982.

15. See S. Dial and D. Taylor, "Parole in Texas: Sentencing Policy and Practice," paper, December 1985.

16. See S. K. Bardwell, "Three Guards at County Units Are Facing Charges," *Brazosport Facts*, 18 September 1985. The prisoners tended to agree with the veteran staff on this score. Over half (56%) of the prisoners surveyed agreed that the quality of the new employees entering guard work has deteriorated in the last several years.

17. S. Ekland-Olson, "Crowding, Social Control, and Prison Violence: Some Evidence from the Post-Ruiz Years," *Law and Society Review* 20, no. 3 (1986): 389–421.

18. State Representative Sam Johnson introduced a bill in the Texas Legislature to resurrect the building tender system. He also had plans to pay the inmates, thus saving the state money it would need to hire guards (see "State Seeks Legal Method to Return to Trusty System," *Brazosport Facts*, 27 April 1985).

19. See D. Black (ed.), *Toward a General Theory of Social Control, Vol. 1: Fundamentals.*

20. The hard-core units are Coffield, Eastham, Ellis I, Ferguson, Darrington, Retrieve, Ramsey I, and Ramsey II.

21. See G. Camp and C. Camp, "Prison Gangs: Their Extent, Nature, and Impact on Prisons," National Institute of Justice, 1985.

22. See ibid.

23. See Jacobs, *Stateville.*

24. See T. Davidson, *Chicago Prisoners: The Key to San Quentin.*

25. See B. Porter, "California Prison Gangs: The Price of Control," *Corrections Magazine*, December 1982, p. 8.

26. See ibid.

27. See J. Irwin, *Prisons in Turmoil.*

28. See Camp and Camp, "Prison Gangs."

29. Interview with George Beto, 1986.

30. Ibid.

31. See K. Price, "The Black Muslims: Prison Problem or Model Inmate," master's thesis, Sam Houston State University, 1978.

32. See Davidson, *Chicano Prisoners.*

33. Interview with Salvador Buentello, gang information specialist of the Texas Department of Corrections, 1987.

34. R. Fong, "A Comparative Study of the Organizational Aspects of Two Texas Prison Gangs: Texas Syndicate and Mexican Mafia," doctoral dissertation, Sam Houston State University, 1987.

35. This description of AB recruiting was obtained from a lengthy document called "The Texas Aryan Brotherhood: It's History, Methods and Mentality," written by two former AB members who turned against the gang.

36. From official gang strength data compiled by S. Buentello and shared with authors.

37. "The Texas Aryan Brotherhood."

38. Ibid.

39. See Fong, "Organizational Aspects."

40. Data compiled by S. Buentello and shared with authors.

41. See "Gang Violence Leaves Three Dead at Darrington Unit," *Brazosport Facts*, 9 September 1985. See also "Gang Slayings Prompt Emergency TDC Lockdown," *Brazosport Facts*, 19 September 1985.

42. See F. Klimko and J. Toth, "Recruiting Drive by Gangs Blamed for Prison War," *Houston Chronicle*, 10 September 1985.

43. See "Prison Gangs Eye Pact," *Brazosport Facts,* 23 October 1985.

44. F. Klimko, "TDC Gangs Unlikely to Call Truce," *Houston Chronicle,* 26 October 1985.

45. See Fong, "Organizational Aspects."

46. This particular murder occurred in 1984 at the Ellis II Unit.

47. F. Klimko, "Paroled Convict Gang Leaders Continuing Underworld Activities, Authorities Allege," *Houston Chronicle,* 26 March 1987.

48. For example, see Engel and Rothman, "Prison Violence and the Paradox of Reform," pp. 91–105; W. Gaylin et al. (eds.), *Doing Good.*

49. Conrad, "What Do the Undeserving Deserve?" p. 319.

50. A note is in order about the question and the time periods used. Prisoners were asked to think about specific time periods and to indicate how dangerous (or safe) the prison felt to them. The scale ranged from 1, very dangerous, to 10, very safe. In Table 11, we have defined responses from 1 through 4 as indicative of a generally unsafe environment and responses from 7 through 10 as a generally safe environment.

Though prisoner responses depended on recall and are limited accordingly, we feel that the time periods presented were sufficiently defined in the respondents' minds to permit a reasonably accurate depiction of levels of personal safety. Those time periods were significant for the following reasons:

1. 1970–1978: period prior to trial and reforms
2. 1979–1981: period of trial, initial court order, and preliminary changes in TDC
3. 1982–1983: period in which TDC initially fought some portions of the ruling, lost, then began implementing the majority of the reforms
4. 1984–1985: period of unprecedented inmate violence
5. 1986–1987: period of thirteen to sixteen months prior to the administration of the questionnaire

51. See "Gang Violence Leaves Three Dead at Darrington Unit."

52. See Fong, "Organizational Aspects."

53. It is safe to assume that violence is not the only problem men in administrative segregation face. Since incarceration there involves placing one man in a cell for more than twenty hours per day (they are taken out for showers and a brief recreation period) indefinitely, the psychological impact of the experience is probably significant and detrimental.

54. That this loss was significant was evident in responses to two questions on the inmate survey. Sixty-five percent of the prisoners (typically "job inmates") agreed with the statement "It's hard to find an officer who can and will make a decision on an inmate's problem." Similarly, 57 percent agreed with the statement "Because of having to do everything 'by the book,' officers won't help inmates solve personal problems (cell changes, phone calls, etc.)."

8. A New Prison Order

1. Governor Bill Clements, State of the State Address before the 70th Texas Legislature, 1987.

2. Some of the elements in our model are analogous to concepts developed by Phillipe Nonet and Philip Selznick in their analysis of the evolution of law in society (see their *The Transition of Law in Society*).

3. J. Vagg, R. Morgan, and M. Maguire stress that prisons cannot be held accountable by such outside agencies as courts unless there is in place a system of internal accountability (see their "Introduction: Accountability and Prisons," in *Accountability and Prisons: Opening Up a Closed World*, ed. M. Maguire, J. Vagg, and R. Morgan, p. 4).

4. Indeed, there is a close parallel between the stages through which the Stateville prison passed, according to Jacobs, and the stages that we observed in TDC. Specifically, our repressive order includes his "anarchy" and "charismatic leadership" stages; our legalistic order includes his "drift" and "crisis" stages; and our bureaucratic order includes his "stability" stage. This parallel underscores the patterned nature of organizational change in prisons (see Jacobs, *Stateville*).

5. For a discussion of some of the difficulties in defining and measuring the success of litigation in prison, see Jacobs, "The Prisoners' Rights Movement." See also Feely and Hanson, "What We Know."

6. In the survey of prisoners, 57 percent agreed with such a statement.

7. This sentiment was reported by approximately two-thirds of the surveyed prisoners.

8. See D. Horowitz, *The Courts and Social Policy*, R. Gaskins, "Second Thoughts," pp. 153–168.

9. S. J. Brakel, "Prison Reform Litigation: Has the Revolution Gone Too Far?" *Judicature* 70 (June–July 1986): 7.

10. See Alexander, "The New Prison Administrator and the Court," pp. 963–1008; Falkof, "Prisoner Representative Organizations," pp. 42–56; Robbins, "The Cry of *Wolfish* in the Federal Courts"; M. Ware, "Federal Intervention in State Prisons: The Modern Prison Conditions Case," *Houston Law Review* 19 (1982): 931–950. Indeed, Kenneth Haas and Geoffrey Alpert argue that recent Supreme Court decisions have created formidable and inflexible barriers that severely limit prisoners' bringing suit against prison officials in state or federal court. See their "American Prisoners and the Right of Access to the Courts," in *The American Prison: Issues in Research and Policy*, ed. L. I. Goodstein and D. L. Mackenzie.

11. *Bruscino v. Carlson*, Civil No. 84-4320 (D.C. Southern District of Illinois, 1987).

12. Significantly, for recent control practices in Texas, this federal lockdown strategy appears to closely parallel TDC's extensive use of administrative segregation for troublesome prisoners.

13. See J. Thomas, "Law and Social Praxis: Prisoner Civil Rights Litigation and Structural Mediations," in *Research in Law, Deviance, and Social*

Control, ed. S. Spitzer and A. Scull; D. A. Timmer and D. S. Eitzen, "Controlling Crime in the 80s: A Critique of Conservative Federal Policy," *Humanity and Society* 9 (February 1985): 67–80.

14. See Jacobs, "The Prisoners' Rights Movement," p. 439.

15. See P. Baker et al., "Judicial Intervention in Corrections." Indeed, Turner points out that some prisons become more constitutional even after prison officials have won a rights suit filed against them (see "When Prisoners Sue: A Study of Prisoner Section 1983 Suits in Federal Courts," *Harvard Law Review* 92 [1979]: 610–663).

16. Quoted in F. Klimko, "The Price of Arrogance: Texas Legal Fees," *Corrections Compendium* 11 (July 1987): 8. In this connection, Estelle recalled that, shortly after he took the Texas post (1972), a friend, during a corrections conference in another state, suggested that he visit with two attorneys active in prison litigation. In that visit, those attorneys, according to Estelle, laid out plans to reform American corrections through the courts. Because of its size and reputation, the Texas system was to be the key to the plan; if it "fell," all the other systems could be reformed without a fight.

17. Interview with Scott McGowan, Enforcement Division of Texas Attorney General's Office, October 1987.

18. C. Robison, "Judge Suspends Fines over TDC, Cites 'Good Faith,'" *Houston Chronicle*, 17 March 1987.

19. This observation is also made by L. Lombardo in *Guards Imprisoned*.

20. For a recent analysis of the problems and the prospects of managing contemporary prisons, see J. DiIulio, *Governing Prisons: A Comparative Study of Correctional Management*.

21. On the elements of due process, see L. Siegel, *Criminology*, p. 421.

22. There are indications that TDC staff still, at times, employ illicit force and that the administration is less than diligent in trying to eliminate these occurrences. In March 1988, the special master reported to the court that TDC was being too lenient on guards who use excessive force on prisoners (see K. Fair, "Report Finds Continued TDC Brutality, Blames Inadequate Guard Punishment," *Houston Chronicle*, 3 March 1988).

23. It has been suggested that, because of the difficulty of enforcing compliance on these values in prison, courts should limit their concerns to such basic matters as safety and health (see Brakel, "Prison Reform Litigation: Has the Revolution Gone Too Far?").

The difficulty of applying social values in prison is illustrated by the problems encountered in efforts to eliminate racial segregation in prison. Many courts, drawing on the same values behind school integration rulings, have held that prison housing units and workplaces must also be "racially balanced." Yet, the close proximity of prisoners in cells and cellblocks, their own preferences and frequently racist attitudes, plus the fact that prison officials might misuse such a mandate (punish a white prisoner by placing him in an essentially black cellblock) argue against the ideal of a completely integrated prison world (see J. Jacobs, *New Perspectives on Prisons and Imprisonment*, pp. 80–98).

24. See "Implementation Problems in Institutional Reform Litigation," *Harvard Law Review* 91 (1977): 428–463; see also J. Handler, *Social Movements and the Legal System: A Theory of Law Reform and Social Change;* Jacobs, "The Prisoners' Rights Movement," p. 451.

25. Martin and Ekland-Olson make a similar point (see their *Texas Prisons,* p. 247).

26. See Sherman and Hawkins, *Imprisonment in America.*

27. The arguments for and against dealing with these two problems by building more prisons are examined in Sherman and Hawkins, *Imprisonment in America.* See also E. Currie, *Controlling Crime,* esp. chap. 3, "The Limits of Imprisonment."

Bibliography

Alexander, E. "The New Prison Administrator and the Court: New Directions in Prison Law." *Texas Law Review* 56 (1978): 963–1008.

Alpert, G., B. Crouch, and R. Huff. "Prison Reform by Judicial Decree: The Unintended Consequences of *Ruiz v. Estelle*." *Justice System Journal* 9 (1984): 291–305.

Baker, P., et al. "Judicial Intervention in Corrections: The California Experience, an Empirical Study." *UCLA Law Review* 20 (1973): 452–580.

Bardwell, S. K. "Three Guards at County Units Are Facing Charges." *Brazosport Facts*, 18 September 1985.

Barrett, W. P. "Lifer." *Houston City Magazine*, 1982.

Belazis, P. "Nineteenth Monitor's Report of Factual Observations to the Special Master." Report on Section IIC of the *Amended Decree* (Use of Force), 1984.

———. "Ninth Monitor's Report of Factual Observations to the Special Master." Report on Section IIC of the *Amended Decree* (Use of Force), 1983.

Benavita, F. "TDC Hard-Hit If Budget Cuts Stand, Panel Told." *Houston Post*, 23 November 1982.

Bertling, T. "TDC Works to Prevent Union." *Huntsville Item*, 4 February 1979.

Beto, G. J. Presidential speech to the American Correctional Association, 1970.

Black, D., ed. *Toward a General Theory of Social Control, Vol. 1: Fundamentals.* New York: Academic Press, 1984.

———, ed. "Social Control as a Dependent Variable." In *Toward a General Theory of Social Control, Vol. 1: Fundamentals.* New York: Academic Press, 1984.

Blassingame, J. W. *The Slave Community: Plantation Life in the Ante-Bellum South.* New York: Oxford University Press, 1979.

Bleeker, A. "An Exceptional Remedy: The Special Master as Administrator in the Texas Prison Case." MPA thesis, University of Texas at Austin, August 1983.

Blow, S. "Inmates Do What It Takes to Survive." *Dallas Morning News,* 30 September 1984.

Blumberg, A. *Criminal Justice.* Chicago: Quadrangle Books, 1970.

Boatwright, L. "Federal Courts and State Prison Reform: A Formula for Large Scale Federal Investigation into State Affairs." *Suffolk University Law Review* 14 (1980): 545–576.

Bowker, L. *Prison Victimization.* New York: Elsevier, 1980.

———. "The Victimization of Prisoners by Staff Members." In *The Dilemmas of Punishment,* ed. K. Haas and G. Alpert, pp. 134–157. Prospect Heights, Ill.: Waveland Press, 1986.

Brakel, S. J. "Prison Reform Litigation: Has the Revolution Gone Too Far?" *Judicature* 70 (June–July 1986): 7.

Brodsky, C. M. "Long-Term Work Stress in Teachers and Prison Guards." *Journal of Occupational Medicine* 19 (February 1977): 133–138.

Bronstein, A. "Prisoners' Rights: A History." In *Legal Rights of Prisoners,* ed. G. Alpert, pp. 19–46. Beverly Hills: Sage Publications, 1980.

Brown, J. "Plantation System Paved Way for Prisons." *Brazosport Facts,* 13 May 1985.

———. "TDC Appoints Two Regional Directors to Aid Management." *Brazosport Facts,* 7 January 1985.

Caldwell, C. "Politics and Prison." *Texas Observer,* 25 February 1977.

Camp, G., and C. Camp. *Prison Gangs: Their Extent, Nature, and Impact on Prisons.* Washington, D.C.: National Institute of Justice, 1985.

Carroll, L. *Hacks, Blacks, and Cons.* Lexington, Mass.: Lexington Books, 1974.

Champagne, A., and K. Haas. "The Impact of *Johnson vs. Avery* on Prison Administration." *Tennessee Law Review* 43 (1977): 275–306.

Cheek, F., and M. Miller. "A New Look at Role Ambiguity." In *Correctional Officers: Power, Pressure, and Responsibility,* ed. J. Tucker, pp. 11–16. College Park, Md.: American Correctional Association, 1983.

Cloward, R. "Social Control in Prison." In *Prison within Society,* ed. L. Hazelrigg. New York: Doubleday, 1960.

Cloward, R., et al., eds. *Theoretical Studies in Social Organization of the Prison.* New York: Social Science Research Council, 1960.

Colvin, M. "The 1980 New Mexico Riot." *Social Problems* 29 (1982): 449–463.

Conrad, J. "What Do the Undeserving Deserve?" In *The Pains of Imprisonment,* ed. R. Johnson and H. Toch, pp. 303–313. Beverly Hills: Sage Publications, 1982.

"Convicts Live in Stinking Filth." *Wichita Falls Record-News,* 23 April 1948.

Copeland, C. "The Evolution of the Texas Department of Corrections." Master's thesis, Sam Houston State University, 1980.

Corrections Magazine 6 (March 1978).

Crouch, B. M. "The Book vs. the Boot: Two Styles of Guarding in a Southern Prison." In *The Keepers*, ed. B. Crouch, pp. 207–224. Springfield, Ill.: Charles C. Thomas, 1980.

———. "The Guard in a Changing Prison World." In *The Keepers*, ed. B. Crouch, pp. 5–45. Springfield, Ill.: Charles C. Thomas, 1980.

———. "Maximizing the Effectiveness of Preservice Training." In *Correctional Officers: Power, Pressures, and Responsibility*, ed. J. Tucker. College Park, Md.: American Correctional Association, 1984.

———. "Pandora's Box: Women Guards in Men's Prisons." *Journal of Criminal Justice* 13 (1985): 535–548.

———. "Prison Guards on the Line." In *The Dilemmas of Punishment*, ed. K. Haas and G. Alpert, pp. 177–210. Prospect Heights, Ill.: Waveland Press, 1986.

———. "Prison Officer Training, Supervision, and Turnover." Report prepared under Grant Number BG-2 from the National Institute of Corrections, U.S. Department of Justice, October 1980.

———. "A Profile of TDC Officers." Department of Corrections Technical Report, no. 5, 1974.

Crouch, B. M., and J. W. Marquart. "On Becoming a Prison Guard." In *The Keepers*, ed. B. Crouch, pp. 75–77. Springfield, Ill.: Charles C. Thomas, 1980.

Crow, H. L. "A Political History of the Texas Penal System." Doctoral dissertation, University of Texas, 1964.

Cullen, F., et al. "The Social Correlates of Correctional Officer Stress." *Justice Quarterly* 4 (December 1985): 505–534.

Currie, E. *Controlling Crime*. New York: Pantheon Books.

Dahl, J. J. "Occupational Stress in Corrections." In *Proceedings of the 110th Annual Congress on Corrections*, pp. 207–222. College Park, Md.: American Correctional Association, 1980.

Davidson, T. *Chicano Prisoners: The Key to San Quentin*. New York: Holt, Rinehart & Winston, 1974.

Deason, B. *Seven Years in Texas Prisons*. Sam Houston State University archives, n.d.

Dial, S., and D. Taylor. "Parole in Texas: Sentencing Policy and Practice." Position paper, Texas Lieutenant Governor's Office, December 1985.

DiIulio, J. *Governing Prisons: A Comparative Study of Correctional Management*. New York: Free Press, 1987.

———. "Prison Discipline and Prison Reform." *Public Interest* 89 (Fall 1987): 71–90.

Diver, C. "The Judge as Political Powerbroker: Superintending Structural Change in Public Institutions." *Virginia Law Review* 65 (1978): 43–106.

Dobray, D. "The Role of Special Masters in Court Ordered Institutional Reform." *Baylor Law Review* 34 (1982): 587–603.

Dunkam, R. "TDC Shuts Doors to New Inmates." *Dallas Morning News*, 11 May 1982.

"8-Time Loser Admits Decapitating Convict." *San Antonio Express*, 16 December 1948.

Eisenberg, T., and S. Yeazell. "The Ordinary and the Extraordinary in Institutional Litigation." *Harvard Law Review* 93 (1980): 464–517.

Ekland-Olson, S. "Crowding, Social Control, and Prison Violence: Some
Evidence from the Post-Ruiz Years." *Law and Society Review* 20, no. 3
(1986): 389–421.

Emerson, R. "Power Dependence Relations." *American Sociological Review* 27 (February 1962): 31–40.

Engel, K., and S. Rothman. "Prison Violence and the Paradox of Reform."
Public Interest (1983): 91–105.

Estelle, W. J., Jr. *For Compliance with* Ruiz *Stipulation Concerning Use of
Support Service Inmates.* TDC Unit Operations Manual, 1982.

"Estelle's Action Termed Insult to Barrientos." *Austin American-Statesman,*
30 September 1975.

Evans, C. "Ellis Moves to Curb Prison Dope Racket." *Houston Chronicle,*
9 March 1948.

———. "Prison Dope Running Is No. 1 Problem." *Houston Chronicle,*
7 September 1948.

Fair, K. "Report Finds Continued TDC Brutality, Blames Inadequate Guard
Punishment." *Houston Chronicle,* 3 March 1988.

Falkof, B. "Prisoner Representative Organizations, Prison Reform, and *Jones
v. North Carolina Prisoner's Labor Union:* An Argument for Increased
Court Intervention in Prison Administration." *Journal of Criminal Law
and Criminology* 70 (1979): 42–56.

Feely, M., and R. Hanson. "What We Know, Think We Know, and Would
Like to Know about the Impact of Court Orders on Prison Conditions and
Jail Crowding." Paper prepared for the meeting of the Working Group on
Jail and Prison Crowding, Committee on Research on Law Enforcement
and the Administration of Justice, National Academy of Sciences, Chi-
cago, October 15–16, 1986.

"Final Ruiz Settlement." *Echo* (TDC), May–June 1985, pp. 1–24.

Fiss, O. "The Social and Political Foundations of Adjudication." *Law and
Human Behavior* 6 (1982): 121–128.

Flanagan, T., D. van Alstyne, and M. Gottfredson, eds. *Sourcebook of Criminal Justice Statistics—1981.* Washington, D.C.: U.S. Department of Justice, Bureau of Justice Statistics, 1982.

Fong, R. "A Comparative Study of the Organizational Aspects of Two Texas
Prison Gangs: Texas Syndicate and Mexican Mafia." Doctoral dissertation, Sam Houston State University, 1987.

Fowler, M. "Prison Inmate Given 50 Years for Assaulting Guard." *Brazosport
Facts,* 14 September 1985.

Fowler, W. "Texas Solution Seen in Model Penal Farm." *Dallas Morning
News,* 4 December 1947.

Fox, J. *Organizational and Racial Conflict in Maximum Security Prisons.*
Lexington, Mass.: Lexington Books, 1982.

Franks, Z. "The Devil-Saint Federal Judge: He Rules, Texans Pay the Price."
Houston Chronicle, 18 January 1981.

Friedrich, C. J., and Z. K. Brzezinski. *Totalitarianism*. New York: Universal Library, 1965.

Friedrich, R. "Police Use of Force: Individuals, Situations, and Organizations." In *Thinking about Police*, ed. C. Klockars, pp. 302–312. New York: McGraw-Hill, 1983.

"Gang Slayings Prompt Emergency TDC Lockdown." *Brazosport Facts*, 19 September 1985.

"Gang Violence Leaves Three Dead at Darrington Unit." *Brazosport Facts*, 9 September 1985.

Gaskins, R. "Second Thoughts on 'Law as an Instrument of Social Change.'" *Law and Human Behavior* 6 (1982): 153–168.

Gaston, E. "Prisons Breed Crime, Says Board Member." *Austin Texan*, 9 April 1948.

Gaylin, W., et al., eds. *Doing Good*. New York: Pantheon Books, 1978.

Genovese, E. D. *Roll, Jordan, Roll: The World the Slaves Made*. New York: Pantheon Books, 1974.

"Get Better Prison System Now." *Tyler Courier-Times*, 3 March 1948.

Goffman, E. *Interaction Ritual*. Chicago: Aldine, 1967.

———. "The Nature of Deference and Demeanor." *American Anthropologist* 58 (1956): 473–501.

"Grand Jury Will Probe Scalding of TDC Guard." *Houston Post*, 15 August 1984.

Guenther, A., ed. *Criminal Behavior and Social Systems*. 2d ed. Chicago: Rand McNally, 1976.

Haas, K. "Judicial Politics and Correctional Reform: An Analysis of the Decline of the 'Hands Off' Doctrine." *Detroit College of Law Review* 4 (1977): 795–831.

Haas, K., and G. Alpert. "American Prisoners and the Right of Access to the Courts." In *The American Prison: Issues in Research and Policy*, ed. L. I. Goodstein and D. L. MacKenzie. New York: Plenum (forthcoming).

Hale, L. "Poor Housing, Pay for the Guards." *Houston Post*, 13 September 1948.

Handler, J. *Social Movements and the Legal System: A Theory of Law Reform and Social Change*. New York: Academic Press, 1978.

Harris, M. K., and D. P. Spiller. *After Decision: Implementation of Judicial Decrees in Correctional Settings*. Washington, D.C.: American Bar Association, 1977.

Hart, W. "Ellis Plan Seen as Long Range Penal Solution." *Austin American-Statesman*, 25 December 1947.

———. "Prison System to Spend $125,000 on Meat, Feed." *Austin American-Statesman*, 8 March 1948.

Harvard Center for Criminal Justice. "Judicial Intervention in Prison Discipline." *Journal of Criminal Law, Criminology, and Police Science* 18 (1972): 200–228.

Harvard Law Review. "Implementation Problems in Institutional Reform." *Harvard Law Review* 91 (1977): 428–463.

Heinecke, H. "Either Him or Me, Convict Declares in Describing Beheading at Prison." *Fort Worth Star Telegram*, 16 December 1948.

Hepburn, J. "The Erosion of Authority and the Perceived Legitimacy of Inmate Social Protest: A Study of Prison Guards." *Journal of Criminal Justice* 12 (1984): 579–590.

———. "The Exercise of Power in Coercive Organizations: A Study of Prison Guards." *Criminology* 23 (February 1985): 145–164.

———. "The Prison Control Structure and Its Effect on Work Attitudes: The Perceptions and Attitudes of Prison Guards." *Journal of Criminal Justice* 15 (1987): 49–64.

"Hobby: Tough Choices Ahead as TDC Lawsuit Settled." *Huntsville Item*, 17 May 1985.

Hogan, W. R. *The Texas Republic: A Social and Economic History*. Austin: University of Texas Press, 1969.

Holbrook, R. "Overcrowding and the 'Tanks' Are the Source of Many Problems Found in Texas Prison System." *Tyler Morning Telegraph*, 29 December 1947.

Horowitz, D. *The Courts and Social Policy*. Washington, D.C.: Brookings Institute, 1977.

Horswell, C. "Women Guards Still a Sensitive Issue in Prisons." *Houston Chronicle*, 21 November 1984.

House, A. *The Carrasco Tragedy*. Waco, Tex.: Texian Press, 1975.

"Implementation Problems in Institutional Reform Litigation." *Harvard Law Review* 91 (1977): 428–463.

"Inside America's Toughest Prison." *Newsweek*, 6 October 1986, pp. 46–61.

Irwin, J. *Prisons in Turmoil*. Boston: Little, Brown and Company, 1980.

Jackson, B. *Wake Up Dead Man: Afro-American Worksongs from Texas Prisons*. Cambridge, Mass.: Harvard University Press, 1972.

Jacobs, J. *New Perspectives on Prisons and Imprisonment*. Ithaca, N.Y.: Cornell University Press, 1983.

———. "The Prisoners' Rights Movement and Its Impact, 1960–1980." In *Crime and Justice: An Annual Review of Research*, ed. N. Morris and M. Tonry, vol. 2, pp. 429–470. Chicago: University of Chicago Press, 1980.

———. "Race Relations and the Prisoner Subculture." In *Crime and Justice: An Annual Review of Research*, ed. N. Morris and M. Tonry, vol. 1. Chicago: University of Chicago Press, 1979.

———. *Stateville: The Penitentiary in Mass Society*. Chicago: University of Chicago Press, 1977.

Jacobs, J., and L. Zimmer. "Collective Bargaining and Labor Unrest." In *New Perspectives in Prisons and Imprisonment*, ed. J. Jacobs, pp. 145–159. Ithaca, N.Y.: Cornell University Press, 1983.

Johnson, E. "Sociology of Confinement, Assimilation, and the Prisons 'Rat.'" *Journal of Criminal Law, Criminology, and Police Science* 51 (January–February 1961): 528–533.

Justice, W. W. Memorandum Opinion: *Ruiz v. Estelle*, December 1980.

King, F. "TDC Cuts Back on Women Guards." *Houston Post,* 9 August 1984.

————. "TDC: Guards Lack Full Control." *Houston Post,* 28 August 1984.

Klimko, F. "8 TDC Employees Arrested in Inmate-Loan Racket, Drug Hunt." *Houston Chronicle,* 8 August 1984.

————. "Paroled Convict Gang Leaders Continuing Underworld Activities, Authorities Allege." *Houston Chronicle,* 26 March 1987.

————. "The Price of Arrogance: Texas Legal Fees." *Corrections Compendium* 11 (July 1987): 8.

————. "TDC Director Gives Tentative OK to Early-Release Plan." *Houston Chronicle,* 16 January 1986.

————. "TDC Gangs Unlikely to Call Truce." *Houston Chronicle,* 26 October 1985.

————. "TDC Plans to Start Moving Inmates into New Dormitories over Weekend." *Houston Chronicle,* 15 July 1982.

————. "TDC Violence on the Rise: Increase Blamed on Younger, More Hard-Case Criminals." *Houston Chronicle,* 5 November 1982.

Klimko, F., and J. Toth. "Recruiting Drive by Gangs Blamed for Prison War." *Houston Chronicle,* 10 September 1985.

————. "TDC Inmate Attacks Guard, Lawyer." *Houston Chronicle,* 8 August 1984.

Klimko, F., and M. Miller. "TDC Suspends Guard after Stabbing." *Houston Chronicle,* 1 February 1985.

Koeninger, R. C. "What about Self-Mutilation?" *Prison World,* March–April 1951.

Krajick, K. "They Keep You In, They Keep You Busy, and They Keep You from Getting Killed." *Corrections Magazine* 1 (March 1978): 4–8, 10–21.

Langston, F. "Behind the Walls." *Daily Times Herald* (Dallas), 20 December 1947.

Lewis, E. *Public Entrepreneurship: Toward a Theory of Bureaucratic Political Power.* Bloomington: Indiana University Press, 1980.

Lieberman, J. K. *The Litigious Society.* New York: Basic Books, 1982.

Lockwood, D. "Issues in Prison Sexual Violence." In *Prison Violence in America,* ed. M. Braswell et al. Cincinnati, Ohio: Anderson Publishing, 1985.

————. *Prison Sexual Violence.* New York: Elsevier, 1980.

Lombardo, L. *Guards Imprisoned.* New York: Elsevier, 1981.

McKinsey and Company. "Strengthening TDC's Management Effectiveness." Final Report to TDC, May 14, 1984.

McWhorter, W. *Inmate Society: Legs, Halfpants, and Gunmen: A Study of Inmate Guards.* Saratoga, Calif.: Century Twenty Publishing, 1981.

Maguire, M., J. Vagg, and R. Morgan, eds. *Prisons and Accountability.* London: Travistock, 1985.

Manning, P. K. "Rules on Organizational Context: Narcotic Law Enforcement in Two Settings." *Sociological Quarterly* 18 (1977): 44–61.

March, R. *Alabama Bound: Forty-Five Years inside a Prison System.* Tuscaloosa: University of Alabama Press, 1978.

Marquart, J. W. "Cooptation of the Kept: Maintaining Control in a Southern Penitentiary." Doctoral dissertation, Texas A&M University, 1983.

Marquart, J. W., and B. M. Crouch. "Coopting the Kept: Using Inmates for Social Control in a Southern Prison." *Justice Quarterly* (1984): 491–509.

Marquart, J. W., and B. Thomas. "Overcrowding and Violence in Texas Prisons: 1927–1939." Paper presented at the annual Southwestern Social Science Meeting, Dallas, 1987.

Marquart, J. W., and J. Roebuck. "Institutional Control and the Christmas Festival in a Maximum Security Penitentiary." *Urban Life* 15, nos. 3, 4 (1987): 449–473.

———. "Prison Guards and Snitches." *British Journal of Criminology* 25, no. 3 (1985): 217–233.

Martin, S. and S. Ekland-Olson. *Texas Prisons: The Walls Came Tumbling Down*. Austin: Texas Monthly Press, 1987.

Mattick, H. "The Prosaic Sources of Prison Violence." In *Criminal Behavior and Social Systems*, ed. A. Guenther. 2d ed., pp. 529–540. Chicago: Rand McNally, 1976.

Messinger, S., and G. Sykes. "The Inmate Social System." In *Theoretical Studies in Social Organization of the Prison*, ed. R. Cloward et al., pp. 5–19. New York: Social Science Research Council, 1960.

Moore, E. "Inmates Can Buy Almost Any Item." *Houston Chronicle*, 19 November 1984.

Moore, E., and F. Klimko. "From Bones to Bombs: Make-Shift Murder Weaponry Limited by Inmates' Imaginations." *Houston Chronicle*, 19 November 1984.

———. "TDC Violence on the Rise: Increase Blamed on Younger, More Hard-Core Criminals." *Houston Chronicle*, 5 November 1982.

Moran, T. "Riot by 1500 Inmates Acknowledged." *Houston Post*, 19 October 1978.

Morgan, R., and A. Bronstein. "Prisoners and the Courts: The U.S. Experience." In *Prisons and Accountability*, ed. M. Maguire, J. Vagg, and R. Morgan. London: Travistock, 1985.

Mouledous, J. C. "Sociological Perspectives on a Prison Social System." Master's thesis, Louisiana State University, 1962.

Murton, T., and J. Hyams. *Accomplices to the Crime: The Arkansas Prison Scandal*. New York: Grove Press, 1969.

Nagel, R. "Separation of Powers and the Scope of Federal Equitable Remedies." *Stanford Law Review* 30 (April 1978): 661–724.

Nelson, T., and R. Vara. "TDC Finances: Out of Control." *Houston Post*, 22 January 1984.

Nonet, P., and P. Selznick. *The Transition of Law in Society*. New York: Harper Torchbooks, 1978.

Nunnelee, D. "TDC Firings: Six Ranking Employees Fired, Others Demoted." *Huntsville Item*, 7 February 1984.

Pack, W. "Guards Admit Accepting Money from TDC Inmate." *Houston Chronicle*, 4 May 1985.

Packer, H. "Two Models of the Criminal Process." *University of Pennsylvania Law Review* 113 (1964): 84–100.

Piliavin, I., and S. Briar. "Police Encounters with Juveniles." *American Journal of Sociology* 70 (September 1964): 206–214.

"Pontesso Sees State Prisons as Failing to Rehabilitate Cons." *Houston Chronicle*, 4 September 1978.

Porter, B. "California Prison Gangs: The Price of Control." *Corrections Magazine*, December 1982, p. 8.

Price, K. "The Black Muslims: Prison Problem or Model Inmate." Master's thesis, Sam Houston State University, 1978.

"Prison Gangs Eye Pact." *Brazosport Facts*, 23 October 1985.

"Prison Oxen Eaten during Scarcity." *Austin American-Statesman*, 8 April 1948.

"Prisons Rotten Says One of Board." *Fort Worth Press*, 5 March 1948.

"Prison System Firings Revealed after Probe." *Fort Worth Star Telegram*, 21 March 1950.

"Procunier Sends Shock Waves through System." *Dallas Morning News*, (*NY Times*), 23 June 1984.

Reavis, D. "How They Ruined Our Prisons." *Texas Monthly*, May 1985, pp. 152–159, 232–246.

Reeves, M. "Problems Toppled TDC Chief." *Dallas Morning News*, 4 December 1983.

Reider, J. "The Social Organization of Vengeance." In *Toward a General Theory of Social Control, Vol. II: Selected Problems*, ed. D. Black. New York: Academic Press, 1984.

Reiss, A. *The Police and the Public*. New Haven, Conn.: Yale University Press, 1971.

Reyes, R. "Estelle Officially Resigns as Director of Texas Prisons." *Huntsville Item*, 8 October 1983.

Reyes, R., and F. Klimko. "Mattox Assigns Lawyers to Audit Probe of TDC." *Houston Chronicle*, 17 December 1983.

Robbins, I. "The Cry of *Wolfish* in the Federal Courts: The Future of Federal Judicial Intervention in Prison Administration." *Journal of Criminal Law and Criminology* 71 (1980): 211–225.

Robbins, I., and M. Buser. "Punitive Conditions of Prison Confinement: An Analysis of *Pugh v. Locke* and Federal Court Supervision of State Penal Administrations under the Eighth Amendment." *Stanford Law Review*, May 1977, pp. 893–930.

Robison, C. "Judge Suspends Fines over TDC, Cites 'Good Faith.'" *Houston Chronicle*, 17 March 1987.

Rocawich, L. "Texas Prisons." *Texas Observer*, 22 September 1978, pp. 1–6.

Rosefield, H. A., Jr. "What's Killing Our Officers?" In *Correctional Officers: Power, Pressure, and Responsibility*, ed. J. Tucker, pp. 5–9. College Park, Md.: American Correctional Association, 1983.

Rothman, D. "The Courts and Social Reform: A Postprogressive Outlook." *Law and Human Behavior* 6 (1982): 113–119.

Sample, Albert. *Racehoss: Big Emma's Boy.* Austin, Tex.: Eakin Press, 1984.

Schneckloth, M. "Why Do Honest Employees React Dishonestly?" *American Journal of Corrections* 21 (March–April 1959): 6, 24, 27.

Schrag, C. "Leadership among Prison Inmates." *American Sociological Review* 19 (1954): 37–42.

Sherman, M., and G. Hawkins. *Imprisonment in America: Choosing the Future.* Chicago: University of Chicago Press, 1981.

Shills, E., and M. Janowitz. "Cohesion and Disintegration of the Wehrmacht in WW II." *Public Opinion Quarterly* 12 (1948): 280–315.

Siegel, L. *Criminology.* St. Paul: West Publishing, 1983.

Silberman, C. E. *Criminal Violence, Criminal Justice.* New York: Random House, 1978.

Singer, S. "New Prison Head Views: Dr. Beto as 'Master.'" *Houston Chronicle,* 6 August 1972.

Skolnick, J. *Justice without Trial.* New York: John Wiley and Sons, 1966.

"Sorry Shape of Prison Farms Told by Sellars." *Cameron Enterprise,* 22 April 1948.

Smith, G. "State Officials Now Appear to Support Prison Reform." *Houston Chronicle,* 13 June 1982.

———. "TDC Investigating Payroll Practices." *Houston Chronicle,* 27 January 1984.

Smith, T. L. *A History of Brazoria County, Texas: The Old Plantations and Their Owners of Brazoria County, Texas.* Angleton, Tex.: Brazoria County Historical Society, 1958.

Stastny, C., and G. Tyrnauer. *Who Rules the Joint?* Lexington, Mass.: Lexington Books, 1982.

"State Prison Program." *Dallas Morning News,* 7 December 1947.

"State Prison Short of Guards—Estelle." *Lufkin News,* 13 August 1976.

"State Seeks Legal Method to Return to Trusty System." *Brazosport Facts,* 27 April 1985.

"Stufflebeme Scores Texas Prison Farms." *Fort Worth Star Telegram,* 3 March 1948.

Sykes, G. *Society of Captives.* Princeton, N.J.: Princeton University Press, 1958.

Sylvester, S., J. Reed, and D. Nelson. *Prison Homicide.* New York: Spectrum Publications, 1977.

Taylor, P. "When Inmates Stopped Running Texas Prisons, Hell Broke Loose." *Washington Post,* 1 October 1984.

"TDC Inmates Testify." *Huntsville Item,* 21 July 1974.

"TDC Names New Director." *Huntsville Item,* 22 May 1984.

"Texan Bawls Like a Baby after Tour of the State's Prison Farms." *Jacksonville Journal,* 4 March 1948.

Texas. General Assembly. House Study Group. *Overcrowding in Texas Prisons.* Special Legislative Report, no. 43, April 8, 1979.

———. *State Employees, Part Three: Public Employee Organizations and Collective Bargaining.* Special legislative report prepared by G. Keith, no. 62, November 1980.

Texas Legislature. Report Made to the 50th Texas Legislature by the Legislative Committee on Investigation of the Texas Penitentiary Including Farm Units. Austin, Tex., Spring 1947.

Texas. Texas Prison System. Annual Reports of the Texas Prison Board of the Texas Prison System, 1927–1947.

———. Biennial Report of the Superintendent of the Texas State Penitentiary, 1900–1902.

———. Biennial Reports of the Directors and Superintendents of the Texas State Penitentiary, 1878–1888.

———. *Guard Record—Texas State Penitentiary.* Books 5, 6, 7, 1920–1929.

———. *Minute Book of the Board of Prison Commissioners, 1914–1915,* p. 547.

———. Minutes of Texas Prison Board Meeting, 10 January 1955.

———. Minutes of Texas Prison Board Meetings, 1914–1927.

———. Report of the 1910 Penitentiary Investigating Committee.

———. *Rules, Regulations, and Statutory Laws,* 1921.

———. Shelby County Penal Farm (Monograph), 1946.

———. Texas Prison Board Meeting, 8 February 1945.

"The Texas Aryan Brotherhood: Its History, Methods, and Mentality." Manuscript in possession of authors, n.d.

Texas Department of Corrections. *30 Years of Progress.* Huntsville: Texas Department of Corrections, 1977.

"Texas Prison Farms Worse Than Nazi Camps." *Galveston News,* 4 March 1948.

"Texas Prisons Called Humanity's Junkpile." *San Antonio Express,* 18 November 1948.

"Texas Prison Story." *Victoria Mirror,* 12 December 1959.

Thomas, C. "The Impotence of Correctional Law." In *Legal Rights of Prisoners,* ed. G. Alpert, pp. 243–260. Beverly Hills: Sage Publications, 1980.

Thomas, J. "Law and Social Praxis: Prisoner Civil Rights Litigation and Structural Mediations." In *Research in Law, Deviance, and Social Control,* ed. S. Spitzer and A. Scull. Greenwich, Conn.: JAI Press, 1984.

Thomas, J., and A. Aylward. "Trends in Prisoner Civil Rights Litigation: A Preliminary Overview." Paper, 1983, presented in part at the Law and Society Association annual meetings, Toronto, 1982.

Thomas, J., D. Keeler, and K. Harris. "Issues and Misconceptions in Prison Litigation: A Critical View." *Criminology* 24 (November 1986): 775–797.

Timmer, D. A., and D. S. Eitzen. "Controlling Crime in the 80s: A Critique of Conservative Federal Policy." *Humanity and Society* 9 (February 1985): 67–80.

Toch, H. *Peacekeeping: Police, Prisons, and Violence.* Lexington, Mass.: Lexington Books, 1976.

Toth, J. "Guard Is Beaten, Stabbed in TDC." *Houston Chronicle*, 8 August 1984.

———. "Team of Last Resort." *Houston Chronicle*, 21 October 1985.

———. "Warden Says Guard Helped Smuggle Gun." *Houston Chronicle*, 24 November 1984.

Toth, J., and F. Klimko. "Possible Hit List, Gun Found in Prison." *Houston Chronicle*, 22 November 1984.

Tucker, J., ed. *Correctional Officers: Power, Pressure, and Responsibility.* College Park, Md.: American Correctional Association, 1983.

Turner, W. B. "When Prisoners Sue: A Study of Prisoner Section 1983 Suits in Federal Courts." *Harvard Law Review* 92 (1979): 610–663.

"2 Guards Assaulted." *Houston Chronicle*, 12 October 1984.

Useem, B. "Disorganization and the New Mexico Prison Riot of 1980." *American Sociological Review* 50 (October 1985): 677–688.

Vagg, J., R. Morgan, and M. Maguire. "Introduction: Accountability and Prisons." In *Accountability and Prisons: Opening Up a Closed World*, ed. M. Maguire, J. Vagg, and R. Morgan. London: Travistock, 1986.

Van den Berghe. *Race and Racism*. New York: John Wiley and Sons, 1967.

Van Maanen, J. "On Watching the Watchers." In *Policing: A View from the Street*, ed. P. K. Manning and J. Van Maanen. Santa Monica, Calif.: Goodyear, 1978.

Vara, R. "Reforms of Prisons Modified." *Houston Post*, 24 June 1982.

———. "Striking Inmates Given Warning of Harm to Trial." *Houston Post*, 17 October 1978.

Walker, D. "Penology for Profit: A History of the Texas Prison System." Doctoral dissertation, Texas Tech University, 1983.

Walter, M. "Overview of *Ruiz v. Estelle:* A Summary of Relevant Orders, Stipulations, Reports, and Issues." U.S. District Court, Eastern District of Texas, July 1984.

Ware, M. "Federal Intervention in State Prisons: The Modern Prison Conditions Case." *Houston Law Review* 19 (1982): 931–950.

Weber, M. *The Theory of Social and Economic Organization*. New York: Free Press, 1947.

Weinberg, J. K. "The Bureaucratic Judiciary: The Future of Court-Ordered Change." *Law and Human Behavior* 6 (1982): 169–181.

West, F., and R. Vara. "White Vows Action if Report of Abuse in TDC Confirmed." *Houston Post*, 30 September 1983.

Westly, W. *Violence and the Police*. Cambridge, Mass.: MIT Press, 1970.

"Wilkinson Describes Texas Prisons as the 'Best in the World.'" *Houston Chronicle*, 4 September 1978.

Wynne, J. M., Jr. *Prison Employee Unionism: The Impact of Correctional Administration and Programs*. Washington, D.C.: U.S. Government Printing Office, National Institute of Law Enforcement and Criminal Justice, 1978.

Zimmer, L. *Women Guarding Men*. Chicago: University of Chicago Press, 1986.

Court Cases

Avant v. Clifford, 67 N.J. 496 (1975).
Bruscino v. Carlson, Civil Case No. 84-4320 (D.C. S.D. Ill. 1987).
Bryant v. Harrelson, 187 F. Supp. 738 (S.D. 1960).
Consent Decree (D.C. S.D. 1977).
Cooper v. Pate, 378 U.S. 546 (1964).
Cruz v. Beto, 603 F.2d 1178 (5th Cir. 1979).
Estelle v. Gamble, 429 U.S. 97 (1976).
Guajardo v. Estelle, 580 F.2d. 748 (5th Cir. 1978).
Lamar v. Coffield, Civil Action No. 72-H-1393 (U.S.D.C. S.D. 1979).
Novak v. Beto, 320 F. Supp. 1206 (S.D. Tex. 1970 aff'd in part).
Ruffin v. Commonwealth, 62 Va. 790 (1871).
Ruiz v. Estelle, 503 F. Supp. 1265, 1277–1279 (S.D. Tex. 1980).
Wolf v. McDonnell, 418 U.S. 539 (1974).

Index

Administrative segregation, 144, 165, 167, 231; "super segregation," 149
Alabama prisons, 4
Alexander, E., 241, 261
Alpert, G., 240, 242, 253, 257, 262
American Correctional Association, 36, 39, 43
Arkansas prisons, 4–5
Auburn model, 13
Austin American-Statesman, 244, 249
Austin Texan, 244
Authority vacuum, 185
Avant v. Clifford, 247, 273
Aylward, A., 239, 271

Baker, P., 235, 258, 261
Bardwell, S. K., 257, 261
Barrett, W. P., 246, 261
Belazis, Paul T., 131–132, 250, 251
Benavita, F., 250, 261
Bertling, T., 253, 261
Beto, George J., 38–43, 117, 205, 224, 225; and building tenders, 91; population growth under, 41–42; and prisoner education, 38, 67; and prison industry, 41; "Walking George," 40, 145
Black, D., 243, 248, 255, 261

Black Muslims, 10, 205
Blassingame, J. W., 247, 261
Bleeker, A., 250, 262
Blow, S., 254, 262
Blumberg, A., 240, 262
Boatwright, L., 241, 262
Bookkeepers, 107–108; selection of, 109–114
Bowker, L., 241, 254
Brakel, Samuel J., 233, 257, 258, 262
Breed, Allen, 234
Briar, S., 248, 269
Briscoe, Dolph, 121
Brodsky, C. M., 253, 262
Bronstein, A., 240, 262
Brown, Eroy, 136, 138
Brown, J., 244, 251, 262
Brown v. Board of Education, 6
Bruscino v. Carlson, 231, 257, 273
Bryant v. Harrelson, 249, 273
Brzezinski, Z. K., 247, 265
Building tenders: authority of, 80–89; as assistant guards, 97–98; control over, 114–115; early lessons of "BT system," 90; elimination of, 131, 185–188; history of, 85–90; as managers, 101–106; as mediators, 98–101; rewarding inmate elites, 108–109; selection of, 109–114; snitching and, 93–

97; stratification of, 92–93
Bureaucracy, as control device, 9
Bureaucratic order, 221, 222–223,
    229–235, 237; and court-prison
    relations, 233–235; and inmate
    life, 232–233; and legalistic re-
    pression, 231–232; and main-
    streaming of TDC, 236–237
Buser, M., 242, 269

Caldwell, C., 249, 262
California prison system, 3, 10, 238
Camp, C., 255, 262
Camp, G., 255, 262
Carroll, L., 242, 252, 254
Champagne, A., 239, 262
Cheek, F., 253, 262
Christianson, S., 243
Civil Rights Act of 1871, Section
    1983, 6, 7
Civil Rights of Institutionalized
    Persons Act of 1980, 7
Clements, William P., 129, 134, 135,
    136, 150, 221, 257
Cloward, R., 241, 262
Coffield, H. H., 38, 42, 140
Colvin, M., 242, 262
Compliance: and charges of fiscal
    mismanagement, 136–137; pres-
    sure toward, 133–139
Compton, C. V., 30
Conrad, J., 215, 242, 256, 260, 262
Consent Decree, 273
"Convict sense," 52–53
Cooper v. Pate, 6, 241, 273
Copeland, C., 244, 246
Courts: and prison reform, 4–10; re-
    sistance to orders of, 128–133
Crouch, B., 242, 246, 247, 249, 252,
    253
Crow, H. L., 244, 245, 263
Cruz v. Beto, 246, 249, 273
Cullen, F., 252, 263
CURE (Citizens for the Rehabilita-
    tion of Errants), 119–120, 122;
    and Estelle, 119–120

Currie, E., 259, 263

Dahl, J. J., 253, 263
Dallas Morning News, 42, 245, 251
Davidson, T., 255, 263
Dial, S., 254, 263
Diver, C., 241, 263
Deason, B., 248, 263
Dilulio, John, 1, 239, 258, 263
Dunkam, R., 250, 263

Echo, The, 30, 251
Eckland-Olson, Sheldon, 240, 246,
    255, 259, 268
Eisenberg, T., 242, 262
Eitzen, D. S., 258, 271
Ellis, Oscar B., 31–38, 117, 224,
    225; and building tenders, 91; and
    Ellis Plan, 32–34; legislative re-
    lations of, 42; order and control
    under, 34–38; "Pappy," 32; re-
    form under, 33–34
Emerson, R., 241, 264
Engel, K., 242, 256, 262
Equal Employment Opportunity
    Commission, and female officers,
    162
Estelle, W. J., Jr., 117, 224, 226, 243–
    244; background of, 43; and build-
    ing tenders, 91; and fiscal misman-
    agement charges, 136–137; and
    prison crowding, 121, 135; repu-
    tation of, with prison board, 140
Estelle v. Gamble, 250, 273
Evans, C., 244, 264

Falkhof, B., 241, 252, 264
Fall, Gerald, 133
FBI, 124
Feely, Malcolm, 1, 240, 242, 257, 264
Field boss, 58–60; control of pris-
    oners by, 70–75; demeanor of,
    72–74
Fifth Circuit Court of Appeals, 128–
    130, 134
Fiss, O., 241, 264

"flatweeding," 21
Fong, R., 255, 256, 264
Formalization of control, 162, 170; and centralization of power, 167–170; and circuit court procedures, 169–170; and control technology, 165–167; and "paperwork," 168; and staff specialization, 164–165
Fort Worth Press, 245
Fort Worth Star Telegram, 244, 246
Fowler, M., 251, 264
Fowler, W., 245
Fox, J., 243, 264
Franks, Z., 250, 264
Friedrich, C. J., 247, 265
Friedrich, R., 248, 265
Frierson, Byron W., 35
Fullbright and Jaworski, 130
Furlough programs, 68

Galveston News, 245
Gaskins, R., 241, 257, 265
Gaston, E., 244, 265
Gaylin, W., 256, 265
Genovese, E. D., 248, 265
Goffman, E., 247, 265
Goodstein, L. I., 257
Good time, as reward, 68–69
Guajardo v. Estelle, 250, 273
Guards: expansion of force, 155–162; female, 161–162; and inmate aggression, 151–155; morale of, declines, 170–172; new, problems with, 156–161; pay of, 19; quality of, 24–26; socialization of, 54–60; and stress, 172–179; as subculture, 47–54, 179–183; unionization of, 177–179
Gunn, Robert, 140, 142, 146

Haas, K., 239, 241, 253, 257, 263, 265
Hale, L., 244, 265
"Hall boss," 56, 57
Handler, J., 259, 263
"Hands-off" doctrine, implications of, 4–6

Hanson, Roger, 1, 240, 242, 257, 264
Harris, K., 239, 271
Harris, M. K., 239, 265
Hart, W., 244, 245, 265
Harvard Center for Criminal Justice, 239, 265
Harvard Law Review, 239, 259, 265
Hawaii prisons, 46
Hawkins, G., 240, 259, 270
Hawkins, R., 240
Hepburn, J., 243, 266
"High rider," 21
High Rollers, 53
Hobby, William P., 135
Hoe squad, 36–37
Hogan, W. R., 243, 266
Holbrook, R., 244, 266
Horowitz, D., 257, 266
Horswell, C., 252, 266
Houston Chronicle, 250
Huff, R., 242, 261
Huntsville Item, 249, 251
Hyams, J., 241, 268

Irwin, J., 255, 266

Jackson, Bruce, 42, 244, 245, 266
Jacksonville Journal, 245
Jacobs, James B., 229, 239, 241, 242, 243, 249, 252, 253, 254, 255, 257, 258, 266
Janowitz, M., 248, 270
Jester, Beauford, 31
Johnson, E., 247, 266
Jones, Ernest, 20
Judicial scrutiny, pre-*Ruiz*, 122
Justice, Judge William W., 11, 117, 123–128, 174, 186, 187, 221, 234, 235, 249

Keeler, D., 239, 271
Keith, G., 253
Keller, Ray, 137, 139
Kerner, Otto, 39
King, F., 251, 252, 267
Klimko, F., 250, 252, 254, 255, 256, 267

Klockars, C., 248
Koeninger, Rupert C., 23, 245, 267
Krajick, K., 246, 267

Lamar v. Coffield, 250, 254, 273
Langston, F., 244, 245, 267
"Lead row," 37, 71
Legalistic order, 221, 222–223, 226–
    229; and organizational change,
    228–229
Legislative Budget Board, 136
Legislative investigation—1974, 118
Lewis, E., 246, 267
Lewis, Gib, 133
Lieberman, J. K., 239, 267
Litigation: impact of, on prison or-
    ganization, 140–150; limitations
    on, 236–237; Office of Internal
    Audits and, 142, 171, 172, 228;
    and prison board control, 140–142
Lockwood, D., 243, 267
Louisiana prisons, 5
Lynaugh, James, 231, 232

McAdams, C. L., 47, 48, 49, 54
MacCormick, Austin, 30, 31, 36, 42
McCormick, Harry, 42
McCotter, Lane, 143, 161, 166; back-
    ground of, 148–149; perceptions
    of, as administrator, 149–150; re-
    sponse by, to gangs and violence,
    149–150, 217
McKaskle, D. V. "Red," 50, 132, 133,
    141, 142, 143
MacKenzie, D. L., 257
McWhorter, W., 248, 267
Maguire, M., 240, 257, 267
Manning, P. K., 247, 248, 267
March, R., 241, 267
Marion Federal Penitentiary, 219
Marquart, J. W., 69, 247, 249, 268
Martin, Steve, 240, 246, 259, 268
Mattick, H., 242, 268
Messinger, S., 241, 268
Miller, M., 253, 262
Mississippi prisons, 5

Moore, Billy, 138
Moore, E., 254, 268
Moran, T., 250, 268
Morgan, R., 240, 257, 267
Mouledous, J. C., 248, 268
Murton, T., 241, 268
Myers, David, 163, 164, 180

Nagel, R., 241, 268
Nathan, Vincent, 127, 129, 130,
    131, 186
Nelson, D., 243, 246, 270
Nelson, T., 250, 268
New Mexico prisons, 143
Newsweek, 240
Nonet, P., 257, 268
Novak v. Beto, 246, 273
Nunnelee, D., 251, 268

Overcrowding, 120–122; and bud-
    get crunch, 133; and "tent cities,"
    134

Pack, W., 252, 268
Pack, Wallace, 138
Packer, H., 240, 264
"Paradox of reform" argument, 215,
    216
"Piddlin'," 68
Piliavin, I., 248, 269
Polygraph, use of, 142, 171
Pontesso, Arnold, 125
Porter, B., 255, 269
Powell, Lewis, 129
Price, K., 255, 269
Prisoner control (pre-*Ruiz* era), 60–
    84; formal controls, 62–65; infor-
    mal controls, 69–84; physical co-
    ercion by guards, 78–84
Prisoner relations: deterioration of,
    188–195; emerging stability in,
    215–219; social fragmentation
    of, 213–215
Prisoner's Defense Committee, 212
Prisoners' rights movement, 6–7, 8
Prisoner violence, 143–144; aimed

at guards, 151–155; crisis level (1984–1985), 195–202; and dispute settlements, 199–202; explanations of, 196–202; and gang activity, 209–213; reduction in, 216–217

Prison gangs: Aryan Brotherhood, 206, 207, 208, 209, 211, 212; insignia, 210; Mandingo Warriors, 206; membership patterns, 206–207; Mexican Mafia, 205, 206, 211, 212; rise of, 203–213; Seeds of Idi Amin, 206; Self-Defense Family, 206; structure of, 206, 207; Texas Mafia, 206; Texas Syndicate, 205, 206, 209, 212; and violence, 209–213

Procunier, Raymond, 142–148, 161, 162, 165, 182, 227; background and style of, 143; efforts by, to control inmates, 143–145; resignation of, 148; staff control by, 145–146

"Public entrepreneurs," 45

Racial segregation, 16

Ragen, Joseph, 4, 36, 39, 40, 41, 42, 249

Reavis, D., 240, 269

Redwine, Clarence W., 20

Reed, J., 243, 246, 270

Reeves, M., 250, 269

Reid, Don, 35

Reider, J., 248, 269

Reiss, A., 248, 269

Reyes, R., 250, 269

Repressive order, 221, 222–223, 224–226; and traditional control, 225–226

Robbins, I., 240, 242, 257, 269

Robison, C., 258, 269

Roebuck, J., 249, 268

Rosefield, H. A., 253, 269

Rothman, D., 241, 256, 262, 269

Ruffin v. Commonwealth, 240, 273

Ruiz, David, 2, 122, 123

Ruiz v. Estelle, 2, 11, 116, 117, 226, 234, 236, 240, 273; final settlement of, 146–148; history of, 122–124; trial and opinion, 124–128

Safety, prisoner perceptions of, 216, 218

Sam Houston State University, 47, 148

Sample, Albert, 70–71, 246, 247, 270

San Antonio Express, 245

Schaedel, C. T., 30

Schneckloth, M., 252, 270

Schrag, C., 249, 270

Self-mutilation, 23–24, 34

Selznick, P., 257, 268

Sherman, M., 240, 259, 270

Shills, E., 248, 270

Shivers, Allen, 38

Siegel, L., 258, 268

Silberman, Charles, 8, 242, 268

Simmons, Lee, 16, 27

Singer, S., 246, 270

Skolnick, J., 240, 270

Smith, G., 250, 270

Smith, T. L., 248, 270

SORT (Special Operations Reaction Teams), 144, 163, 164, 165

Spiller, D. P., 239, 265

Stakes, Douglas W., 19, 24, 31

Standards for the Use of Force, 142

Stastny, C., 239, 241, 270

Stateville prison, 39, 40, 41, 229

"Stuck out," 133

Stufflebeme, B. A., 31, 33

Sykes, G., 241, 252, 268, 270

Sylvester, S., 243, 246, 270

"Tail row," 37, 71

Taylor, D., 254, 263

Taylor, P., 254, 270

Texas Adult Probation Commission, 136

Texas Civil Liberties Union, 122

Texas Criminal Defense Lawyers

Association, 122
Texas National Guard, 134
Texas prisons: farms, 15–16, 26–29, 90; leasing and contract era, 14–15; life in tanks, 16–24; reform efforts, 2–4, 29–31; reputation of, 43, 46
Texas Public Employees Association, 177–178
Texas State Employees Union, 178
Thomas, B., 249, 268
Thomas, C., 242, 271
Thomas, James, 239, 257, 271
Timmer, D. A., 258, 271
Toch, H., 242, 269
Toth, J., 252, 255, 267
Training Academy, 47
Tucker, J., 247, 272
Turner, William Bennett, 239, 258, 272
Turnkeys, 106; selection of, 109–114
Tyler Courier-Times, 246
Tyrnauer, G., 239, 241, 270

United States Department of Justice, 124, 129
Useem, B., 242, 272
Utah prisons, 143

Vagg, J., 240, 257, 267
Van den Berghe, P., 247, 272
Van Maanen, J., 247, 272
Vara, R., 250, 272
Victoria Mirror, 246
Virginia prisons, 143

Walker, D., 243, 244, 272
Ware, M., 257, 272
Washington, Craig, 138
Waters, Mittie, 30
Weber, M., 254, 272
Weinberg, J. K., 239, 272
West, F., 250, 272
White, Mark, 128, 129, 130, 134, 139, 141, 150
Whittington, Harry, 141
Wichita Falls Record-News, 244
Wilkinson, Fred T., 125
Windham School District, 43, 67
Windsor, Wilbur C., 31, 32
Wolf v. McDonnell, 126, 247, 273
"Work buck," 117, 180
Wynne, Jim, 243, 253, 272

Yeazell, S., 242, 261

Zimmer, L., 243, 253, 272